How Do We Know We're Doing It Right?

Pandora Sykes is a journalist and broadcaster. She has written for the *Sunday Times*, *Vogue*, *ELLE* and the *Telegraph* amongst other publications, and was the co-host of *The High Low*, the UK's No. 1 podcast for women. She lives in London. This is her first book.

How Do We Know We're Doing It Right?

and other thoughts
on modern life

<small>P</small>ANDORA <small>S</small>YKES

WINDMILL

1 3 5 7 9 10 8 6 4 2

Windmill Books
20 Vauxhall Bridge Road
London SW1V 2SA

Windmill Books is part of the Penguin Random House group of companies
whose addresses can be found at global.penguinrandomhouse.com.

Penguin
Random House
UK

First published by Hutchinson in 2020
First published in paperback by Windmill Books in 2021

www.penguin.co.uk

A CIP catalogue record for this book is available from the British Library.

ISBN 9781786091000

Typeset in 11.1/13.86 pt Garamond MT Std
by Integra Software Services Pvt. Ltd, Pondicherry
Printed and bound in Great Britain by Clays Ltd, Elcograf S.p.A.

The authorised representative in the EEA is Penguin Random House Ireland,
Morrison Chambers, 32 Nassau Street, Dublin D02 YH68

Penguin Random House is committed to a
sustainable future for our business, our readers
and our planet. This book is made from Forest
Stewardship Council® certified paper.

To Z, S and O. Three things I know I got right.

In this short Life
That only lasts an hour
How much – how little – is
Within our power
        Emily Dickinson

Contents

Prologue

February 2021

'How much – how little – is within our power,' wrote Emily
Dickinson in her beautiful poem 'In this short Life'. I keep a
scrappy little cut-out of it taped to my computer and looked
at it every single day during the writing of this book, like a
guiding light. It was a shoe-in for the epigraph. Even though
it was written almost 150 years ago, it succinctly observes
what I was writing about: the compulsion to control each and
every tentacle of our lives and, as a result, to spend more time
weighing up our choices than actually living them.

There is an irony to writing a book about choice just before a
worldwide pandemic made us feel like all our choices had been
stripped away. How could we have *decision fatigue* when there
were no decisions to make? But this is the great hoax of the
pandemic. We are making more decisions than ever before,
because the way we did everything – even the most basic
things – has been obstructed. You no longer take your kids to
school, or hug your mum. It takes an entire afternoon to run
minor errands: the queues at Sainsbury's are like going to see
Robbie Williams at Knebworth; the post office has become an
easyJet counter in August. The result is a constant and frenzied
re-routing; each of us like Google Maps in a dead-end. What is
left is the flatbread of choice, unleavened by details: what to

eat, what to believe in, how to breathe. Without the distractions we used to rely on, we are left with only ourselves.

In the beginning, there was an attempt to use the situation to find common ground. There were some memorably lofty endeavours, most famously actress Gal Gadot's Hollywood sing-a-long of John Lennon's 'Imagine', which seemed to unite people not in harmony, but in their dislike for the montage. Debates raged across social media about *who had it worse*. Was it the parents home-schooling, exhausted and stressed but surrounded by miniature people they love; or the person living alone, with all the time in the world to binge Netflix, but wreathed in loneliness? Those in cities, in smaller homes but with proximity to other people; or those in the countryside, physically isolated but with plenty of fresh air and green space? Such comparisons were pointless, amounting to a straw man. 'The misery is very precisely designed, and different for each person, and if you didn't know better you'd say the gods of comedy and tragedy had a hand in it,' wrote Zadie Smith of (our first) lockdown in *Intimations*. The debates very rarely centred on those who actually did have it worse: the immuno-supressed, isolating even between lock-downs; women locked in with violent partners; the single mother with one tablet to home-school five children. We are not in the same boat. We are not even in the same sea.

In the course of one day, news outlets would dizzyingly flip-flop between optimistic entreaties that we were 'almost there' and proclamations that we have 'years of this left'. It made me feel like I was living in a version of Katy Perry's 'Hot N Cold'. I stopped buying the papers for the first time in thirteen years and avoided the news on the telly. I put up my blinkers – some-thing I had always cautioned against, no matter how bad the news cycle was. But how could anyone absorb all this uncer-tainty, multiple times a day, without spiralling? 'The special trouble with uncertainty is that it's a doorway to infinity,' wrote the human-behaviour expert Oliver Burkeman. 'When you've no idea what tomorrow will bring, it's easy to fill that gap with fantasy, and the world of fantasy knows no bounds. It's possible to imagine things getting limitlessly bad.' I'd felt myself teeter shortly after having my second baby and, having come through a mercifully brief period of post-natal depression, I couldn't afford to teeter again. I know I'm not alone. I know people spiralling so fast that they have become human helixes: just a whirr where bone and flesh once were. Those who were not religious found themselves grappling for a belief system, in the hope it would bring them answers. I looked to the sky for my conviction – a sort of mystical take on pathetic fallacy. If it rained, we had a while longer to go before All This was over. If the sun shone, I felt change was afoot.

'We're grieving the world we have lost,' says the psychiatrist David Kessler, a collaborator of Elisabeth Kübler-Ross who founded the not-uncontroversial grieving model, the Five Stages of Grief. 'Everything has changed. And change is actually grief – grief is a change we didn't want,' he notes. To those who have lost loved ones, this talk of a collective, shared grief was jarring. Several close friends of mine lost immediate family during lockdowns and bearing witness to their devastation, I realised the importance of language around grief. The psychotherapist Julia Samuel suggests the term 'living losses', to differentiate between the loss of a life, and that of a life*style*. 'But you cannot qualify loss,' she caveats. 'We can't ever tell someone how great or small their loss is.' Grief and loss are subjective, and the knowledge of what other people were going through made many feel guilty to be struggling at all. To some people, the pandemic has been an inconvenience. To others, it has been earth-shattering. It is not up to us to decide for whom it is one, or the other.

There was recently a flurry over the story of a Japanese man who rented himself out 'to do nothing'. For £70 you can rent him for a meal, where he will eat, drink and give simple responses. He isn't a friend, he clarifies, but he can ease your loneliness. It should be noted that he is in extremely high demand. Like tears on a clown, this story is both absurd and devastating. A social crisis distilled into one dining companion for rent. For some people, the mere presence of another body can ease loneliness. But loneliness is not just a personal feeling, born of physical objects. It is also a political issue; a social crisis. It comes from feeling disempowered, voiceless and purposeless. However many wonderful incidences of local social cohesion we have seen, like Clap For Our Carers, community grocery shopping and pandemic heroes such as Marcus Rashford and Captain Tom, there are those who have had their already deprived lives reduced further. Those who had been abandoned socially and politically before the pandemic, and who will continue to be alone after. Individuals, but institutions too. It is wonderful that Captain Tom raised £33m for the NHS before he passed away, but he should not have had to. (Long before the pandemic, my GP wept to me that his NHS surgery was 'a sinking ship'; the clapping is lovely, said my midwife sister, but being able to pee during a shift or park for free in the hospital car park would be even better.) It is wonderful that Marcus Rashford raised over £20m to fund free meals for schoolchildren, but he should not have had to. (Even then, this not-insignificant amount could only go so far. A free school meal plan consisting of little more than a Frube and half a pepper, will be a sorry symbol of this year.) There were wonderful things, but their very existence could also make your blood boil.

A number of scientific studies argue for the idea of emotional contagion – that we mimic the emotional behaviour of those around us. On my daily walk, I'd spy friends engaging in short, feverish bursts of conversation at a two-metre distance. Eyes bugging, bodies jittering, like two tectonic plates moving away from another, they had lost the ease with which they once conversed. It was laughably dramatic and yet we all did it. It was not just Covid that was catching, but low mood too.

Strong relationships became more important than ever, but they faced their own challenges. Friendship works best in tandem, when one is a little more up (to pep) and the other is a little more down (to be pepped). So what happens when *everybody* is frazzled, *everybody* is weary, and *everybody* is frightened? Who the heck props up whom? Loneliness can bond people together, but it can pull us apart. When everyone needed each other the most, a lot of people felt neglected. It can take a lot less than a pandemic to throw that balance off; an actual pandemic, it turns out, can bring clashing friendship codes to breaking point. 'He wants to break lockdown because he is low,' one friend despaired to me. 'And I'm low *because* people are breaking lockdown.' But amid the confusion, there was also new-found clarity: When you were shattered, who picked up the pieces? Who did you help put back together? Who do you want to walk this scorched earth with?

It will take years, perhaps decades, to metabolise the last year. The pandemic will leave not so much scars but craters, etched into the DNA of future generations. (For the twin babies born in the Indian state of Chhattisgarh last March, named Covid and Corona, it is a literal nameplate.) I'm wary of the entreaty for us all to 'learn something from this', even if on a personal level the opportunity to retreat allowed me to attend to my mental health and consider the ways in which I was navigating this so-called life. The painful reality is that many people may never recover from what the pandemic has wrought. But social truths have inevitably been laid bare: that key and care workers are woefully underpaid and overworked, that women are disproportionately impacted not just due to 'shecession' – globally, women's job losses are 1.8 times that of men – but also because they shoulder the majority of care work. I do not know what the future holds because, for the first time ever, I refuse to slip into the skin of future me. I feel almost aggressively present – rooted somewhere I haven't inhabited since I was a child. 'To come' is a land I no longer allow myself to stroll to. I was humbled by the words of writer and artist Josie George, confined to her home due to illness long before the rest of us became locked down – and without the respite of park walks and supermarket trips. 'I have learned not to treat life as a waiting room,' she writes. 'Instead, I look at this new day in front of me.'

No sane person would wish for Covid, but now it's happened, perhaps we should use this moment to take stock. We are not psychologically, emotionally or cognitively able to keep up with the frenetic pace of this modern world we have created. Just because it is *possible* to do things or to live a certain way doesn't mean we have to. Doesn't mean we should. Not everyone lives with their heart in their mouth – overwhelmed with decisions, pressured to have an opinion on things they don't know, multi-tasking every minute, constantly feeling like they are getting it wrong – but many do. This book is for those of you that do.

Many people ask me what I would have written differently had I known what was coming. The answer is everything and nothing. At first, I was worried that reading this book might feel like you were being trolled with a version of your former life. But I hope that with a critical distance, we are more able to assess some of the ways in which we lived. To think about what served us, and to live lives that may serve us better. 'Approach the future with fervent curiosity, not with an ideology of the future,' writes entrepreneur Margaret Heffernan, but with questions. 'What do we do now? What do we need to *be* now? What must we preserve at all cost?' I don't know what 'normal' means, but let's not go back to it. Instead, let's think about where we could go instead. Above all, let's be ambitious – not with our optimism, but with our hope.

'"Hope" is the thing with feathers –' wrote Dickinson. 'That perches in the soul – And sings the tune without the words – And never stops – at all –'

Introduction

It is a surprisingly hot Easter Sunday when I begin writing this book. From my desk, I observe passers-by caught off-guard by the April heatwave – mottled legs, self-consciously stripped of their winter casings, roam free in outfits better suited to the Med: embroidered smocks, booty shorts. I am wearing leggings with a tasteful rip at the groin, an oversized T-shirt and furry clogs. I have been alone in the house for two days – my baby, at her grandparents'; my phone, on airplane mode – before I venture out into the sunshine. 'You are wearing your slippers,' notes the cashier at the newsagent. Easter brings a dip in business; I am his entertainment for the day. 'I am not wearing my slippers,' I correct him. 'They *look* quite slippery, I grant you, but look at their ridged rubber bottoms,' I continue, plonking a clog up on his counter. 'They are outside shoes.' And then I trot home in my inside-outside shoes – a strangely singular figure on this celebratory weekend – the happiest or, rather, the most content (because they are *not* the same thing) that I have been for a long time.

There is no specific reason why I feel so content today. Why I am alone, but not lonely. Possibly it's because everything is quiet and the weather is lovely, I am free of responsibility and enjoying writing. Possibly I just woke up on the right side of the bed. Who knows? And yet we live in a world where we expect to know everything about ourselves, like hyper-vigilant self-guards, in order to live our *most optimal* lives. As a generation, we've been rushing towards this moment since we could walk. We grew up alongside the positive psychology movement of the '90s, also known as the study of 'the good life', telling us that the key to happiness lies within. We were raised by boomer parents and the constant reminder that, unlike them, we have So Much Choice. We were safe in the knowledge the ceiling had been broken and that we had all the tools at our disposal. We can be whoever we want to be! And yet there is a widespread feeling of restlessness among millennial women. Like something is not quite adding up. Like we might be getting life wrong.

The *paradox of choice* is a theory coined by the psychologist Barry Schwartz to describe how choice has become just as much a straitjacket as a liberation. 'The official dogma of all Western industrial societies runs like this,' he says. 'The more choice people have, the more freedom they have. And the more freedom they have, the more welfare they have.' Having no choice is unbearable, he writes in his book of the same name, but having too much choice can be dizzying, especially when it's over things that shouldn't matter. No one's life was ever improved by 175 different salad dressings, or scrolling through 88 pages of black dresses.

Schwartz's theory feels especially significant for millennial women, brought up thinking that 'since choice is good, it's only good'. That with maximum choice comes maximum chance of getting life right. More economic, psychological and social freedom – hard-fought for by previous generations – has led to an overall better quality of life for the vast majority of us. But for many women, it has also led to conflicting pressures: we can work full-time, but we are also still assumed to be the primary care-givers; we are free from retro beauty standards and yet the avenues to self-improvement have intensified through the lenses of wellness, surgery and social media. Rather than being satisfied with what Schwartz calls 'the good enough', we are vulnerable to a socially enforced perfectionism. Success has always been relative (recall the fable about the farmer who, on finding his only cow dead, prayed to God for his neighbour's cow to also die). The difference is now we no longer compare ourselves with our peers past whom we stroll, but the perfect strangers past whom we *scroll*. A whopping 83% of women say that social media negatively impacts their self-esteem. *Quelle surprise*. We are drowning in a sea of *comparisonitis*. As we splash in the lives of others, options begin to feel like obligations. The adage 'strive for progress, not perfection' has been flipped on its head. In the *Goop Lab* documentary, Gwyneth Paltrow, queen of self-polishing, unwittingly sums up the pressure we feel to eternally strive for something better: 'You only get one life, so why not milk the shit out of it?' she crows delightedly.

With more choice, the parameters for what makes a good life – and what makes a good *woman* – narrow. The grey area is too large to navigate and so we tread the familiar, claustrophobic ground that has dogged women for centuries. I was struck with this realisation when I participated in a Radio 4 segment about the row between Coleen Rooney and Rebekah Vardy (a pop culture moment dubbed 'Wagatha Christie'). The presenter, Paddy O'Connell, chastised me for being 'too equivocal'. We were talking about two women and so obviously I had to pick a side. Was I *for* Rebekah, or *for* Coleen? Who was *right* and who was *wrong*? This is not to throw shade at O'Connell – black-and-white morality, particularly when it comes to young women, is consistently reinforced. And I think *that* is where our disconnect comes from. Women have been told for so many years that either they are the right type of woman or the wrong type of woman; that they have the right set of opinions or the wrong

3

set of opinions; and so with what seems a surfeit of choice (and avocados), comes a sort of confidence collapse.

As someone with considerable privilege – able-bodied, white, privately educated, married with children – I clearly do not face all the same struggles as other millennial women. This book is a subjective piece of work, written by a Middling Millennial (I was born in 1987), not a finite conclusion on What Millennial Women Want. Many of the anxieties I write about are, somewhat inevitably, middle-class anxieties. If you struggle to feed your children or can't afford the bus fare, then you likely do not give a toss about wellness or WhatsApp or what you are wearing. But the global middle class is a socio-economic group growing at tremendous speed, comprising more than half the world's population. Worrying about the kind of life you lead is a privilege, to be sure; but it is not a niche concern. It is one that many women, in their many different circumstances, share. 'Am I living the right life? I'm as filled with anxiety as anyone else,' said Zadie Smith last year, in a live conversation with fellow novelist Diana Evans.

The problem with writing about a specific generation is that there can be a tendency to write about their worries as if they are the first generation to have them. Spoiler alert: the struggles millennial women face are no different to the struggles women in previous generations faced. Their *form* is different (we are no longer fighting for the vote, for example, but for parity in the workplace) but their *intention* is the same: to have a purpose, to feel valued, to seek contentment. As Betty Friedan said in *The Feminine Mystique*, a book about the restlessness of 1960s suburban housewives, it is the responsibility of every generation to sift through the weeds. To look at the lives we are living and to think about how they serve us.

This book is my attempt to sift through the weeds. To analyse the tools we use and have pressed upon us in order to navigate the effluvia of modern life. And how, in our various attempts to make life easier for ourselves, we often make it harder. Virginia Woolf wrote in *A Room of One's Own*, 'I thought how unpleasant it is to be locked out; and I thought how it is worse, perhaps, to be locked in.' I see this as a reminder to resist complacency and impotency by keeping clear-eyed about the choices that we want to make, and those that do not matter. This book does not offer answers. It won't help you nail *the right life*, assembling pieces as if it were a Pinterest board. But I hope that by asking the right questions, we can start to find comfort and cohesion in the good enough.

The Dream Catchers

There is only one corner of the universe you can be certain of improving, and that's your own self.

Aldous Huxley

I.

We called them *the dream catchers*. Stretched out across the white sands of Tulum beach like Instagram ideals, they looked the definition of health and wealth. The deeply tanned women in delicate swimwear, coiled into yogic positions; the men all loose curls and layered silver pendant necklaces. They were from New York (or Central America *via* New York), wore their iPhone chargers around their wrists like friendship bracelets (because your phone and body can be charged simultaneously) and spoke in languorous Spanglish: 'I'll take that *con gowacka-molayyyy*. We'll eat it on the *plyahhhhh*.' They represented a moneyed elite who alternate gong baths and green juices with cocaine and Botox. This hypocrisy is the key to Tulum's appeal. As local businesswoman Melissa Perlman says, 'They drink their water and eat their salads and get their dose of feeling like they're in balance, then they go and get toasted.'

We'd been looking for somewhere to spend two weeks of doing nothing with our baby daughter, and Instagram told me Tulum was the place. The reality was we were about ten years too late. The Caribbean town on Mexico's Yucatán Peninsula has transformed from a rustic seaside idyll into a key destination on the 'wellness tourism' map. It is an expensive and bountiful centre of modern wellness – and a gigantic EDM festival. All-night syncopated beats have been given an *ohm*-over of pseudo-spirituality, so that DJs are now 'shamans' and dance parties are 'rituals', as Reeves Wiedeman puts it for *The Cut*. (The minimal house music sounded less shamanic than it did, well, exactly the same as the minimal house music that plagued my university days in the late noughties.) As I wandered down the beach early each morning, my daughter wriggling in her sling, groups of partygoers would wave and coo at her. Everyone wants to see a baby when they haven't been to bed. Babies give the illusion of wholesomeness, as if the world is on your side. A bit like wellness.

Welcome to Wellness Inc., an industry worth $4.2 trillion worldwide and growing twice as fast as the global economy, according to the Global Wellness Institute. Wellness is not the same thing as health. Health feels rudimentary (the absence of major sickness) while wellness is *exceptional*. In 1959, the doctor Halbert Dunn defined wellness as 'a holistic approach to health, encompassing physical, mental, social, cultural and spiritual dimensions'. In his book *High Level Wellness*, Dunn described wellness as being just as much about family, community and the environment as it is about the self: 'an exchange between the inner and the outer world'. Social wellness, he wrote, cannot exist in one group if it does not exist in another. Sixty years later and wellness has become a class-cue. It has turned inward and upward.

As I watched this glossy posse shuffle their oils and elixirs on the beach, I started thinking about how *nebulous* the concept of wellness is. Under the guise of self-help, self-improvement or – the latest buzzphrase – *self-optimisation*, wellness now comprises anything and everything that makes us look and feel good, or like we are good people (which have become one and the same). At the heart of wellness lies the equally vague concept of self-care, which refers to the talismans, tinctures, rituals and therapies that preserve and/or restore our mental and physical zen. These range from the ancient to the frankly dystopian. 'Yoga in the park is wellness. Yoga at work is wellness. Yoga in Times Square is peak wellness,' writes Taffy Brodesser-Akner for the *New York Times*. 'When people give you namaste hands and bow as a way of saying thank you ... So is: SoulCycle, açaí, antioxidants, the phrase "mind-body," meditation, the mindfulness jar my son brought home from school, kombucha, chai, juice bars, oat milk, almond milk, all the milks from substances that can't technically be milked, clean anything. "Living your best life." "Living your truth." Crystals.'

It is also: jade eggs up your noony, BulletProof coffee, celery juice, transcendental orgasms, turmeric lattes, pink Himalayan salt lamps, activated charcoal, kefir, gratitude journals, colouring books, detox cleanses, face masks, perineum sunning, placenta pills, chia seeds, matcha powder, selenite wands, alkaline water, raw water, rose quartz water, the water consciousness movement. Oh, and: oxygen therapy, cryochambers, flotation therapy, infra-red saunas, pillow spray, mindfulness apps, massage, CBD oil, standing on your head, anything prefixed by 'green' or 'raw', forest bathing, dry bathing, bath salts, gong baths, sound baths, bubble baths, running a bath, just *looking at* the bath.

Observing the wellness elite in their only-sort-of-natural habitat of Tulum™ became my holiday obsession. My name for them came from the early-noughties fondness for dream catchers that cost a tenner from Ebay (hung above your bed to complement your lava lamp and your inflatable chair – it was a dicey time for interior design trends). Removed from their Native American spiritual origins, these dream catchers became flimsy protectors; wisps of cheap beads and synthetic feathers. In Tulum, wellness was similarly fluttering in the warm breeze. Inoffensive and ineffective. *'Do people really believe in the power of a sound bath?'* I whispered feverishly to my husband. Can an oat-free diet and rearranging your pretty pink crystals like they're Pogs cancel out the Botox and cocaine? It wasn't just Tulum, either – back home, wellness was flourishing even in the humble supermarket. Morrisons and Lakeland now sell kombucha (Lakeland also sells a kit to make your own), while Sainsbury's has an entire wellness aisle. Wellness feels like the manifestation of everything we have been heading towards: a seven-chakra band-aid to cover our fears, desires and unedifying habits. Am I the only one not drinking the green Kool-Aid?

II.

'You're all here because you're misfits,' declared the comedian-cum-holistic guru Russell Brand at the 2018 Wellspring Festival in Palm Springs, California. 'You wouldn't be here if there wasn't something you're trying to fix, now would you?' At the heart of wellness is deficiency. The idea that we are broken, suffering from a sort of *neurasthenia* – a nervous exhaustion caused by the stress of modern, urban life, where symptoms include tiredness, aches and irritability. Though it dates back to the nineteenth century, it's not unlike the way we feel today, writes the political economist William Davies. We need fixing and wellness tells us that this fix can come from within, if we find the right tools, or listen to the right gurus. Self-optimisation challenges the idea that we are trapped in our own bodies – instead, our bodies can be upgraded like smartphones, if we just commit to the change. By 2030 we will all be 'regularly going into body shops for upgrades', insists the transhumanist campaigner Zoltan Istvan. This reminds me of an advert shown in North America in 2017 for the '5-hour ENERGY' drink, which showed people going about their day with little red battery icons hovering above their heads. Once they downed the energy shot, their charge zoomed up to a full green battery alongside the peppy tagline 'Because isn't life better at 100%?' *Is* life better at 100%? It sounds exhausting. What are the consequences of living – or of trying to live – a fully optimised life?

Self-optimisation is about tweaking yourself so that you can operate harder or faster, while self-care is about taking time to recharge and restore your body. Recently, our leisure time has taken on a political dimension. You must have something shiny and bright to show for how you spend your time and that something is you – so that self-care is now the *key* to self-optimisation. Self-care isn't a new concept, but for millennials it carries a new-age aspiration that wasn't a part of the self-care of, say, Apple inventor Steve Jobs, who liked to relieve stress by soaking his feet in the loo. (Not even his *own* loo, either – he'd do it in the company bogs.)

According to the Pew Research Center, millennials spend twice as much as boomers on self-care (including gym memberships, diet plans and therapy). Modern self-care comes in many forms: basic and homely (a warm cuppa); highfalutin biotechnology (a freezing cryo chamber); and hippie-dippie hogwash (rose quartz water). Such a vague definition serves us well. It means we can include under the wellness umbrella 'nearly any activity people use to calm, heal and preserve themselves in the face of adversity', writes André Spicer, the co-author of *The Wellness Syndrome*. There are plenty of challenges facing us right now – the housing crisis, the mental health crisis, the political crisis – but the 'obstacle' that modern self-care often addresses is minuscule. That being tired, for instance, can be overcome with the 'self-care ritual' of taking a long bubble bath.

The dictionary defines 'selfish' as 'for one's individual profit or pleasure'. It could very well also describe modern self-care, which is frequently thrown around as a Get Out of Jail Free card. 'Doing it for my self-care' has become a phrase that makes anyone challenging your choices cruel and unfeeling. Cancelling on someone an hour before you are meant to meet doesn't make you a shitty friend, but a woman who is *prioritising her self-care*. Or, as a user called @AnnieKNK quipped on Twitter, we 'use self-care language to justify increasingly sociopathic behaviour'. Don't get me wrong, prioritising self-care over socialising is not necessarily a bad thing. In the last few years, I've set much-needed boundaries in the name of self-care. While writing this book, I think of nothing but writing, mothering and self-care – ordering in food so I don't have to cook; taking muscle-soak bubble baths; ignoring my entire social life so I can focus. In this instance, self-care is a justifiable expense because it allows me to continue to monetise my *own* output as seamlessly and efficiently as possible – it is both profit *and* pleasure. That self-care and the self as a marketable product are related is a crucial pillar of Western wellness.

Since Google appointed its own mindfulness motivator, Chade-Meng Tan (aka the 'Jolly Good Fellow') in 2013, wellness has gradually become a part of corporate workspaces, with many companies holding wellness retreats (although there is a question mark over the 'wellbeing' of a compulsory 'retreat' that takes place over a weekend). Various universities in the US – such as the American University in Washington, DC – have introduced wellness contracts to encourage students to self-regulate. There are wellness summits – like the aforementioned Wellspring Festival, costing $1,000 for the weekend – and wellness residences – such as the Delos building in Manhattan, which features a 'posture-supportive flooring system' and focuses on the 'core wellness principles' of, erm, air, water, light and sleep. The penthouse apartment is currently on sale for $26 million. In these instances, wellness simply means: extremely expensive.

This cost sits at the heart of moneyed Western wellness. It is impossible to talk about wellness without namechecking Goop, Gwyneth Paltrow's 'aspirational lifestyle brand', valued at $250 million in 2018. It is both the greatest advocate and the darkest spectre of the wellness industry – depending which end of the yoga mat you lotus at. Goop started in 2008 as a newsletter about cleanses and detoxes and yoga – now Basic Wellness 101. Over the next decade, Goop – like wellness itself – blossomed into an ideology. Goop's biggest export is that wellness is something that money can buy; that, as Amanda Mull writes in *The Atlantic*, 'having nice things and being a good person are achieved through the same means'. There are stores (I went to its fragrant London location last week and cooed over a £550 dress) and festivals and a podcast and a Netflix docuseries – which I devoured, alternately bemused (watching a woman have an on-screen orgasm) and mystified (cold therapy to unlock trauma) by what Paltrow, clad in a roster of chic, tactile outfits and gold jewellery, calls the 'healing modalities'. Goop has launched dozens of wellness trends into the mainstream marketplace and not without controversy. In 2018, it was fined $145,000 for making 'unsubstantiated claims' about the benefits of inserting jade and quartz eggs into the vagina (which it said could balance hormones, regulate periods and improve bladder control) and the Inner Judge Flower Essence Blend (which it claimed could cure depression).

It is hard not to be cynical about the scores of wellness trends that aim to unify the 'mind-body' while actually unifying the holistic and the commercial. Take the Californian retreat of Esalen, which birthed the 'human potential' movement in the '60s, and has hosted visitors including Aldous Huxley, Bob Dylan and Joni Mitchell. Writing about it, Andrew Marantz recalls an episode of *Mad Men*, where 'Don Draper sits, cross-legged and ill at ease, on the Esalen lawn. He closes his eyes, relaxes, and smiles. Has he achieved satori? Not even close. He has used his mental clarity to think up a new way to sell sugar water.' Perhaps Draper felt better after visiting Esalen. More importantly, he felt richer.

III.

Take a raisin in your hand. Look at it. No, *really look at it*. From all angles. Observe its raisiny … raisin-ness. Try and ignore the fact that your palm is getting sticky. Sniff the raisin. Inhale its mildly sweet raisin smell. Trail your fingers over its teeny-tiny wrinkly body. Don't stop thinking about the raisin for one second. Nothing exists in this moment except you and the raisin. After several minutes of raisin love, put it slowly in your mouth. Savour every single morsel of this dried fruit. Focus on the flavour. Chew until that raisin is no more. And then think about how you felt doing all that.

The Raisin Consciousness is perhaps the most famous and mockable form of mass-marketed mindfulness. Devised by the psychologist Jon Kabat-Zinn, it is an exercise to get you to focus on the present, without distraction. Kabat-Zinn first introduced his theory of Mindfulness Based Stress Reduction (MBSR) in the 1970s, after he noticed that our 'entire society is suffering from attention deficit disorder'. In the last decade, concerns about our diminishing attention spans have bloomed into an anxiety epidemic, with the practice of mindfulness growing in response. Stress-busting has moved beyond something to read about (although there are hundreds of thousands of books on mindfulness, should you be so curious) into something you access on your smartphone. There are currently 280 mindfulness apps in the iTunes store, most notably Headspace and Calm – worth £255 million and £787 million respectively. It feels ironic that the cure for our tech-addled anxiety could lie in an app. The founder of Headspace, Andy Puddicombe, calls it 'unplugging by plugging in' – which feels aligned with the contradiction of wellness.

Modern mindfulness has its critics. Many question Kabat-Zinn's secularisation and commodifying of Buddhist *dharma*, or teachings. Ron Purser, the author of the brilliantly brutal *McMindfulness*, notes that the mass-marketing of Buddhist practice wouldn't be tolerated with any other religion: imagine taking something from Jewish culture and then selling it as something made much better without any of the 'mumbo jumbo' of Jewishness. Stripped of the 'moral worldview' of Buddhism, writes David Forbes, mindfulness doesn't provide a way out of human suffering – it is just a tool to muddle through. But is there anything wrong with that? Don't we all want to get better at coping with modern life? Isn't acceptance a pretty key part of human happiness? Buddhist monks themselves disagree on this. The American monk Bhikkhu Bodhi warns that without 'sharp social critique', Buddhist practices risk 'becoming a reinforcement of consumer capitalism'. On the other hand, Gelong Thubten, author of *A Monk's Guide to Happiness*, warns of detaching mindfulness from compassion but sees no great harm in the secularising of Buddhist principles. 'Are we to exclude people from discovering the benefits of a calm mind?' he writes to me.

Mindfulness, like other meditative activities such as reading and yoga, is presumed to lower your cortisol and reduce stress. Neuroscientific research has shown that mindfulness positively modulates the impact of external experiences of the brain, though we need to be wary of grandiose claims of 'brain rewiring'. 'As if anyone could reach directly into their own moist brain tissue and "resculpt" it in a calmer, more attentive direction,' scoffs Barbara Ehrenreich, a writer and political activist, and the author of *Natural Causes*.

I like the sound of mindfulness – my mother once said that the only thing more exhausting than raising me must be *being* me – but something seems to stop me from embracing it. I've had Headspace on my phone for nearly two years and have never opened it, not even in my most frantic moments. Perhaps that in itself is proof that I need mindfulness more than ever. My flow is clearly off. Or is it my chi? While writing this, I receive an email out of the blue from the cognitive hypnotherapist Jessica Boston, who offers me a complimentary mindfulness session. Boston specialises in harnessing your unconscious to help you separate what you think of yourself from what others think of you (something I'm not very good at). I spend two peaceful hours horizontal on her sofa, stroking her tiny dog as she calmly encourages me to imagine a house where all the rooms are in different states. Some are beautifully finished while others are wrecked – crooked pictures, blown lights, mangy carpets. She tells me to move through the house gradually, spending an equal amount of time in each of the rooms; to see the house (spoiler: the house is my mind) as a work in progress, rather than something that runs flawlessly in all areas.

After the session, Boston sends me an eleven-minute recording for me to listen to twice a day. She talks me through the house, with a bit of colour therapy thrown in on the side. I like the recording. She has a nice, reassuring voice. And yet in a month, I have listened to it only once. I have no idea why – except that I seem to forget. Of course, forgetting is not coincidental. We forget the things we don't prioritise. So even at a time when I really need mindfulness, I just can't commit to it. I hold some disbelief – most likely inherited from my pragmatic mother – about how much power I have over my mind, or body, or mind-body. I am like a bloated spider, dangling off the web of the dream catcher, convinced that it is too fragile to bear my weight.

IV.

The wellness dream catcher is a filigree which shimmers from a distance, but up close is riddled with loose threads – tug at one and the whole thing comes loose. Wellness presents itself as forward-thinking – with its wearable gizmos and performance apps – and yet it is based on one of the oldest principles of patriarchy: that women are dirty and that a woman's virtue depends on being perfect inside as well as outside. Juice cleanses and other self-care rituals aim to scrub us filthy femmes pristine, bringing purity and benediction. 'Not only is this bad feminism,' gynaecologist and Goop critic Jen Gunter told the *Guardian*, 'it's bad science.' Nothing challenges the myth of women being 'clean' more than birth: an act which quite literally turns you inside out. Thought you'd never shit in front of your beloved? Yeah, me too.

We live in a society that fetishises emptiness. The ideal body is a scooped-out temple. First came colonic irrigation (Princess Diana was supposedly a fan) and then the Squatty Potty: a stool that angles you into a pooposition that causes less strain for a more fulsome crap. The potty is proof that even ablution can be done in a more efficient, leaner way. 'The implicit notion seems to be that ridding ourselves of "bad" foods, unthoughtful thoughts and every last pellet of faeces can help us achieve not only health, but something approaching a state of purity,' writes Alex Blasdel about the potty's phenomenal success (more than 5 million were sold between 2011 and 2018). 'Elimination is love,' proclaimed the actor Bryan Cranston, somewhat bafflingly.

Cleanliness is next to godliness, but my generation increasingly identifies as agnostic (52% in 2017 compared to 31% in 1983), which leaves us seeking new belief systems and new ways of redeeming ourselves. The psychologist Jean Twenge – author of *Generation Me*, a book about millennial narcissism – argues that we reject religion because of individualism (there's no 'I' in 'we'!), but I disagree. I think a lot of women struggle with religion because it fails to support so many of our rights, particularly those around family planning. Wellness offers an alternative to religion: devotion without divinity. A community, a sense of purpose and a belief system free from dogma and doctrine. Except, of course, it isn't – no mass-marketed enterprise can be. 'Wellness comes with its own set of doctrines that decree how certain lifestyle behaviours enable wellness disciples to ascend to enlightened wellbeing,' notes the science writer Maxine Ali.

Instead of religion, many women are moving towards heterodoxy – where you combine your own set of spiritualities. I am about as likely to go for a crystal reading as I am to have a coffee enema, but a surprising number of my friends are into astrology, tarot readings and all things woowoo. 'I love them, but not as a couple – *they're both Leos*,' a friend sighed recently. Another told me that she goes to a psychic once a year, in order to be reassured that her choices and desires are valid. 'I pay her to agree with me; to tell me that I can have everything that I want.' That says a lot about the kind of comfort and validation we crave. Heterodoxy is a key part of our paradox of choice. No need to place all of your (jade) eggs in one basket, when there are so many to try. In our 'on-demand' era, when we are encouraged to personalise every choice to make it *right for you* (with the capitalist subtext that what is right for you is also right for a lot of other people), it makes sense that we should have a hand in our destiny; that we can line up our crystals like we can line up our life goals. It offers an illusion of control, that everything is within reach, if we just pivot the right way. 'The minute the phrase "having it all" lost favor among women, wellness came in to pick up the pieces,' writes Brodesser-Akner. 'It was a way to reorient ourselves – we were not in service to anyone else, and we were worthy subjects of our own care.' But of course that is not true. We have pledged eternal servitude to self-improvement.

V.

Millennial women may be moving away from religion, but conventional medicine can also often leave us disappointed. Various studies have shown that women are less likely to be taken seriously in A&E than men; that they are less likely to be prescribed painkillers, and that when they are, they have to wait longer to receive them; and that they are more likely to be referred to psychologists for unexplained pain than given medical tests. In particular, women's reproductive organs are seen as shadowy and unpredictable (although, in response to this gender gap in healthcare, there has been a huge rise in both the diagnoses of and dialogue surrounding endometriosis and vulvodynia in the last few years), or even as something that works against them. A miscarriage being blamed on an 'inhospitable womb', for example, implies that a woman's own body is a hostile place. Women who struggle with fertility or fatigue or digestion go and see their doctor again and again and again, and they ache and they worry, and still they are told nothing is really wrong. It is easy to become dispirited when you can't find answers, and I think that's truer now than ever before, because we have been raised to see life as a series of questions that can be answered. 'You're tired, you're stressed, you're anxious, you've had a baby – *of course you feel depleted!*' say the doctors. '*It's normal!*' And yet, it doesn't feel like the *right* way to live. Not in the age of wellness.

Though it existed long before, quackery really took off in the nineteenth century, with the Dutch-named 'quacksalver' who peddled 'miracle' cures around a choleric Victorian London. Often made of opium, alcohol and/or honey, these tinctures gave a jolly buzz and did absolutely zilch (but the buzz ensured the customer returned to buy more). 'There is a current opinion among women, which every year causes the death of many young women – that acids, especially vinegar, are preventives of obesity,' wrote the French lawyer, politician and epicure Jean Anthelme Brillat-Savarin in 1861. 'I knew, in 1776, at Dijon, a young lady of great beauty … [who was] in the habit every day of drinking a large glass of vinaigre. She died at eighteen years of age, from the effects of these potions.' The 1858 Medical Register dramatically reduced health fraud, and yet ludicrous stories like this still take place. The Victorian quack has evolved into the millennial wellness grifter, who uses social media and a smiley, telegenic face to sell dubious health tips.

In 2017, the creator of the alkaline diet, Robert Young, was jailed after demanding $77,000 from British army officer Naima Houder-Mohamed in order to cure her breast cancer. He treated her on his 'pH Miracle Ranch' in the States, with a diet that included baking soda and avocado (which Young called 'God's butter'). She died two years after her treatment. In 2014, the Australian blogger Belle Gibson claimed she cured her multiple cancers through a regimented diet and alternative therapies. The self-proclaimed 'wellness guru' wrote in her book, *The Whole Pantry*, that she had been free of cancer for two years. Doubts started arising when her claims got loftier and she was unable to name any of the doctors who supposedly treated her. It turned out she'd never had cancer. Gibson was charged $AU410,000 for breaching consumer laws. Gibson's grifting was outrageous – the Fyre Festival of the wellness world – and it was certainly dangerous, yet it took an alarmingly long time for her to be busted.

Gibson was a proponent of the controversial Gerson Therapy – a cure for cancer invented by the physician Max Gerson in the 1950s, it involves a vegetarian diet, hourly juices and up to five coffee enemas a day. It was denounced almost immediately by the National Cancer Institute and Gerson eventually lost his medical licence. Yet many, sadly, still have faith in it. In February 2015, Gibson attended the funeral of another Australian wellness blogger, Jessica Ainscough (aka The Wellness Warrior), who died after attempting to cure her soft-tissue cancer with Gerson Therapy, among other alternative therapies. Her commitment to 'natural healing' over medical intervention (doctors advised her to undergo a complicated and disfiguring amputation of her arm, shoulder and shoulder blade) involved eating clay to 'detoxify' herself. Detoxification, which most frequently involves the sweating out of 'evil toxins', is a popular concept in wellness – and one vigorously contested by medical professionals, who maintain that the only effective form of detoxification is already taken care of by our liver and kidneys. What's even more devastating is that Ainscough was not the first woman in her family to fatally invest in Gerson Therapy. Her mother had died of breast cancer, two years before.

Where Gibson's cancer con differs from the vinegars of the nineteeth century is in its scale and the intensity with which it spread. *The Whole Pantry* made a whopping $1 million in book sales and app downloads before small rumblings turned into public inquiry. Unlike the title of 'dietician', 'nutritionist' is not yet protected (even for those with a robust, evidence-based practice) – so it is not hard to find welly-wallies making unfounded, ambitious claims on social media. I could shovel 'nutritionist' into my Insta bio tomorrow. This world of food fact and fiction is so shadowy that dieticians and scientists have created a hashtag with which to discredit wellness myths: #nutribollocks. The botanist James Wong regularly tweets pictures of gluten-free cakes adorned with toxic, non-edible flowers, with the wry hashtag #StaySafe. 'Reading that Gwyneth Paltrow's "clean beauty" regime means she starts every day with a refreshing glass of alkaline water + a spritz of lemon,' he wrote in 2019. 'Which makes the alkaline water no longer alkaline & highlights the magnificent level of BS that people will swallow from celebrities.'

In 2017, toxicology chemist Yvette d'Entremont wrote the boldly titled 'The "Food Babe" Blogger Is Full of Shit' for *Gawker*, after the food blogger Vani Hari warned her followers to stop ingesting chemicals. 'I wonder if anybody's warned her about good old dihydrogen monoxide? (AKA water),' seethed d'Entremont. Defendants argue that the science of food is not objective – even among themselves, dieticians often disagree. But the accessibility and wilderness of the internet – where science and gobbledygook co-exist on a level playing field – has led to an erosion of trust, where we simultaneously trust everyone and no one. When we scroll through the internet and social media, we don't read so much as spot keywords that function as positive reinforcement for our choices: good, well, health, happy, fulfilled. And isn't it tempting to believe that a 'Cosmic Ginger Rose Activated Charcoal Latte', devised and beautifully photographed by someone called Moon and Spoon and Yum, could pull toxins from the body, relieve indigestion, lower cholesterol levels *and* brighten teeth? Why deny yourself the joy of this 'healthy, flavorful brew' that comes complete with an Instagrammable petal-strewn surface?

The thing that often strikes me about my generation is that we are savvier and more cynical than ever – with a meticulous eye for wrongdoing and injustice – but we are also incredibly naive. We are *desperate* to believe that there is a universal cure for the incurable human condition. And that the solution may be available through ancient alternative elixirs of wellness rather than the scientific advances of medicine. That is not to say that alternative medicine does not work in some instances – and I would never tell anyone what they should or shouldn't have faith in – but rather that wellness plays into a dangerous purity myth where the good are well and the bad are ill. That sickness is retribution for moral failure, and that the 'good vibes' of wellness, notes Laura Thomas, nutritionist and author of *Just Eat It*, could cure you 'if you just try hard enough'.

VI.

In the 1970s, the French philosopher Michel Foucault coined the term *biopower* to refer to the ways in which capitalism encourages people to self-regulate and self-discipline their bodies to make them 'docile'. We like to think this kind of obligation has been eradicated by a neo-liberalist emphasis on personal choice over collective regulation. ('My body, my choice' is a common motto for the millennial woman.) But wellness *enforces* rather than liberates us from self-surveillance, so that there is now an extremely narrow script from which women may talk about their bodies. Despite the fact that up to 50% of women are trying to lose weight at any one time, a diet is now *persona non grata*. A woman who admits to wanting to be slimmer is seen as betraying the sisterhood, even if she has been medically advised to lose weight.

A recent survey revealed that two-thirds of young women hide their weight-loss plans, perhaps unsurprisingly, given that when the singer Adele lost three stone she was highly criticised for no longer being a body-positive role model, despite having lost weight through a balance of exercise and healthy eating. 'A woman's body is everyone's business but her own,' writes Brodesser-Akner. 'Even in our attempts to free one another, we are still trying to tell one another what to want and what to do. It is terrible to tell people to try to be thinner; it is also terrible to tell them that wanting to lose weight is hopeless and wrong.'

Any public attempts to hone your body should be done under the guise of health rather than anything as gauche as Kate Moss's infamous line, 'Nothing tastes as good as skinny feels'. This move towards 'clean eating' rather than dieting is particularly prevalent on social media: at the time of writing, the hashtag #cleaneating has over 45 million posts on Instagram. The link between social media and an obsession with healthy eating in women has been scientifically proven – a 2017 science paper by the registered nutritionist Pixie Turner revealed the shocking statistic that orthorexic tendencies were present in 49% of heavy users of Instagram, in comparison to 1% of the general population.

Orthorexia nervosa is an obsession with healthy eating. 'Sufferers may appear to friends as simply "a bit fussy" or, like me, as "health-conscious",' writes the author Scarlett Thomas. Thomas spent two decades obsessing over food trends and diet plans 'in search of the perfect hack for a good life': vegan, vegetarian, paleo (aka the caveman diet), keto (low-carb), raw food, sproutarian (seeds and raw veg), juicearian, macrobiotic (grains and beans), pegan (paleo combined with vegan), low-GI, low-carb, 16:8 (where you fast for sixteen hours of every twenty-four), the warrior diet (one meal a day). Thomas cultivated friendships based on storytelling and food obsessions, so that her quest became almost poetic: self-improvement through language as much as food. One macrobiotic friend would recommend listening to Shakespeare to anyone with heart trouble, 'because the iambic pentameter will stabilise you'.

It was as a teenager – when over a third of my classmates at an all-girls school developed an eating disorder – that I realised how fortunate I am to have a body I am largely content in. It's easy for me, with a socially accepted body type (slim), to dismiss food trends and fads. But I have witnessed body struggles my entire life: I am the only member of my family not to battle with their weight and be in a cycle of restriction and gorge. We never had snacks in the house when I was growing up, so that whoever was on a diet wouldn't feel tempted. I have seen the impact that not being able to buy clothes on the high street can have on a woman's psyche – the agony of feeling like if you could *just drop these pounds*, you might feel good about yourself. Might feel accepted. Might feel worthy of love. That these thoughts often come from women who are so obviously loveable no matter their clothing size, causes an ache deep in my bones.

The social critic and psychoanalyst Susie Orbach says that the only difference between the diet culture of 1978 – when she published her seminal book *Fat Is a Feminist Issue* – and now, is language. 'Instead of saying "this is going to make me thin," the language takes on an almost moral quality. We talk about purity, about "healthy," "natural" and "clean" foods. We use euphemisms (like saying we're undertaking a "transformation") to signify that we're going on a diet. But the effect, and the impact on us, is much the same.' Weight maintenance was much less cloak-and-dagger in the '70s – people used words like 'fat-free' and 'low-fat' and tended to mean what they said – while modern wellness is founded on the language of fortitude and feminism. Instead of talking about dress sizes and diets and shedding weight, we praise the benefits of a *strong* and *empowered* body.

Victoria's Secret supermodels – whose tanned, slender and toned bodies look exactly the same as they have for the past twenty years – now diligently share via social media and workout vlogs their desire for a 'strong body', which is athletic, they stress, *not* thin. There is no doubt that this is part of a PR strategy. During the pre-show interviews from Victoria's Secret catwalk shows past – an annual spectacle that cost over $26 million to execute and was axed last year due to the brand's 'pivot in marketing' (read: being out of date and haemorrhaging both sales and viewers) – beauty editors observed nervous models clutching notecards with empowered, feminist, motivational mottos prepared by the lingerie brand. A clear example of this change in rhetoric is the 2019 rebranding of Weight Watchers to WW (which doesn't stand for anything) and their new tagline, 'Wellness that Works'. Such fuzziness is fundamental to the success of wellness: it means that it can be marketed to everyone. It means everything and nothing.

In April 2019, Twitter CEO and biohacker Jack Dorsey revealed how he stayed 'performant' and 'clear': ice-cold baths, a standing desk and no food over the weekend. Dorsey is a fan of the ancient Greek philosophy of Stoicism, where you endure pain and hardship with no complaint. He embraces a sort of conspicuous asceticism, where one shows off their wealth not through cashmere and helicopters (so 2000) but extreme denial. Dorsey eats one meal a day, between 6.30 p.m. and 8.30 p.m. At the weekends, he eats nothing at all (water is allowed). Fasting is as old as mankind: the Ancient Greeks loved a fast, and the Ayurvedic diet, promoting better health for the mind and body, can be traced back to 6,000 BCE. Dorsey's fasting is not even the most extreme out there. The Himalayan Fast requires sixty consecutive hours – almost three days – of not eating; even the fast's own website warns that the diet is hard to sustain. No shit, Sherlock.

Fasting in itself is not necessarily bad. From testing carried out on mice, some experts believe that the 5:2 diet (where you eat normally for five days and consume a max of 500–600 kcal a day for two) *could* be sustainable and life-lengthening. But intermittent fasting is different from Dorsey's daily food deprivation, which instead reflects the gendered attitude towards diet culture and wellness. Dorsey was mocked when he posted about his biohacking, but imagine the fury that would have been levelled at him had he been a woman. The differing responses tap into the insidious idea that men can't possibly starve themselves because they are strong, not weak – a cultural myth that damages men as much as it does women. 'When teenage girls [fast] before prom, it's an eating disorder,' Virginia Sole-Smith, the author of *The Eating Instinct: Food Culture, Body Image, and Guilt in America*, told her Instagram followers. 'But when very rich Thin White Guys do it, it's … still a fucking eating disorder.' And so a new term has emerged for the caveman-meets-high-tech eating deprivation that occurs in Silicon Valley: techorexia.

Many of our new attitudes to food centre on the possibility of not having to eat at all. WeFast is a powder that promises you will live as long as possible, while meal replacement shakes Soylent and Huel are designed for those who see any kind of mess, time-wasting and chewing as an attack on their wellbeing. 'This home manufacturing center has been by far the most liberating thing to eliminate,' wrote Rob Rhinehart, the founder of Soylent, on his blog, about his decision to get rid of … his kitchen. Rhinehart isn't the first American to get rid of his home manufacturing centre – Carrie Bradshaw, after all, used her oven to store her sweaters. Plenty of people, including me, don't like cooking. But Rhinehart wants to do away with the pleasure of food entirely. Soylent, he says, comes in three different flavours (cacao, mocha, unflavoured) but its taste is not supposed to bring enjoyment. It is a 'utility', like water. 'There is a curious privilege in actively choosing not to eat,' writes Laura Thomas. 'While food banks across the UK are struggling to keep up with demand, swathes of people who have the resources to achieve adequate nutrition are giving food a hard pass.'

Since the dawn of time, my family have gathered around the gingham-clothed kitchen table every weekend for lunch at 2 p.m. When I was younger, I found it hugely irritating. I didn't always *want* to eat lunch at 2 p.m. (I still don't – I like to eat earlier.) I didn't always want to come back from a shopping trip or from a friend's house in order to attend an enforced family meal. Now, I have nothing but fondness for this special part of the day, where we eat 'as much food as one's hand can hold', to quote Samuel Johnson. A family meal is never just about the food, it's also about the emotional impact of all being together, grounded in ritual and routine. Recall Charles Dickens' Scrooge eating his 'melancholy dinner in his usual melancholy tavern', compared with the happy Christmas dinner of the poor but loving Cratchits. Meal times have a purpose beyond survival: the act of buying, preparing and consuming food is meditative and restorative in its repetition. How can we comfort or soothe ourselves when, rather than idling over a meal with those we love, we are downing a shake in the same time it takes to sneeze? And yet 'eating around a table' can be a form of elitism. For parents who work long or difficult hours (one in nine employees now works nights), sitting down together as a family is impossible. Public Health England's proposed ban on eating on public transport is a further example of this 'bias' from governing bodies, write the dieticians and authors of *Is Butter A Carb?*, Rosie Saunt and Helen West.

I find the homogenisation of wellness – as if we can a i afford to make the same choices; as if we even *want* to – equal parts infuriating and concerning, particularly when it comes to the demonisation of basic foodstuffs, like bread, pasta and cow's milk, which are cheap and easily accessible staples for many households. The most mainstream food trend is the avoidance of wheat. While writing this sentence, I receive a press release regarding the launch of a podcast about why 'we' can't 'stomach' bread any more, which is 'privileged pseudo-science', says Saunt – unless you have a diagnosed intolerance or coeliac disease. (How can anyone but you know what you can or can't 'stomach'?) With 29% of adults and 20% of children classified as obese in England, food is clearly a pressing political issue. But it is also a complex one, and it has much more in common with poverty than it does with the consumption of cow's milk. Social inequality cannot be saved by wellness – at least not in its current form.

The issue is not that Huel or Soylent are bad for you – the drinks can provide an 'affordable, nutritious, easy and potentially environmentally sustainable option to eat on-the-go', notes Saunt – but that they encourage an unhealthy workism. How long, I wonder, until companies offer free Huel to encourage employees to streamline their lunch-breaks? You can imagine it built into a corporate wellness contract: *We care about YOUR health, and we want to make sure that you consume all the nutrients you need to be a happy worker* ☺ . And when I use the word 'work', I don't just mean in the professional sense. I also mean the 'work' of the self, which carries an ethical and economic implication: that relentless self-improvement will endow you with the health and wealth of the Tuloonies. 'I suspect that next is "the sustainability diet" where we are encouraged to restrict our diet under the auspice of saving the planet,' notes Laura Thomas. While this motivation may be genuine for many, for others it way to moralise a diet so that we become better ... nd a better person – which, under the guise of ... s, are one and the same.

... on one end of the wellness spectrum we have the high- ... n biohackers of Silicon Valley, on the other end sits the homely 'earthiness' of the yoga-loving baby-mama of five who makes her own deodorant, drinks turnip chai and favours the crystal ball emoji (and shares all of it on social media). Politically, these two figures are poles apart, although both rely on the internet. One wants to make the entire world as efficient and lean as possible through saving time. The other believes that salvation comes in the *stilling* of time: a slowing of everything, from the making of our own toiletries to the rearing of children. But both embrace the notion of optimisation, in their conflicting ways, with an assumption that life, with its infections and toxins and flab, is *just not good enough*.

VII.

Lying under my Zzznest blanket, I feel like a goldfish stuck under the stones of its bowl. Every fidget is like ploughing through a bog barefoot. Heaving the blanket *off* and my heavily pregnant belly *out* of the bed for my hourly pee-breaks proves an almost insurmountable task. My restless legs are crushed by the velvety-soft elephant squatting across my chest and thighs. In the darkest moments of this physical oppression, I imagine the plush grey quilt with a trunk. It becomes a gladiatorial battle of wills, which hampers rather than facilitates my attempts to sleep. By the morning, the weighted blanket with its trillions of tiny glass beads lies pathetically across the floor like poured cement.

I feel deeply disappointed with my failure to 'respond' to my new quilt. Initially developed for autistic children with anxiety and sensory problems, it has proved tremendously popular as a sleep aid. The original weighted Gravity Blanket was named one of *Time*'s best inventions of 2018, and research has shown that it can reduce anxiety by a third through 'deep touch pressure' that can 'earth' or 'ground you'. The Gravity is a hefty £150, so I opted for a copycat, which arrived the next day in a box so solid my husband struggled to lug it up the stairs. 'I actually don't know if you'll ever get out of this,' he said presciently. Sleep specialists have compared it to being swaddled like a baby, or like receiving a very long hug. The problem is, I don't know anyone who could sleep in a hug all night long. And the idea of being mummified is terrifying. Babies are swaddled because of something called 'the fourth trimester' – the theory that they are born three months before they are ready to face the world (it's why they like being close to their mother's heartbeat: it makes them feel like they are still in the womb). Are anxious millennials stuck in an eternal fourth trimester? It's not a total stretch. After all, Freud compared sleep to being back in the womb.

The blanket was not my first rodeo into the world of sleep hacks. I'd already tried the basics – no screens at night, sleepy tea, a hot bath, ear plugs, white noise – as well as prescription pills. (Some sleep specialists dismiss pills as inducing 'junk sleep', but without them, I might as well be if not six, then at least three feet under.) After two years of on-off insomnia – at its worst, I slept for forty-five minutes and the next day felt both jacked up as if on amphetamines and fog-dog dead – I sometimes wake up nine or ten times a night, with a two- or three-hour dawn window during which I am wide awake. It is not uncommon for me to read an entire book in this time. I don't like sleep-tracking apps – what can they tell me, except that I haven't slept? *Which clearly I already know.* I'm suspicious of wearable tech (I've never been remotely tempted by a Fitbit, or a ring that can tell me when my phone is ringing), which meant that the Oura Ring sleep-tracker was out. I'd already tried, and then sold on eBay, the Lumie Bodyclock, which wakes you up with natural light rather than the harsh abruptness of an alarm. But my problem is never the waking up – it is the staying asleep.

To sleep is to dream; to dream is to escape. A vital part of the dream catcher's armoury – and perhaps the only part I am not cynical about – is to be well rested. Even the kooks and the trads agree on this: sleep replenishes the body more than any trendy tincture can (although I know many anecdotally testify to the efficacy of CBD – of which I have been sent vast amounts of press samples, but have not able to try when pregnant). It is an irony universally acknowledged that the more you seek the dreamscape, the more it eludes you. As the joke goes: the greatest cure for insomnia is sleep. It is a special kind of torture not to be able to sleep when you are extremely tired and everyone else is asleep. 'You'll sleep when you're really tired,' someone once told me. In fact, I've found the opposite to be true. For a long time, those who could not or chose not to sleep were revered for their resilience. Vladimir Nabokov dismissed sleepers as 'the most moronic fraternity in the world', and Margaret Thatcher and Ronald Reagan famously slept only four hours a night (incidentally, both died of Alzheimer's, which has been tentatively connected by neuroscientific research to a lack of sleep). Now, the morons are those of us who *don't* sleep.

Millennials are obsessed with sleep. You don't have to be an insomniac to want to talk about it all the time. We chase it, resent it, pathologise it. There is even a name for sleep obsession: *orthosomnia*. (Though perhaps our naming of everything makes it easy to escalate anything to a critical issue.) Our 24/7 culture is ruining our sleep because 'we are constantly entertained' and unable to properly shut off, writes

Stuart McGurk in *GQ*. 'We've never known more about the impact of sleep and yet we've never slept less.' The sleep industry is now worth £100 billion, with £30 billion lost per year in sleep-related productivity issues. In 2017, the World Health Organization declared us to be in the midst of a global 'sleep-loss epidemic'. But is that really true? According to the Centre for Time Use Research, we get more sleep now than ever before – an average of 8 hours and 30 minutes for women. It could be that we think we get less sleep because sleep specialists and many sleep aids rely on 'self-report' data. And as we all know, it is nigh impossible to be objective about our own sleep log ('I didn't sleep the *entire* fourteen-hour flight!').

The issue is not the quantity of sleep, but the quality. One theory for its decline is that we now live on a range of schedules. In the '60s, most people went to bed and got up at the same time. Nowadays, we work extremely varied hours: people lead less 'conventional' schedules because they're having children later, or not at all; the number of freelancers in charge of their own work hours is rising together with a corporate culture of flexible working hours; and many people work multiple jobs. We socialise outside of home a lot more than we did fifty years ago – '*You're out, again?*' I hear my mum lamenting – which means we might be out late one night and in bed early the next. Our lives are full of irregularities, so is it any surprise that our sleep is too?

In *The Nocturnal Brain*, neurologist Guy Leschziner describes a patient who believed her insomnia had returned because she had not been *good enough* at following the strict sleep routine he had set her. Leschziner didn't doubt that his patient was following her schedule with diligence. Rather, he thought she had become so preoccupied with optimising her recovery from insomnia that it started overshadowing her primary goal of sleeping. This anecdote says a lot about the frenzied manner in which we (I) approach sleep, but also about how millennial women operate today. Instead of focusing on the task itself, we focus on how well we are doing it. Wellness has claimed sleep as part of its relentless self-optimisation. When we inevitably come up short (because if it isn't perfect, then it isn't good enough) we see it as a failure. Even in our dreams, we are not free from self-regulation.

VIII.

The day after that long night of forty-five minutes' sleep, I went on the Radio 4 programme *A Good Read*, where guests discuss their favourite books. The host chose *Neuromancer*, a seminal work of science fiction written by William Gibson in 1984, which I had read that morning with eyeballs that felt so dehydrated they might as well have been shrink-wrapped. In the book, there is a cyborg named Julius Deane who is 135 years old with 'a seamless pink face' and a 'warped metabolism' maintained by 'spending each week a fortune in serums and hormones'. Even as someone in dire need of an upgrade that day, I didn't like the book. I don't enjoy stories about cyborgs in cyberspace (I prefer books where people do mundane human things like fall in love and/or die). Julius Deane reminds me of Dorsey and his biohacking companions' quest to take super-health a step further and achieve immortality. Peter Thiel, the founder of PayPal, thinks death could soon become 'optional', and the co-founder of Google, Sergey Brin, hopes to 'disrupt death' with his biotech company, Calico. (That is the biggest difference between the biohackers and the amethyst mums, who care about curating a life that feels 'at one with' the earth more than they do about living forever.) Perhaps that's why I don't get on with wellness. It melds together the human and the inhuman without any sort of empirical proof, in ways that feel terrifying.

Just as we respond differently to men and women who control their eating, there is a gendered element to how biohacking men and wellness women are seen. When Gwyneth Paltrow talks about stuffing parsley up your cooch to induce a period (in a now-deleted post for Goop), she is called a dangerous kook; but when biohacker Ben Greenfield writes a piece for his website called 'How To Make Your Penis Stronger With a Private Gym', there is zero criticism – just hundreds of giddy new subscribers, writes Alex Kuczynski for *Harper's US*. Both crotch-based hacks sound like total hokum. Yet one hack is validated because it is about the penis! And they are strong! But can always be stronger! Meanwhile the other is dismissed because vaginas are seen as soft, apologetic and pliant. The wellness lens transforms men and women differently: lean, mean, fighting machines versus flighty, formless narcissists.

Wellness can also divide us on an individual level. There is a 'curious self-alienation' brought around by self-optimisation, writes Ehrenreich, where 'there is the self that must be worked on, and another self that does the work'. Such splitting encourages self-surveillance, where you are watching yourself improve *while doing* the improving. 'Transcendent Oneness does not require self-examination, self-help or self-work. It requires self-loss,' Ehrenreich continues. This self-loss is what makes us human. It should not be a gloomy thought that we 'cannot levitate ourselves into that blessed condition by wishing it', but a *comforting* one. It reminds us that we are fallible, and that only so much is in our control. There is a perverse idea among millennial women that everything can be bent to our will, even our fertility. I've lost count of how many conversations I've had with friends who tell me when they are planning to conceive their child, to the month. But acknowledging that we are sometimes powerless is a relief. If we are no longer in control of everything, if we are not fully in charge of our destiny, then we can't blame ourselves for everything that does not 'manifest' itself as we hoped. We can, to an extent, relax the reins. Or at least accept that they may on occasions become twisted beyond our grasp.

The irony of wellness is that most enthusiasts are, as Mull writes, the 'wellest among us', with enough money left over at the end of the month to invest in the tools of the well-being trade. Telling someone who can barely pay the bills, or who faces sustained prejudice because of their race, gender or geography, that they could be happy *if they just want it enough* is as unhelpful as it is insulting. Purser nods to cultural theorist Lauren Berlant's concept of *cruel optimism* – a neo-liberalist fantasy that privatises stress and malady, so that the good life becomes something that we as individuals could – and *should* – manifest in ourselves. It alleviates pressure on societal structures and institutions to make any systemic change. For instance, lack of affordable housing is often undercut by the suggestion that young people nowadays are no good at saving – that they spend all their money on avocados and face masks – and that in order to get on the property ladder, they merely need to approach their finances with the same austerity and diligence of boomers. When in truth, one in three UK millennials will never own a house because the average price has risen by 281% across the UK, and 501% in London since 1996.

If we encourage ourselves to turn inwards and only invest in acts that make us feel better, we risk turning health into 'self-coddling', writes Spicer. 'If we spend all our time caring for ourselves, it is likely we will have no time and energy to challenge ourselves. This could easily leave us feeling safe and cared for but also stunted, while doing little to reduce the anxiety about the world around us.' Much has changed since Audre Lorde wrote that self-care is an act of 'political warfare'. In *A Burst of Light*, written after she was diagnosed with cancer for a second time, Lorde says that 'Caring for myself is not self-indulgence. It is self-preservation.' This is a sentiment echoed by writer Evette Dionne, who writes in *Ravishly* that self-care is a 'radical feminist act for Black women because we've spent generations in servitude to others ... in many communities of color, the responsibility of rearing children and offering support to multiple members of the village falls upon the shoulders of Black women. We're conditioned to believe that we're obligated to nurture others at our own expense.' The concept of self-care may have hardened into a Botoxed eyebrow or an expensive spa weekend, but that is not to say it can only ever be superficial. When my sister had breast cancer, beauty products were the one thing guaranteed to make her smile: thick luxurious moisturisers to slake parched skin; muscle soak and bath oils to relax the tendons in painful feet strung out by radiotherapy.

Yet even the most 'worried well' yearn for self-care – albeit from a different vantage point. 'Continued political shocks mean even relatively privileged people have started to feel that the world is against them and the best they can hope for is to endure,' writes Spicer. Is it any coincidence that many people feverishly invest in self-care after a break-up or when they are grieving? It's worth noting that Paltrow started Goop after her father died of cancer. Self-care has become a default way to maintain a sense of control in a chaotic world. I don't think the world has necessarily become *more* chaotic, but the idea of choice certainly has – there are so many options thrown at us daily, from both the marketplace and the internet – and amidst this chaos of choice, we double down: less willing to relinquish control over ourselves, our bodies, our careers. We are so terrified of things slipping from our grasp, that we think having a bad day is a reflection of our failure to harness something – rather than a shitty day being a life staple, often to do with uncontrollable external conditions and not some inner failing. As technology makes so many aspects of our life quicker and more efficient, instead of enjoying this liberation, we are now able to spend – or rather, feel like we *should* spend – more time on improving ourselves.

The ambition behind wellness – even in its least radical state – is an entirely human one. *Of course* I want to feel brighter and lighter in my thoughts and body. *Of course* I want to throw off the anxiety that fringes each day. Next to the bath, I keep two books about self-care by the writers Nadia Narain and Katia Narain Phillips. I recently met them when I hosted a panel conversation on self-care. I turned up with eyes narrowed, cynicism radiating from my every pore. And yet, dipping into their book about self-care for the 'real world' during one insomniac middle-of-the-night soak, I found myself immensely comforted by their tips. Light a candle on a dark winter's morning instead of turning on all the bright lights. Spend five minutes massaging your face when you feel tired. This type of self-care is about acceptance, not fixing something that's broken.

I am not against trying new things, particularly things that I may enjoy, or that might make me feel better – I imagine I'd like flotation therapy (a cool £55 for 60 minutes) because I like floating in warm water-holes. I even give my weighted blanket another chance – groaning as I heave it off the floor and back onto the bed – and, thrillingly, this time enjoy an undeniably improved night of sleep. It doesn't work every night – but then, what does? These small changes in my life are about comfort and calm; they are not tied to my fundamental being. But wellness envelops everything in a seamless false perfection that doesn't allow women to live lives full of contradiction. I refuse to accept the supremacy of wellness, as if without it you are shapeless and slovenly. Eat the açaí bowl, sure; but don't view it as redemption.

Tulum is not always flawless. As the dawn breaks, before the Instagrammers descend upon its pristine shores, men with wheelbarrows are busily clearing vast mounds of smelly, rotting seaweed. Away from the beach, things are worse. According to Mexico's Ministry of Environment and Natural Resources, 80% of the underground swimming holes (known as *cenotes*) in the Yucatán Peninsula bear traces of cocaine, Viagra, and ibuprofen. That is not to say that you shouldn't go to Tulum (although, to be frank, I wouldn't go back). Or that we shouldn't invest in the wellbeing of ourselves, and of others. But it's important to remember that Wellness Inc., and the notion of an optimised self, comes with a much higher cost than a dream catcher from eBay.

In her 1961 essay 'On Self-Respect', Joan Didion writes that, 'there is a common superstition that "self-respect" is a kind of charm against snakes, something that keeps those who have it locked in some unblighted Eden, out of strange beds, ambivalent conversations, and trouble in general. It does not at all. It has nothing to do with the face of things, but concerns instead a separate peace, a private reconciliation.' It strikes me that what we should be seeking is not self-care, but self-respect. Dignity and faith in ourselves which is more than skin-deep. Something that does not offer a dream catcher – a false protection against ambivalence or trouble – but that seeks a sense of peace and private reconciliation.

Get The Look

I celebrate by buying more clothes than I can afford.
I must be rich, my void is always building a bigger room to accommodate new things.

Theresa Lola, 'Black Marilyn'

I.

In the summer of 2019, a £39.99 Zara dress became a wardrobe phenomenon and the unofficial uniform for the millennial woman. Long-sleeved, polyester, polka-dot-patterned, 'The Dress' – as it was rapidly christened in internet parlance – was as bland as it was malleable. The breezy fit and midi length made it the perfect foil for the heatwave, but with enough coverage to qualify as modest-wear; smart enough for work when teamed with a tailored blazer and low heels, it was easily dressed down with trainers and a leather jacket. Occasionally, the dress wearer was an older lady, but mostly she was your quintessential, easily pilloried, middle-class millennial.

'She loves a bottomless brunch, food markets, day festivals, tennis, baby showers (sometimes hers), hen dos, polo, work parties, weddings, rooftop bars and poolside prosecco,' noted the London stylist Faye Oakenfull, who created the Instagram account @hot4thespot, where she uploads pictures of The Dress as spotted around the UK for her 26,000 followers. (The account is not without controversy: the uploading of photographs of women without their permission has a chequered and misogynistic history.) The account relies on crowd-sourcing, as people eagerly submitted their pictures of The Dress en masse. One image captured three women gathered outside a London pub, clad in identical monochrome spots. In another, a group of eight women, all wearing identikit frocks, crowd somewhat inexplicably around the politician John Bercow.

The Dress's ubiquity in Britain (its popularity did not extend to America or Continental Europe) became near farcical. It also revealed a strange paradox about modern womanhood: despite the unprecedented choice that exists in retail, despite the bold affirmations – strewn across social media, posted on whiteboards at the entrance of tube stations and scrawled on chalkboards outside cafes – that women are queens of their own universe and centres of their own solar system, many are increasingly dressing like facsimiles of one another. And, despite a subtext of 'basic bitchery' (a basic bitch being someone who 'engages in typical, unoriginal behaviours, modes of dress, speech and likes'), women are dressing the same both *intentionally* and *joyfully*. At a time when popular culture is extensively documenting and celebrating the individuality and liberation of the millennial woman, her look – like her lifestyle – is morphing into something curiously homogenous. The Dress's ubiquity became itself a reason to have it. 'Part of my love of the dress is the idea that I shouldn't wear it because so many other people have it,' a dress wearer told Sirin Kale for the *Guardian*. 'But that just makes me want to wear it more.'

When I was growing up, it was considered agonisingly gauche to turn up in the same outfit as someone else. That is no longer a prevailing anxiety for my generation, who are far more concerned about looking like they belong than they are fearful of looking the same as someone else. Where the worry once was that you might not stand out, it's now about not fitting in. There is reassurance and relief to be found in this mimicry. It is a 'modern variation' of 'homosocial grooming behaviour', writes cultural historian Pamela Church Gibson in *Fashion and Celebrity Culture*. Young women have moved on from 'combing, brushing and dressing each other's hair [and] assisting each other in their toilettes', to dressing similarly, becoming both a mirror and refraction of each other.

The way women copy one another's style is driven by a phenomenon that I call 'Get The Look'. It is a movement driven by the overproduction of affordable – if not extremely cheap – clothes, and the ease of acquiring them; an emphasis on looking presentable and camera-ready at all times; a capitalist exploitation of collective self-esteem; and the impact of celebrity and influencer culture. The confluence of these factors renders 'discussions of "agency" problematic,' writes Church Gibson. 'Self-expression through dress is to some extent eroded, a fortiori subversion. More and more people actually seek sameness.' This seeking of sameness is not static; it is constantly refreshed, with one in three women now considering something worn more than twice to be 'old'. Compulsive shopping is rising in tandem with our Kondo-cued urge to purge, so clothing is moving through our homes more quickly than ever before, like a kind of bulimic impulse. Dana Thomas, author of *Fashionopolis*, calls the 'absolute avoidance' of being seen or photographed in something twice 'Cinderella Syndrome'. Fuelled by our constant visibility in the digital age, it has become entirely normal to buy something not just for a specific event, but for *every* event. Fashion has become omnipotent and the acquisition of a new look a salve, salvation and purpose.

By 2014, the average British woman was buying twice as many clothes as she had bought in 1980. By 2019, she was buying more clothes than any other woman in Europe, with the average lifetime for a piece of clothing just two years. J. D. Salinger, who popularised the term *neophilia* for describing our thirst for new things, may have been writing over fifty years before the 'New In' tab was invented, but he got to the heart of the way we shop now: with an attentional bias towards things that are new. The feeling of having 'nothing to wear' is an experience every woman has had: flinging open the wardrobe and yelping in dismay. But in our present day of hyper-visibility and self-surveillance, this anxiety has become frenetic. It is now better to look like someone else than to risk looking again like you're failing at modern life. The feeling of not having enough, of not *being* enough, is quelled only by a battery of outlets that in their multitude – too many to possibly sift through, activating Schwartz's paradox of choice – act as further fuel to the flame. Clothes shopping has become like a perpetual hangover: slaked, briefly, by a swig of orange juice, before the quivering doom of inadequacy returns minutes later.

A self does not exist in isolation: it is informed, among other things, by the talismans we collect. But where once we collected talismans, now we collect clothes. In the 1950s, the writer Philip K. Dick coined the word *kipple* to describe pieces of rubbish and detritus that build up seemingly without human intervention. If Dick were writing now, he might very well have reworked his definition of kipple to cover the tat that mysteriously accrues in our wardrobe, reproducing itself. Given that the typical British woman wears each item of clothing an average of only seven times total, we effectively treat our clothes like food wrappers anyway.

For a long time, these piles of wrappers built up in our wardrobes with minimal disruption. Though there had been rumblings after the Rana Plaza tragedy in 2013, where 1,129 garment workers were killed by an eight-storey factory collapse in Bangladesh, it wasn't until 2018 that the dialogue around fast fashion kicked into mainstream consciousness. The BBC released its documentary, *Fashion's Dirty Secrets*; the news came out that Burberry had shockingly chosen to burn £30 million of stock rather than sell it at discounted price; and we saw the explosion of the hashtag #WhoMadeMyClothes from the global movement Fashion Revolution, calling for greater transparency in fashion. Legislative changes – a tariff, a policy or a levy – will have to be put in place to manage overproduction. (The most recent proposal from the MPs on the Environmental Audit Committee – to tax every garment by 1p in order to raise £35 million to improve garment sorting and collection – was rejected by government ministers in June 2019.) But for now, despite being questioned, the vast consumption of clothes continues to rise.

There's no denying that excessive consumption is a middle-class problem. But in twenty years, the global middle class is expected to grow by 3 billion people – making it a very large problem indeed. Leaving aside the pressing issue of sustainability and the impact of fast fashion on the environment – for which I thoroughly recommend the work of Lucy Siegle and Orsola de Castro – I want to look at some of the *whys*. *Why* did we start shopping so voraciously? *Why* are we so obsessed with new clothes? And *why* do we want – nay, need – to look like other women?

II.

The idea of shopping as entertainment was born in the economy boom of the 1980s, flourishing under mall culture in the US and the local high street in the UK. The high street had been a feature of British life since the 1960s, but by the '90s it had grown beyond the merely functional, into an unforeseen mecca of shopping for teenage girls and young women. The jewel in the crown was Gap. It was Gap that got millennials hooked on shopping, writes Elizabeth Cline in *Overdressed*, opening 570 stores in 1999 alone. That year, I turned twelve and emerged from my eleven-year-old chrysalis as a walking Gap sandwich board, in denim flares and a baby-pink polo shirt. Meanwhile, the uptick in catalogue culture – and particularly that of Next – planted the idea that shopping could be done in large quantities and remotely. I distinctly remember that in 1999 it was rare for a week to go by without the arrival of a Next package for my Gen X sister.

In 2000, heralding the start of the new millennium, the novelist Sophie Kinsella prophesied our contemporary shopping appetites with the first of her wildly successful *Shopaholic* books, which I inhaled in a matter of hours. The narrative centres on financial journalist Becky Bloomwood's insatiable thirst for new clothes and her daily attempts to hide purchases from her flatmate, her boyfriend, and her long-suffering accountant. And while Bloomwood might seem like a product of her time, in many ways she is a modern-day version of Lily Bart in *The House of Mirth*. 'Her whole being dilated in an atmosphere of luxury. It was the background she required, the only climate she could breathe in,' writes Edith Wharton evocatively of Bart's need for new clothes back in 1905. 'That instant when your fingers curl round the handles of a shiny, uncreased bag … It's like going hungry for days, then cramming your mouth full of warm buttered toast. It's like waking up and realizing it's the weekend. It's like the better moments of sex,' exalts Kinsella's protagonist, with similar lust. What has changed in the two decades since Kinsella started publishing her *Shopaholic* books, of course, is that Bloomwood is no longer an anomaly among women.

The early noughties were a seismic time for pop culture. It was, quite frankly, a brilliant time to be a teenager: loads of telly, bonkers fashion and no social media. The turn of the millennium birthed the twin ideas of ordinary people as celebrities (with the first series of *Big Brother* debuting in 2000) and of celebrities as shoppable entities. The celebutante Paris Hilton was the congruence of both. She rose to fame starring on the reality show *The Simple Life* in 2003–2007 with BFF Nicole Richie. Hilton's slogan, 'I love it, do you love it?', delivered in a deadpan Valley Girl monotone, made her the fallen angel of reality television, while her panther-thin, biscuity-brown body proved the perfect canvas for the sexified fashion trends of the '00s: pubis-defying Miss Sixty low-riders; pastel-hued Juicy Couture terry cloth tracksuits; and tightly cropped slogan tees stretched across petite, pert breasts. It was an impossible look to pull off unless you were cardboard-thin. In 2003, an illegal DVD of the seminal California-set teen drama *The O.C.* made its way into my panting possession. I wanted, so badly that I could taste it like taffy on my tongue, to be a) American and b) shopping for a halter-neck at Abercrombie & Fitch.

In 2005, Paris and Nicky Hilton were at the sartorial forefront of the biggest love triangle modern celebrity culture had ever known: when Brad Pitt left *Friends* actress and girl-next-door Jennifer Aniston for Hollywood sexpot Angelina Jolie. Paris hit the streets in a ladybird-red and black TEAM JOLIE T-shirt, arm-in-arm with her younger sister, who had opted for a white and frog-green TEAM ANISTON. It was a super-cute photo opportunity (I loved it, did you love it?), and the baseball shirts became a pop-culture phenomenon, with eighteen-year-old yours truly endlessly trawling through eBay in order to pledge my allegiance to Aniston. (Instead, I ended up inexplicably buying a T-shirt that read: THIS IS THE SHIRT I LOST IN LA. I didn't go to LA until I was twenty-six.) It was in this climate that ASOS blossomed, stocking the very same Truffle Shuffle slogan tees that Paris had been seen slinking around in. The website had been around since 2000, trading on celeb-u-like props and fashion, with the acronym standing for 'As Seen On Screen' (early products included the purple photo frame on the back of Rachel and Monica's apartment door in *Friends*). At its zenith, ASOS had over 18 million customers.

While American pop culture began its thrilling invasion of Britain, two things happened from within the UK that forever changed the way we dress. In 2005, the Multi-Fibre Agreement (a decades-old tariff that imposed quotas on textile exports) expired, leading to a 100% increase in Chinese imports to the West and the establishment of Bangladesh as a primary force in fast fashion. Meanwhile, the British paparazzi evolved, and beardy men with visible bum cracks upped their coverage of young, beautiful, stylishly dressed women, thus offering the public an unprecedented access to celebrity fashion (a genre previously dominated by Liz Hurley's 1994 safety-pin Versace dress, and not much else). Through their long lenses, these men inadvertently began to predict and shape fashion trends.

Their coverage mainly focused on two blonde white women: Sienna Miller and Kate Moss. (That they both are blonde, skinny and white – thus conforming to the entrenched Eurocentric beauty standard of the time – is as relevant in their going 'mass' as their clothing choices.) After Sienna was papped sashaying across the Glastonbury fields in 2004 sporting a low-slung coin-studded leather belt and UGG boots, I dashed to New Look and bought a leather-effect coin belt and a pair of fake UGG boots. When Kate mooched around the same, albeit muddier, terrain in 2006, Pete Doherty hanging off her arm, wearing a black waistcoat and silver micro hot pants, I immediately combed the local vintage stores for a black waistcoat. (Even celebrities are not immune to Get The Look: Moss accused Miller of stealing her style, before Marianne Faithfull accused a 'vampirical' Moss of doing the same thing to her.) A few years later, along came the lissom Alexa Chung and her seemingly simple sartorial equation of Breton tee, cut-off denim shorts, a Barbour and over-the-knee socks, and the same thing happened all over again.

Young British style icons weren't a new phenomenon – there was Twiggy in the 1960s, Princess Diana in the 1980s – but the combination of the internet, paparazzi and the evolution of shopping turbo-charged this generation's ascent. Combined with the new format of weekly women's magazines that blended celebrity and fashion, functioning predominantly to highlight the good, the bad and the ugly of celebrity fashion with forensic gusto – such as *Grazia*, which launched in Britain in 2005, and *Heat*, which launched in 1999 – Get The Look clicked into full throttle.

Not every celebrity was ripe for emulation – Angelina Jolie's glacial beauty and minimalist style has always been seen as too alienating to adopt. But Moss made it oh-so-easy. In 2007, the supermodel solidified her much-copied style into something seriously profitable when she became the face of the high street's first celebrity collaboration, Kate Moss for Topshop. The partnership neatly nudged Get The Look away from something to strive for and towards something you had direct access to. Previously, you would have had to undertake a high-risk journey. (In 2005, on trying to purchase Miller's blue Chloé dress for my sixth-form ball, I bought a fake Chinese import from eBay that was three sizes too big and made of what appeared to be tissue paper.) But with this collaboration, you no longer had to hunt tirelessly, only to endure shoddy replicas as reward. *You could look exactly like Kate Moss!*

Kate Moss for Topshop opened the floodgates to a slew of subsequent duds (Jesus *still* weeps for Madonna for H&M) and is preserved in hallowed terms, with many women breaking out the floral tea dress come summer, even now. I was in my first year at Leeds University when the collection dropped, and I set my alarm for 4 a.m. so that I could queue outside the store, with my day-glo time-slot wristband, before the doors opened at 7 a.m. On my way into town from uni halls, I passed friends on their way home after a night out. Too embarrassed to admit where I was going, I mumbled incoherently about forgetting something at someone's house. But in truth, I was more excited about that launch than I had been about anything else all term.

III.

While these milestones were undoubtedly fundamental, the biggest benefactor to Get The Look was the arrival of the internet as a medium for style documentation – via fashion blogs, street-style and social media. In 2007, the first fashion blog, *Fashin Fags*, was launched by a user called 'lolmodelbitch'. Thanks to easy-to-use publishing services such as WordPress, LiveJournal and Blogger (my preferred platform), fashion blogs paved the way for a 'fashion news cycle' – not only instigating the idea that fashion even *had* news, but that it could be updated daily, or even at multiple points throughout the day – and later, with the rise of Instagram, opened the door for influencers. (Due to influencer culture – providing a quicker and easier way to profit from personal style – fashion blogs have largely died out now, or have transformed into industry-defining media businesses like *The Business of Fashion*, *The Blonde Salad* and *Man Repeller*). Street-style was born when the American photographer Scott Schuman began taking pictures of women (and occasionally of men) outside fashion shows and uploading them to his blog, *The Sartorialist*. For the first time, 'normal' people were being photographed for style inspiration and so began to govern trends as well as simply following them. Soon, every single magazine, website and newspaper was running its own street-style pages. It was not just celebrities who had become shoppable, but also regular women without any kind of industry authority or clout. Women like me.

For the purpose of this essay, I traversed the exquisitely embarrassing and frequently baffling trove of Google Images of myself, in order to find my first ever street-style photo. In it, I am wearing a blue vintage velvet coat, a polka-dot shirt from Nasty Gal, patched jeans from Zara, black pointed multi-strap heels from Kurt Geiger, a strange sort of 'crystal waterfall' necklace from a website whose name I can no longer recall, and a neon orange beanie from American Apparel. I'm exhausted just looking at it. I'm not sure which is the straw that breaks the camel's back, visually speaking; the crystal necklace and neon beanie both vie for the prize. (The only piece I still own, incidentally, is the vintage coat.) It was 2012, I was twenty-five years old and attending one of my first ever fashion shows as the editor of a now-defunct fashion-sharing website called Today I'm Wearing, created by the *Daily Mail*. To use the website, you uploaded a picture of your outfit, whereupon other women could 'heart' it and follow your looks. (Unlike Instagram, there was no opportunity to tell someone you *didn't* like their look.) I remember telling someone about the website and she asked, confused, 'But why on earth would you upload your outfits to the internet?' I secretly agreed, despite being obligated to share pictures of myself on the site and post them on the then-nascent start-up Instagram in order to drive traffic back to the site. Said woman now has almost

900,000 Instagram followers and regularly shares pictures of her outfits.

By 2015, the convergence of shopping and the internet led to a vast rise in online fashion aimed at young women, and to the birth of social commerce. Today, 43% of clothing shopping is 'social shopping': shopping executed on your phone and mostly via a retailer's app, featuring moving stimulation, digital rewards and models who look like (and sometimes are) social media influencers. The commerce model of social shopping follows the highs of social media and is based almost entirely on the excitement of acquisition. This kind of shopping activates the 'hunter gatherer instinct' in our brain, says the writer Lucy Siegle. 'It is about the kill.' Every single aspect of social shopping is built towards making the purchasing process friction-free, with handy tricks like thumbprint login and PayPal checkout to ensure the *quickest* and *easiest* transaction.

With swifter delivery times than ever before – the lure of Next Day Delivery often too tempting to resist – social shopping has removed the dreaded sense of delayed gratification. At the same time, it has also managed to create a feeling of anxiety through an illusion of scarcity. *Scarcity?* I hear you repeat, baffled. These are websites with up to a thousand new products dropping every single week. *Where the hell is the scarcity?* But these e-tailers have achieved the impossible: flooding the market with thousands of pieces – and then making those pieces a limited edition. A 'new drop' can sell out within hours, giving the customer no time to prevaricate; to apply any deliberation tactics like 'Will this really suit me?' or 'What else in my wardrobe could I wear this with?' Instead, her gaze is isolated to this one item among thousands: the item that could ensure she remains part of the crowd. A viable member of team Get The Look, rather than out in the cold, all alone, without those must-have boots.

IV.

Get The Look is not limited to one socio-economic bracket. In luxury fashion, cult brands *du jour* repeat across the fashion pages and street-style albums so much so that the pictures become almost interchangeable: in 2016 it was Gucci; 2017, Vetements; 2018, Balenciaga (though Celine ran through all of them); and in 2019, Bottega Veneta, with its padded clutch bags and quilted mules. The fashion buyer Tiffany Hsu noted that the £1,730 pouch, like Dior's saddle bag and the Chanel 2.55 handbag before it, has become pop-culture royalty – 'You see them everywhere and they're instantly recognisable' – but that their being everywhere on Instagram and the fashion-week circuit only adds to their value, rather than making them less desirable. (If you're wondering how so many people can afford such an expensive handbag, it's most often down to 'gifting' or press loans.) It's a similar story across the 'contemporary market' – clothing that sits on luxury e-tailers like Net-a-Porter and MatchesFashion.com but that costs about one quarter of luxury fashion – where each season sees a series of 'hits' unfurl across Instagram. In the summer of 2019, this included Danish brand Ganni's neon green checked sundress and a surprising revival of Havaianas rubber flip flops (high fashion trends do not always cost the earth: they just need to be obscure enough, as rubber flip flops surely are, to qualify as outside of the mainstream and, thus, as 'fashion'.)

A price-tier down from contemporary fashion and you have the fast fashion of the high street. Most prominently, there's Zara, which has a retail model so 'nimble' that it makes 'roughly four times more profit than its peers,' notes Thomas. Zara inspires the same rapacious shopping appetite and obsessive brand loyalty that Gap did in the early noughties. (Where once her catnip was a Gap logo hoodie, the millennial woman now appraises a pair of mules, or light-weight blazer, with that same delight). The Zara customer shops the store an average of seventeen times a year. Not *visits* the store; *shops* the store. This kind of shopping is so constant that it almost becomes unconscious. It is lunch-break shopping, where a pair of sandals can be bought in the time it takes to eat a Pret salad. At some point, the Zara customer realises less that she does not *want* to shop anywhere else, but that she simply does not *need* to.

Just as the Get The Look epidemic is not limited to a single socio-economic group, fast fashion is not restricted to one age bracket. In *Fashionopolis*, Thomas describes the women shopping fast fashion as being aged 18–24. But the reality is that women in their thirties also shop at fast fashion outlets (and not necessarily any less rapaciously) – they just do so differently to an eighteen-year-old. A generation contains multitudes, after all; there are some women who eschew millennial trends altogether. Mid- to older millennials tend to shop faster fashion via the 'old guard' (high street stores such as Zara and Mango), whereas younger millennials (born 1995 to 1997) and older Gen Z-ers (1997–2003) are more likely to purchase from the sexier, online e-tailers such as Boohoo.com. These women like to think that they are very different from one another – the Zara customer in her mid-thirties likely considers herself a discerning, chic woman, who would not *dream* of shopping at Boohoo.com or dressing like anyone on *Love Island*, thank you very much. Yet they have more in common than she might care to admit: both subscribe to a mode of dress that comes pre-approved by other women and adheres to what Professor Brenda Weber calls an 'economy of sameness'.

While Get The Look exists up and down the fashion food chain, it is most prevalent in the cheapest, internet-specific category. I call it 'faster' fashion (it is also known as 'ultra-fast fashion', 'instant fashion' or 'furious fashion'): a category you might be only vaguely familiar with, and yet which is the fastest-growing retail sector, accounting for 66% of online fashion traffic in the first half of 2019. *Faster* fashion makes *fast* fashion look almost slow. While Zara can take a product from design, through production and onto the shop floor in as little as fifteen days, faster fashion's turnaround can be under a week.

This rapidly increasing sector comprises a slew of sassily monikered e-stores, which spring up like dust motes on a floordrobe and trade solely via the internet: Pretty Little Thing, MissPap, Nasty Gal, Boohoo (which has majority stakes in all three of the previous brands, as well as new ownership of both Coast and Karen Millen), Never Fully Dressed, Missy Empire, Missguided, Rebellious Fashion, Vivichi, PrettyLittleThing, Oh Polly and Fashion Nova (the only one to originate as a bricks-and-mortar store and Google's most searched-for fashion brand in 2018). Since writing this, more will have inevitably popped up. So specific are they to their young audience that even the keenest shopper in her thirties might not have heard of more than one or two. But their impact on the high street has been enormous – the profit losses of trad stores like Topshop and Dorothy Perkins are not unconnected to the wild growth of the faster fashion e-tailer (although a select few, such as Zara, Mango and Next, have proved resistant).

There is little to no difference between the sites themselves, which churn out unexpectedly constructed, reality-TV-reactive clothing – aggressively latticed swimsuits, neon cycle shorts, corset mini dresses, lace body-suits and giant puffer coats – that range from the very cheap to the exceedingly cheap. At Vivichi, the Kendal crop top and shorts co-ord rings in at £17.60, which is positively astronomical compared to Boohoo's £2.85 red minidress, or Missguided's One Pound Bikini, a minimal black '90s-style string bikini that retailed for

£1 in June 2019 and, despite the media uproar, quickly sold out in sizes 4–24.

Faster e-tailers do not give a toss about what is happening on the Milan catwalk or in the pages of glossy magazines, because their consumers do not give a toss. These brands correctly subscribe to the notion that most young women want to wear what celebrities and influencers are wearing – not what some lofty Italian fashion designer tells them they should wear – and that they will shop online to get it at the lowest possible price. What they stock is informed not through any kind of planned schedule, but through micro-trends that change weekly and are responsive to Instagram, festivals, music videos, reality TV, a meme, what one Victoria's Secret supermodel wore in one paparazzi shot. The trigger point can be almost undetectable and is most often ephemeral.

Journalism student Keira Harris sends me screenshots of influencer looks that she plans to replicate during the winter of 2019. The majority of the women are from the reality show *The Only Way Is Essex*, and Harris dutifully lists the pieces she wants – 'I like Georgia Kousoulou's puffer jacket, Frankie Sims's leather trousers and Chloe Brockett's bouncy blow-dry' – as well as what she has already nabbed, like Georgia's 'small feature bag'. Harris had found the items on I Saw It First and Missguided (helpfully, the items are typically tagged on Instagram, sending her right through to the brand's page, or even the page of the item itself). But she is not entirely welded to Get The Look – she also enjoys the process of going to 'little markets and boutiques to get something similar', not the exact same. Knowing where 'the piece' is from is mandatory – so much so that there are now Instagram fashion accounts *about* Instagram fashion accounts. The Instagram accounts @ferragnezoutfit and @chiara-ferragnioutfits, for example, regram pictures from the Italian super-influencer Chiara Ferragni's page, spliced with flat-lay cut-outs of the pieces themselves. Their followers are quick to the keyboard if there are any products or prices missing. 'Splendid!' writes one. 'But what about the hairband???'

The impact of the Kardashians on Get The Look is almost incalculable; the meteoric rise of faster fashion and of the sisters themselves go hand in hand. 'Brands that affiliate themselves with the Kardashians, whether officially or unofficially, experience mega-growth,' notes Kale. Arguably, the entire *point* of shopping these sites is to look like a Kardashian, such is their pop-culture pull. The Kardashians themselves know and exploit this, teaming up with various e-tailers on collaborations – Boohoo.com's UK sales rose by a third after a collaboration with Kourtney Kardashian in 2018 – and suing them when they get too cocky. (Or, rather, when they do not profit from the collaboration.) In July 2019, Kim Kardashian West demanded $10 million from Missguided after they copied a gold foil cut-out swimsuit and side-tie sarong that her husband had had made for her. 'Fast fashion brands, can you please wait until I wear this in real life, before you knock it off [crying emoji]?' she captioned her Instagram post, to which Missguided, living up to its name, replied, 'The devil works hard, but Missguided works harder [eyeball emoji]. @kimkardashian you've only got a few days before this drops online.' Kardashian West won $2.7 million in damages.

These are not clothes designed for the daily grind – grocery shopping, cleaning, working, taking a piss. These are outfits for festivals and hot (or very cold, preferably ski) holidays; pool parties and clubs; for being admired inside the home (in a sparsely decorated bedroom, or perched upon a super-sized sectional sofa), or just outside of it (urban scapes only, no trees unless palms). Kardashian West's self-proclaimed 'minimalist monastery' is the aspirational apex: clad in a copper-coloured spandex crop top and matching tube skirt, she not so much stands out in her ginormous, empty, concrete home as she shines, lit up like an Oscar. These are clothes designed for a fantasy, but it is a fantasy that both allows for and encourages your participation. In this sense, operating via a sort of *enclothed cognition* (where clothes have an influence on your psychological state), Get The Look becomes a route to Get The Life. By buying a crop top and matching tube skirt, you too can exist in this minimalist monastery: a beacon of your own desire.

The homogenisation caused by Get The Look extends beyond fashion and into body shapes and beauty routines. This is where the 'copyquette' of the Zara or the Bottega Veneta customer differs from that of Missguided et al. The faster fashion customer understands that clothing is only *part* of the longed-for look. The clothes pivot around a woman's body, not so much encasing it as showcasing it, testing its resistance. Can your breasts stay within a swimsuit designed to cover only the top half of your chest? (This is not swimwear for typical underboobs, forgotten and apologetic, lying soft against the ribcage – but for furiously tanned, alert underboobs. No sleeping on the job here, gals.) The clothes have to be cheap, because the beauty routine that goes with them – a certain sleek, airbrushed glam that may or may not feature hair extensions, fake tan, Shellacked nails and injectable fillers – is as important, if not *more* important, than the outfit itself, and certainly more expensive. It has many names – 'Instagram face', 'filter face' and 'rich girl face' – but without Instagram, which normalises an amplified aesthetic, this look would likely never have broken out into the mainstream.

Kylie Jenner and Huda Kattan have formed billion-dollar companies out of Instagram face, and epitomise the look itself. Jenner is white and Kattan is Middle-Eastern, but when fully made-up they look extremely alike. (This part, this sameness, is not coincidental.) The irony of what Yomi Adegoke dubs a 'Mr Potato Head' approach to beauty, is that for all its competing influences – 'Latin, Black, Arab, or Asian extraction', notes Joanna Fuertes – the result is a paper-chain of identical-looking women. Jenner and Kattan blur the lines between make-up and surgery (both have admitted to having fillers put into their face, but nothing else) with a canny vagueness, allowing fans to persuade themselves that all they need is a pair of Kattan's mink eyelashes or Jenner's lip kits in order to Get The(ir) Look. What was once considered an extreme representation of beauty has now become the everyday, with the average young woman taking five and a half hours to get ready for a night out. Time aside, these beauty procedures cost a lot of money – infinitely more than a £15 dress. As she forks out pennies on her hair, her lashes, her lips, it is not so much that this Get The Looker cannot afford to spend more on a dress, but that she does not *want* to.

A positive element of what is commonly considered the spectre of fashion is that the sizing of faster fashion e-tailers is far more inclusive than that of the high street, whose limited sizing instead insinuates that women should apologise for being an entirely average size 16 (an L in Zara actually only fits a UK size 14.) For the iffily named 'plus-size' shopper, the sizing options of Pretty Little Thing et al (which stock up to a size 26) encourage a celebration of their bodies. The casting of the models showcasing the clothes is similarly diverse. But while the representation of different ethnicities is something to be commended, there is again an economy of sameness at play, with the 'diversity' presented on these sites not always a celebration of form or skin colour, but of one single melting-pot. With diversity at the top of the cultural agenda – in rhetoric if not always in action – there is the uncomfortable idea that, for some, representation is merely a trend, like a new trainer to slip on and take off again when it is no longer in style. (That not being white is something that could win you favour in marketing circs, has led to the phenomenon of 'blackfishing', where white women present as black or mixed race, such as the Instagram influencers Aga Brzostowska and Emma Hallberg.)

Though these e-tailers initially promise – and to some extent deliver – diversity, a new impossible ideal is also perpetuated. With its teeny-tiny waists, big bums, pert boobs and loose silky curls, this look – which plucks the 'best bits' of different racial body stereotypes, much like the Mr Potato Head of beauty – 'is as unattainable as white runway model thinness', writes the author Reni Eddo-Lodge. This ethnically ambiguous body type is a departure from the long-held *Sweet Valley High* Western ideal of a slim white woman with long straight blonde hair. But it has led to a 'collective cognitive dissonance' for black women, continues Eddo-Lodge, who have gone from an absence of representation in popular culture to being seen exclusively as 'black Jessica Rabbits'. With their waist-trainers – creating exquisitely tiny waists, on top of very large, very round, surgically enhanced bottoms – the Kardashians and their krusaders are accused of creating and propagating a look that is impossible for women to achieve naturally, even for the women of colour whose bodies they are said to be appropriating. This type of body, so different to what has been lauded for decades as beautiful, attempts to defy convention – and yet it has itself become a mainstream ideal, less revolutionary than exhaustively and endlessly high-octane.

V.

Love Island is a reality TV show which, to the lamentation of many a male politician, has captured the zeitgeist to an extraordinary degree (an impressive 3.8 million viewers tuned in to the finale of the 2019 series). In this gameshow environment, Get The Look becomes almost dystopian: an immersive experience where you can shop the show live, thanks to an accompanying app. Most, but not all, of the clothes worn by the contestants hail from the show's official sponsor. In 2018, this was Missguided, who saw their sales leap by 40%. In 2019, it was I Saw It First, a relatively new e-tailer, whose multimillion-pound sponsorship entailed an almost constant stream of adverts before, during and after the nightly show, featuring a trio of lethargic models moving with seeming reluctance between various rarefied scenes: from Jeep to beach to Ibizan club.

Television's first but inevitably not its last shoppable show, *Love Island* is ostensibly a series about finding love, but is more accurately a reflection of a collective surrender to Get The Look. With such regular exposure – an hour of television, six nights a week for eight weeks – few of us are safe. I experienced it first hand when I caught myself gazing longingly at contestant Molly-Mae Hague's pale pink satin minidress, which featured a high neck and a ruched skirt (£31.50 from Missguided) and which was later worn by axed contestant Jordanne to the finale show – a neat example of Get The Look, live in action. (The dress sold out, thankfully, before I let myself make my first-ever faster fashion purchase.)

These future celetoids enter the villa as contestants and leave as fully fledged social media influencers (each contestant has a talent manager before they even enter the villa, with their details posted in the contestant's social media biography). These women 'are not necessarily influential icons of style', writes Church Gibson – certainly not in the same way that Moss and Miller were, and still are – but they are immensely influential online and *intensely* copied. Just two months after the series ended, 20-year-old Hague launched a collaboration with Pretty Little Thing, for a rumoured sum of £500,000, and the 2019 winner, 22-year-old Amber Gill, signed a £1 million deal to be the face of MissPap. Meanwhile, their fellow Islander Maura Higgins became an official ambassador for Boohoo.

Television is the birthplace of only a very small minority of influencers: the rest (of whom there are hundreds of thousands) emerge through social media, forging a path via happenstance, grit, or both. According to Tech Jury, the scale is thus: micro-influencers have 25,000–100,000 followers, big influencers track up to 1 million, and macro-influencers are 1–7 million. After that, they're celebrities. How efficiently they peddle clothes is not so much down to their numbers, but their engagement. The Parisian influencer Jeanne Damas has an angora-clad, lace-slip-selfied, red-lips-around-a-Beaujolais *je ne sais quoi* that sends the women who follow her into even wilder paroxysms than the men. She has cleverly parlayed the female longing to look like her into a pared-back, vintage-cued fashion label, Rouje – which she wears almost exclusively. Damas's label is not faster fashion – prices average the €130 mark – but a dress typically sells out within two hours of Damas posting a picture of herself wearing it on Instagram. Like Alexa Chung, Damas is in a small minority of appealing to women who prefer *fashion* over *glam* yet, most likely on account of being very pretty and very sexy, also holds a mass appeal.

Every morning, the presenter Holly Willoughby shares a picture of her outfit for that day's episode of ITV's breakfast show *This Morning* with her 6.3 million Instagram followers. In keeping with Willoughby's brand of sunny homeliness, the colourful, feminine dresses and flared midi skirts are a mix of high street (Warehouse, Topshop, Joie) and contemporary fashion (Sandro, Reiss, Maje). Willoughby is catnip to retailers – everything she posts quickly sells out, not only because she is gorgeous, but also because she is 'relatable'.

She isn't trying to pull off awkward high-fashion looks, or pout through glossed lips in a neon cropped twin-set. She is straight-backed, smiley and often shot against a dreary wardrobe (showing that background only really matters when you aren't properly famous). Willoughby's Instagram feed plugs a genuinely helpful gap – styling advice without needing to go into a store. And because she never wears the same thing twice and posts on every single weekday, this translates to *a lot* of styling advice.

That her followers flock to her Instagram because they want to shop, is a no-brainer. But to thrust Willoughby forward as a poster woman for Get The Look's rabid consumerism is to miss out a crucial part of the story. Television budgets are famously tight, and the more clothes a talent can get for free, or on loan, the healthier and happier the production piggy bank. If Willoughby stopped posting her daily #hwstyle looks, brands would be less willing to loan to her (negatively impacting the ITV budgets), and it would infuriate her fans who not only *want* to know what she is wearing but feel like she *owes* them that.

Would Willoughby wearing something twice be a disservice to the *This Morning* viewers? Or do cultural arbiters have a responsibility to try and dim the bright shiny light of new things? To use a still-pristine silk-printed swingy-skirted floral dress to ask: does it actually matter if it's not new? Perhaps what we need is a middle ground, like the one lightly prodded by the Duchess of Cambridge. She often repeats a dress, an act made easier by the fact that she does not follow trends except in their broadest sense (she might wear splashier florals in the spring and more delicate buds in the winter). She does not participate in micro-trends, but instead rotates a wardrobe of classic looks, lent a buoyancy by her exuberant blow-dries.

The narrative around Kate's 'wardrobe recycling' (daft fashion parlance for *wears something more than once*) has traced an interesting arc. It started in 2006, when she was mocked for repeating formal outfits. *How boring*, crabbed the commentators. *Like those nude courts she always wears.* It is only in recent years (as she redeemed herself by popping out three adorable children in quick succession – who cares if she is boring when she is bountiful!) that the dialogue has stilled into something kinder. Kate is modest, humble, beatific and thoughtful. (The public opinion has grown gentler towards Kate as it has soured towards her sister-in-law, because in order for one woman to go up, another must go down.) She wears clothes twice because she knows how influential an act like that can be. It really shouldn't seem as radical as it does. And yet when a celebrity wears something twice, it still makes headlines. 'We are obsessed with famous people daring to wear something more than once, as it feels relatable' writes Adegoke. 'A "celebs – they're just like us!" moment of fashion faux pas or frugality. But if anything, in recent years we *have* become "just like them", with insatiable appetites for new outfits, our wardrobes slowly morphing into ceaseless conveyor belts of polyester.'

The undeniable truth is that Get The Look, particularly in its fastest sector, hinges on newness: pristine, chemical-scented and flat-packed. 'It's important to have a lot of styles because our customers post so much online and need new clothes,' said Fashion Nova's bearish CEO Richard Saghian last year, showing a curious interpretation of the word *need*. Saghian reads (or rather, shapes) the zeitgeist with accuracy: Brits now spend £700 million a year on single-use holiday clothes and £800 million on single-use wedding outfits (with an average spend of £80 per outfit). So rapacious is this online obligation for single-use wear that over a third of millennials now buy, wear, and then return clothing, in a form of returns fraud known as *wardrobing* or *snap and send back*.

'The stresses of taking clothes outside and being super paranoid about getting anything on them/rain starting!' exclaims twenty-year-old fashion blogger Common Toff. In her post, 'Instagram Illusions', Common Toff writes of the pressures young women face in feeling like they need to constantly be wearing new things but not having the funds to support it, and the role that influencers play in this perverse cycle. 'When you're more indebted than ever, and your hobby involves the upkeep of an appearance of wealth … Well, desperate times call for desperate measures.' Common Toff is aware of the false economy of what she is doing. 'The lifestyle I present on my Instagram is somewhat impossible for the average student (I mean it would be for me), and that is why I find it so very necessary to expose the illusion on here. It's a fine balance,' she concludes. 'I want to offer inspiration; I want people to access my style if they so wish, but I equally hope they can be aware that I am posting my own dream life.' Common Toff alludes to something that the novelist Upton Sinclair once noted: 'It is difficult to get a man to understand something, when his salary depends upon his not understanding it.'

In 2018, it was reported that personal borrowing on credit cards, loans and car finance is rising at almost five times the rate of growth in UK salaries. Newspaper headlines regularly inform us that young women are bankrupting themselves by chasing Get The Look. 'Woman racks up $10,000 debt after trying to become "Instagram famous"' read a 2018 headline in the *Independent*. Much of this is facilitated by a new payment system called Klarna – which is referred to on social media as if it were a person, not an online bank.

*Think I need to whined it in with the klarna purchases fuck
sake getting dangerous now @hanwashingtonx
I need to block myself from klarna @hannahmcguiganX*

Klarna is a dangerous bad bitch but a canny help myself
  @danielleforsyth
Klarna is ruining my life @emsbell97

Klarna allows you to 'try before you buy' and is rolled out across typically youth-skewed websites, for credit-averse young millennials. It is the socially acceptable form of debt for the 18–34-year-old woman, with zero interest (instead, they charge merchant fees from retailers), and requires only a 'soft' credit card check. It also increases basket size by a whopping 30–40%. Unlike credit cards, Klarna and similar payment systems like Clearpay and Laybuy benefit from trendy marketing: they are packaged as the means to enable a *lifestyle choice* that is yours to have, to hold and to wear. It is debatable whether these payment systems are actually worse for a young person's pocket than credit cards, but either way, Klarna has done something that credit cards never managed. It has integrated itself into the sexified shopping experience and earned itself tweet status as a 'bad bitch': the Regina George of credit.

VI.

My own role in Get The Look is one of complicity. When I was twenty-seven, I assumed the slightly saucy-sounding alter ego 'Wardrobe Mistress' as a columnist and editor for the *Sunday Times Style* magazine. My two-page column would solve the 'fashion dilemmas' of readers, flag new brands and interpret a different trend on a weekly basis. It was considered poor service to the reader to repeat a brand more than once in each column, meaning that every single week I was compiling products from approximately thirty different brands. Everything I featured had to be immediately shoppable – meaning it had to be brand new, so as not to have sold out in any sizes, and in the current season. From memory, I never shot clothing from Primark or from faster e-tailers – which were still in their nascence when I was the Wardrobe Mistress from 2014 to 2017. Even before I became aware of Get The Look, I believed clothes should not be that cheap. The column was mostly comprised of high street and contemporary brands, and was based on a notion of affordable covetability and relatable aspiration.

During this time, I noticed a strange pattern: everywhere I went, friends – and sometimes people I didn't know – would ask me if they were getting it *right*. I was bewildered. How is personal style something you can get wrong? Surely by definition, personal style is yours and only yours. It was only later, when I thought back to those conversations, that I understood this anxiety is the cornerstone to Get The Look, and one that feeds into the larger theme of this book: most women feel that getting dressed, that their appearance, is something they can get right or get wrong.

The purpose of my role at the *Sunday Times* was instructive: to help my readers. There is a certain responsibility and authority bestowed upon fashion editors that is absent from influencer culture. But that does not make fashion magazines guiltless. The influencer economy has been under the Advertising Standards Authority's spotlight for some time – to ensure every post accurately states when it is an ad or sponsored – but it remains largely unknown that consumer magazines comply with a credit system whereby advertisers see themselves 'appropriately represented' in response to their ad spend in the magazine. (Should a magazine fail to shoot the product from an advertiser, the brand could threaten to 'pull' their spend.) Magazines also profit from your attempts to Get The Look – you buy something that they have featured because they are paid to do so. This shouldn't be surprising. As their name suggests, *consumer magazines* are designed to encourage you to consume, with a specific parlance that reflects the regularity of that endeavour: 'this season's must-haves'; '10 hot new trends'. Often the language is inverted to give the *appearance* of longevity – '10 Pieces That Will Last Forever' – a feat undermined by the quarterly regularity of that segment.

But many editors are starting to rub against their consumerist constraints. Last year, the *Guardian*'s Fashion Director, Jess Cartner-Morley, decided that having an entirely shoppable column no longer resonated with her growing concerns with neophilia. 'When I buy clothes, I am trying to buy a better-looking, cooler, more exciting version of me,' she wrote. 'Same as it ever was, nothing new in that. But what has changed is that the chasm between the reflection in the mirror and our Instagram-fed aspirations yawns ever wider.' Cartner-Morley's column now consists of a couple of shoppable pieces, plus vintage items and often decades-old pieces from her own wardrobe. 'My aim with my column is not simply to rail against fast fashion,' Cartner-Morley tells me, 'but to interrogate the culture that has embraced it. It seems to be that there's a self-esteem gap. What is it that we are *really* craving when we wander into a high street store, to buy a new dress?' As the American economist Theodore Levitt once said, 'People don't want to buy a ¼ inch drill. They want a ¼ inch hole.' It is not just a new dress that women want. They want to *feel* new.

Cartner-Morley's column hints at the idea of consumerist mindfulness. A recollection of a time when fashion was about inspiration just as much as acquisition, and involved pieces you'd owned for ages, or that belonged to someone else. But not everyone can be bothered to shop second-hand. It takes too long. The sizing can be tricky (the offering tends to run small, which makes it a not particularly inclusive medium). It's impossible to replicate. In short, it makes Get The Look so much *harder*. 'Vintage is great,' someone wrote to me recently, in response to my increasing efforts to wear more vintage. 'But how are we meant to go buy it?'

I no longer write shopping stories or collaborate with fashion brands (mostly because my work has moved into non-fashion-related areas). But even without that, even without posting on Instagram as much as I used to, I am associated with clothes and shopping by dint of my large social media following, and of my history as a fashion columnist. (The extreme alternative – *not* wearing clothes – is not exactly a viable option.) I also occasionally accept freebies, benefiting from the industry's 'gifting cycle' that negatively fuels the unattainable idea of how many clothes a woman should, or could own, and that feeds the wardrobing crisis. I don't feel exempt from this narrative. My friends and family don't understand this inner conflict as to whether or not I should accept free things. 'Get the free shit!' they screech. 'Give it to us!' So that they, in turn, may Get The Look.

VII.

'The things we buy and buy are like a thick coat of Vaseline smeared on glass,' wrote the novelist Ann Patchett. Many people are now seeking a guilt-free solution in the rental business, a global market predicted to grow to $2.5 billion by 2023. The bigwig in the US is Rent the Runway, while in the UK we have Girl Meets Dress, Wear the Walk, My Wardrobe HQ, Onloan, Front Row and By Rotation, the first ever 'peer-to-peer' rental service where the platform itself holds no stock. The upside to rental is obvious – fewer clothes purchased equals fewer clothing in landfills, less clutter in your home, less debt, and it is especially useful for temporary periods of life such as pregnancy. But rental does not tackle the psychological crisis at the heart of the epidemic:

that in order to feel like we are getting it right, we need to wear something *new*.

Rented clothes are not *literally* new, but they are new for the customer receiving them. They subscribe to a wardrobe pattern that she is now well-versed in: In. Out. 'Can things really change when businesses are increasingly intent on absolving shoppers of responsibility in a purchase?' ponders the *New York Times* journalist Elizabeth Paton in an email to me. Rental is expensive – not as expensive as buying the clothes themselves, which are from the contemporary and luxury fashion category rather than high street, but certainly out of the budget of most women. The customer who can afford to subscribe to these platforms can often afford to buy semi-designer clothes outright. The idea that rental is a sustainable, even virtuous alternative hits a barrier when you consider how few people can spend £70 a month (if not more) on clothes they do not own. (Girl Meets Dress has a monthly fee of £99 for unlimited dress hires.) 'Our subscribers spend nineteen hundred dollars a year, and last year the average subscriber got forty thousand dollars' worth of value,' the CEO of Rent the Runway, Jennifer Hyman, told the *New Yorker*. 'That's a lot of money to spend on not buying clothes,' notes the article's author, Alexandra Schwartz. 'Is it worth investing money in your self-image if that image is just on loan?'

There is something odd about spending so much money to *not* possess something. I have never rented clothes before. That's not to say I wouldn't consider it, but I do find the idea of sending my clothes back strange. It's a no-brainer that we should own less. But the pathology is not just in owning too many clothes, it's also in *spending* too much on clothes. Yes, it might help you own fewer clothes, but rental doesn't stop the drive to spend. The rental economy is not inherently good or bad; certainly, it fills a gap – especially for those who only need a piece of formalwear once every two years. But the rental market – with its regular dopamine hits of newness and temporal ownership – has more in common with the Get The Look phenomenon than it does not.

It may cut down on waste, but you could argue that the rental economy also fosters a wardrobe dissonance that harms, rather than alleviates, Get The Look. You're still *getting the look*. It's still a transient acquisition. The only difference is you're not bearing any responsibility for it. But perhaps I'm missing the point. In a piece about her new clothes-renting habit, the *Times* journalist Harriet Walker explored how renting clothes, which promises 'newness' without 'gluttony', has enabled her to experiment with her look in a way that felt too risky when actually purchasing clothes. She notes that a rented Mother of Pearl shirt is 'more fun than the sort of thing I usually buy'. Could the rental economy be the invention we need to liberate us from homogenous fashion? Maybe, says Walker. But maybe not. On presenting her rented wares to a friend over dinner, she asks her if she might consider renting her clothes too. 'I might,' the friend replies. 'But it's much easier just to go to Zara, isn't it?'

VIII.

In the three months since I started writing this essay, the seasons have changed, but people are still wearing 'the' Zara dress. Perhaps this dress defies the odds with not only its virality, but also its *virility*. Various editors have been trying to predict the next Zara dress to blow up. But I'm yet to see any translated to the streets around me, and part of me thinks nothing can ever quite do what the polka dots did. Perhaps this is just the start. Perhaps we will become almost Gilead-like in our fashion: instead of Pearl Girls, we will be

Polka Dot Girls, walking in a line, hand-in-hand, into the nearest Zara.

The marketing expert Phil Barden says that there are different neural circuits regulating our feeling of 'wanting' and 'liking'; that we could want something without actually liking it. With clothing now accompanied by such overwhelming visual cues, it becomes impossible to truly determine how much of our shopping is about liking the item itself, and how much of it is about wanting a look. It has become increasingly difficult to shop to your own agenda, without any kind of conditioning. It is a sort of algorithm-based free will, whereby sartorial choices are made under a bombardment of mindset targeting – a marketing term for when brands appeal not just to a demographic, but to a psychographic too (a person's personality and interests). You may wonder why you scroll through social media thinking, *I do indeed love those shoes! How did they know?* Mindset marketing, mate.

The idea of choice is further complicated by the concept of social approval, whereby we buy something because it comes pre-approved by someone else. Someone we trust. Someone with a lot of followers. 'We choose what other people are choosing,' as the sociologist and philosopher Renata Salecl puts it. In our digital age, this peer-to-peer marketing is as persuasive as it is lucrative. You may think you are buying something on your own terms, but in reality you are responding to a shopping experience that millennial women have been socialised in: that of the *experiential economy* (you are going out to have a good time) and the *visibility vector* (you will be seen, appraised and perhaps photographed).

Clearly this does not apply to everybody. Generations, as I said, contain multitudes. For every sweeping statement (Gen Z only shop sustainably! Millennials only wear fast fashion!) there is an opposition. Eighteen-year-olds are not all Greta Thunberg; plenty of Gen Z-ers shop faster fashion. And not all thirty-year-olds are getting the look of their favourite Instagram influencer; some of them are going to clothes-swaps and combing vintage markets. But avoiding social media and resisting fast shopping does not make you impervious to this culture shift. If you feel even remotely addled when you go shopping for a new dress – if you feel even slightly self-conscious – then you'll understand that this surfeit of choice is a paradox. There are exceptions to this metric – there always are. But they are fewer than you might think.

We are verging on becoming post-fashion. The democratisation and proliferation of fashion means that it is no longer a singular category. It is everywhere. It is in the ether. As a result, we are in an era of *chaos fashion*, where the '60s, '70s, '80s, '90s and '00s are all in style at the same time. The way I can best describe it is: all of the Spice Girls at once. That's great, right? That you can be anyone you want to be? I certainly enjoy that freedom. But then after years as a fashion journalist, I have acquired a confidence in dressing how I want, even if it's not the popular option. (Now that I work from home and socialise a lot less due to young children, my mode of dress has increasingly become the antithesis of any kind of 'look' at all.) But for most women, this surfeit of clothing, trends, influencers and eras to copy is frankly overwhelming. Amid this chaos of choice, it becomes harder to know what your style is, and, perhaps, who you are.

But the truth is, for all my supposed confidence in my own style, I am not immune to Get The Look. I saw a picture of a friend in a simple black dress – functional yet cool – and with longing, I asked her where it was from. I waited for a work break to surf the & Other Stories website (it didn't feel like much of a break, it felt like work, which says a lot about how we may feel about getting dressed now). Holding my breath, I scrolled through their selection of black dresses. I looked through 174 dresses and it wasn't there. Exhale. Relief. Crisis averted. Next, I headed to the Arket website, another Scandi high street brand with an aspirational quality (they call their HQ their 'atelier'), to locate a pair of sandals that I'd seen in a weekend supplement. I found them quickly, and put two different colourways in my basket so that I had *options*. Ready to race through the checkout, I paused and considered the weight of the words I had written. I cast my mind back to two years previously, when a friend was wearing those very same Gurkee sandals. *She looked great,* my subconscious whispered. *Yes, but have you forgotten how flat your feet are? These sandals are not your friend. You'll wear them once, they'll make your feet look like sad pancakes, and then you will never wear them again. You only want them because she has them.* Thirty seconds later, I closed the tab and returned to writing. I felt better not buying them than I would have if I'd bought them. But I can't pretend this always happens.

When will Get The Look break its power over us? Individuals are not responsible for this state of affairs (we did not invent the internet; we did not end the tariffs or reject the levies), and real change will require policy and systemic change. But it is not true that we cannot consider our choices as our own – even if it's simply psychological. Perhaps we should no longer see The Look as owing us something, but place the onus on ourselves as the consumer and think: *What can I give that look?* Freighting ourselves with responsibility may prompt a pause that currently eludes us. Instead of wondering if we can afford something, what we will throw out in order to house it, or if we even like it – we could consider whether we have the energy not just to possess it, but to wear it.

Little Pieces Everywhere

*Inside us as women we have a little harem of
female voices, coexisting and competing.*
Elif Shafak

I.

In her comedy drama series, *Fleabag*, about a messy millennial
Londoner, Phoebe Waller-Bridge delivers an empathic monologue on what it is like to be splintered by indecision – and
a million women swallowed their hearts whole. 'I want
someone to tell me what to eat. What to like, what to hate,
what to rage about, what to listen to, what band to like, what
to buy tickets for, what to joke about, what not to joke about,'
she says. Fleabag's ambivalence goes across the keys, from
minor (what band to like) to major (what to believe in). As
a way out of this indecision, she begs to be flattened into
someone else's ideal. Screw all my choices, she appears to
say, for there are too many to make; tell me how to think
and how to live. *Tell me how to get it right.* Fleabag seeks direction from the Hot Priest partly because he is a 'man of the
cloth' and therefore (she believes) of total conviction; partly,
because she fancies him. Seeking completion in men we fancy,
or fear – or both – is a pattern women are well versed in.

We have had our parts sifted through, siphoned off and shaped into female flatbread for so long that sometimes, like Fleabag, we crave it.

I watched the finale in exquisite agony – wringing it for every last drop. The almost-unprecedented level of praise the show received was largely due to the fact that 'Fleabag neatly inverts the idea of success', as Gaby Hinsliff wrote in the *Guardian*. For millennial women, 'under constant pressure to excel at things all the time; to jump through endless hoops without even questioning who put them there in the first place', Fleabag's flagrant admission of her insecurities was a comfort. She made so many of us feel seen, in all our ill-defined anxiety.

In exposing the fragmentation and flattening of women, Waller-Bridge has a lot in common with female writers of modern literature. It's not an issue limited to our times, despite sometimes feeling that way. In Virginia Woolf's *Mrs Dalloway*, 1920s society wife Clarissa views herself not as a distinct entity, but as a compilation of relationships – 'so that to know her, or anyone, one must seek out the people who completed them'. Forty years later, in *The Feminine Mystique*, Betty Friedan contemplated the impact of female fragmentation on women's happiness. Calling it 'The Problem That Has No Name', she identified the moment when the idealised image of the American housewife – waving her husband off to work, dropping her children at school, before returning to gaily clean the kitchen floor – 'burst like a boil'. It left women with a hole 'that food cannot fill' – a desire to be a complete self rather than an appendage of her husband and family. In 1980, the protagonists of Mary Gaitskill's genre-defining short-story collection, *Bad Behavior*, are extravagantly emancipated in comparison to those who came before. The tough-on-the-outside, fragile-on-the-inside New Yorkers engage in creative work, have sex with people they are not married to, and take drugs. But they are still seeking human connection and fighting their own fragmentation. 'One half of the face was alertly contemplating the world with expectation and confidence, while the other had fallen under the weight of it,' Connie observes of Alice in 'Other Factors'. 'The eyes expressed the fatigue and rancor of a small, hardworking person carrying her life around on her back like a set of symbols and circumstances that she could stand apart from and arrange.'

There are myriad ways in which women are fragmented and flattened. Fragmentation happens when a woman feels forced by the expectations placed upon her in a patriarchal society to publicly reject various parts of herself, in order to become more manageable or appealing. 'There's always someone asking you to underline one piece of yourself,' said Audre Lorde in 1981. 'Whether it's *Black, woman, mother, dyke, teacher*, etcetera … that's the piece that they need to key in to.' A woman's flattening happens when one of those fragmented parts absorbs the rest of her identity. This can be physical: a woman with big boobs is isolated into just those boobs. Cultural: a single woman is a roving and lonely soul. Sexual: a woman who has an affair with a married man is nothing more than a slut. Racial: a woman who is not white is defined only by the colour of her skin. And biological: she becomes someone who has either produced a child or not. A woman can be fragmented without being flattened, but she is rarely flattened without being fragmented first.

From day dot, women are taught to see their body in slices. It becomes the lens through which we watch ourselves and other women grow. I remember sitting on the radiator at primary school, in a line of little girls idly kicking their legs out, and casually observing that my legs were thinner than Rachel's but fatter than Sophie's. 'Breasts, feet, hips, waistline, neck, eyes, nose, complexion, hair, and so on – each in turn is submitted to an anxious, fretful, often despairing scrutiny,' wrote Susan Sontag in 'A Woman's Beauty: Put Down or Power Source?'. 'In men, good looks is a whole, something taken in at a glance … nobody encourages a man to dissect his appearance, feature by feature.'

The grim slang that exists around female bodies simply does not exist around those of men. A woman with pert boobs and a great bum is a T 'n' A (tits 'n' ass), or a woman in possession of a banging body but average face is a 'butterface' or 'prawn'. How often have you heard a man called a D 'n' A? Well, quite. For those who think that such isolation is not political, I offer up a *Daily Mail* headline from March 2017, which crowed, 'Never mind Brexit, who won Legs-it!' next to a photograph of Scottish First Minister Nicola Sturgeon and then-Prime Minister Theresa May. Both had been so bold as to bring their legs with them to a meeting. Sturgeon's crossed pair, encased in flesh-coloured tights, feet in neat courts, were a 'direct attempt at seduction', hooted journalist Sarah Vine.

Fragmenting a woman is a way to keep her at bay; to allot her a certain space. When that woman is not white, the picking off of her parts becomes another way to 'other' her. In Candice Carty-Williams' *Queenie*, Queenie's exboyfriend's grandmother hopes that their future child will have Queenie's big hair and dark eyelashes – but not her nose. Queenie is constantly eroticised, like a contemporary Sara Baartman – the South African Khoikhoi woman put on display at nineteenth-century freak shows under the name Hottentot Venus so that Europeans could marvel at her large buttocks. Queenie is splintered into a bum, a pair of tits, a mouth to be colonised. 'Is that big bum ready for me? It's looking bigger, you know,' caws her married neighbour Adi, while the charmless Guy uses the same technique to thwart her attempts to see herself as a whole person.

'"Guy, you know I'm a person, don't you?"' says Queenie. '"With thoughts and feelings and—" "And a big gob, but most of all, a big arse." He laughed.' Carty-Williams describes the attitude towards Queenie's body as something she has 'seen and understood my whole life. It happens to me so often that I end up seeing myself in that way. A little while ago I said to a (black) guy I'd slept with, "That's me, right? Big mouth and a big bum," and he was shocked and said, "Er … no? You're a lot more than that." The ways that I have been fragmented and fetishised have impacted me in ways that I'm still realising.'

II.

The flattening of women is a key element of consumer capitalism: women who have been flattened are *so* much easier to sell to. In turn, these branded tropes, as ridiculous as they sound, can make us feel like there are only so many acceptable ways to be. The choices include: *Manic Pixie Dream Girl* – gorgeous, ditzy, young, bewitches geeky men; *Yummy Mummy* – slogan T-shirt that reads MUM-IN-CHIEF, brood of golden-haired children in tow sucking on Ella's Kitchen fruit pouches; *Angsty Twenty-Something Millennial* – broke yet stylishly dressed, prolific on Instagram, constantly looking for a new therapist; *Career Bitch* – brittle, thin, suited, Botoxed, breaking deals at midnight from the bath while a gigolo massages her feet; *Badass Black Gal* – hypersexual, sassy sidekick, never the main role (her only alternatives as a black woman being *Angry Black Woman* or *The Mammy*); *Nutty Lesbian* – loves drugs and clubs, eyeliner crusted under her eyes, a feminist book tucked under her arm. Then there's *Asian Nerd* – head to toe Uniqlo, scurrying about with a laptop. Or the classic *Thin White Parisian Girl* – striped Breton, basket bag, stylish fag. And, of course, there's always *Cool Girl*, brilliantly decimated by

Amy in Gillian Flynn's thriller *Gone Girl*. 'Being the Cool Girl means I am a hot, brilliant, funny woman who adores football, poker, dirty jokes, and burping, who plays video games, drinks cheap beer, loves threesomes and anal sex, and jams hot dogs and hamburgers into her mouth like she's hosting the world's biggest culinary gang bang while somehow maintaining a size 2, because Cool Girls are above all hot. Hot and understanding … *Go ahead, shit on me, I don't mind, I'm the Cool Girl.*'

Once a company has identified its variety of woman, it sells the hell out of its product to her. She is branded by what she chooses to buy, becoming part of a Rolodex of women: categorisable and flippable. The comedy Instagram account @StarterPacksofNYC arranges a flat lay of clothes and objects that signify a certain tribe of woman, accompanied by short yet super-specific captions that are snarky but never cruel. 'Liberté égalité follow mé' reads a caption on a Jane Birkin lookalike starter pack, which includes a French slogan T-shirt, hand cream and red lipstick. I had a wincing recognition at the The Divisionista, who sips from a reusable water bottle, wears Glossier face cream and totes a beaded Susan Alexandra bag. In her 1998 book, *Bitch*, the late Elizabeth Wurtzel describes the launch of Calvin Klein's fragrance, Contradiction, as 'mass production's first acknowledgement of a woman's desire for her warring factions to find peaceful co-existence'. But the powdery, musky, floral scent never reached cult status like Eternity. I'm not sure mass production could ever sincerely acknowledge a woman's contradictions. It is so much easier to accept the flattening of consumerism. 'Once upon a time,' says Zadie Smith, 'we used to fear that the robots were coming. But what if we *are* the robots?'

Of course, men are not exempt from being categorised. You'll likely recognise Beardy Hipster, Football Lad, The New Man, Power Gay, Hot Dad, Tech Bro and Silver

Fox. A recent *New Yorker* article entertainingly grouped Hollywood's leading men into the following categories: 'sad-eyed brooders (Ryan Gosling, Jake Gyllenhaal), muscled he-men (Channing Tatum, Dwayne Johnson), sophisticated gents (Benedict Cumberbatch, Eddie Redmayne), high-spirited underdogs (Michael B. Jordan, Ryan Reynolds), bug-eyed misfits (Rami Malek, Jared Leto) and the inter-changeable hunks known as the Chrises: Evans, Hemsworth, Pine and Pratt'. But the tropifying of men is done with a lightness and is rarely enforced in any political or social sense. A woman who has recently had a baby understands it's her duty to shed her 'mum tum' as soon as possible. Meanwhile, a man with a 'dad bod' is thought of fondly – he is providing an empathic softness to complement his post-partum wife. Male tribes primarily exist within the confines of a humorous *Buzzfeed* listicle or an Urban Outfitters newsletter. 'Men are less likely to feel the need to subscribe to these marketing-led roles because they aren't taught from the off that their identity will make them less desirable,' says Carty-Williams. But then neither have men found the space to 'interrogate the roles that have been carved out for them', she notes.

Trying to resist flattening can feel futile. As a one-time fashion editor, people would frequently assume the only thing I want to talk about is shoes. 'Stick to "Wardrobe Mistress", love,' tweeted someone when I wrote about mental health, because a woman is not allowed to be more than one thing. I am a posh girl, so how could I empathise with the world around me? I am married and thus have no concept of what life must be like without a live-in partner. I enjoy talking about celebrities and therefore have no clue about politics. I am a mother and so wilt in the face of anything beyond four soft walls. I have been flattened and, at times, have willingly flattened myself. For as long as I can remember, I've tried to shave off the louder, messier, more abrasive parts of my personality. And with the bits I cannot change no matter how hard I try, I trail apologies behind me – 'I'm sorry I'm anal; I'm sorry I'm too sensitive' – desperate to be thought of as nice and sweet. I know we are told that women are now ready to be seen as angry and assertive and that we no longer crave modifiers such as 'sweet' and 'nice' – but I do. Not just because men expect it of women, but because so many women still rate each other based on how sweet they are, and I mostly look to other women for acceptance. This is one of the most crucial aspects of the flattening of women: while the desire to be seen as graceful and gracious is the by-product of a patriarchal society, *that does not mean that the messaging only comes from men*. When women have been conditioned from birth that the easiest and best way to move through the world is to present their shiniest shards, they both absorb and radiate that.

In *Recollections of My Non-Existence*, Rebecca Solnit describes her desire as a young woman to 'disappear and to appear, to be safe and to be someone, and those agendas were often at odds with one another'. I receive this line like a thud in the chest. Like so many women, I feel the pressure to stand out – but assimilate. To be visible – but unseen. It's a feeling closely connected to Imposter Syndrome, which two-thirds of women in the workplace are said to experience. This contradiction is at the heart of a woman's fragmentation. *Be the best, touch that glass ceiling,* women are told from a young age. *But do it modestly and, preferably, quietly.*

Solnit's work refers not just to emotional safety, but to the physical too. In a world where violence against women is still so prevalent, we become aware at an early age that our body makes us visible and vulnerable. I remember the pride I felt stepping out in my denim Miss Sixty miniskirt for the first time when I was fourteen, only to spend the entire Tube journey desperately pulling it down, face burning, after I realised it wasn't just my friends who were noticing my outfit. I am 'lucky' in that the worst thing that has happened to me on the Tube is when a man cupped my vagina from behind; or that time when another man pressed himself behind me on the escalator, whispering in my ear in Portuguese. But the baseline of anxiety persists. Even now – in my thirties, with infinitely greater reserves of fury and confidence and infinitely fewer denim miniskirts and crop tees – if I am wearing a short-ish dress with bare legs, then I do not risk the Underground. I will drive. I will walk. I will do everything I can to not find myself *almost* alone in a carriage, without the protection of hosiery or a mate. This feeling that your body is either 'a good danger or a bad danger' is so constant, writes Sophie Heawood, that it is a shock when you hit a certain age (not an old age, incidentally – anything, really, above forty) and that baseline stills into quiet ambivalence. 'Don't get me wrong: it's not that I want to be sexually harassed,' she writes. 'If such a phenomenon had never occurred in the world, I'd hardly be inventing it to give us ladies a little treat. But after a lifetime of being pushed up against those reminders that I was a woman, or perhaps that I was meat, it's as if the pressure I was leaning against has gone, and I might fall right over.'

III.

If it is possible to find a woman unfragmented by motherhood, I am yet to find her. Writing this at nine months pregnant, my prominent belly button nudging hungrily at my desk, I feel simultaneously unmoored and berthed by my body. As with my first pregnancy, my body is on loan – swollen and roiling inside with the zealous kicks of my son – and appears in the mirror nothing like the body I think of as my own. And yet when I am pregnant, I am mentally and literally grounded by my physicality in ways I have never been before. I am sore enough as to be almost sedentary. I am also extremely conscious of my physical parameters. Writing about the then-pregnant Meghan Markle in 2018, I defended what was seen as her ostentatious bump-cradle. '"It's not going to fall off," scorched Twitter of Meghan's rictus arms, to which I say – well it f*cking *feels* like it could,' I wrote furiously, thinking less of Markle and more of my own hands, which during pregnancy can be found cleaved to my round belly like furious clams. The irony of pregnancy is that at a time when many women would really rather be rendered invisible, you become extraordinarily conspicuous. In turn, you find yourself flattened into the archetypal pregnant woman. You know the one – you'll have seen her in movies: wears dungarees, sleeps, weeps, paints, has extremely funky cravings like charcoal. I wear dungarees, sometimes, but I don't sleep, I work harder than ever before, I succumb to irritation more than I do tears, and I prefer Coca-Cola lollipops to charcoal. This sense of being both deeply within myself and hovering outside of myself, waiting for *the real me* to return, is further cut loose by birth and, most permanently, by motherhood itself.

Like me, my daughter was born in a throat-chokingly bright March snowstorm. When we brought her home, my neighbour took a photograph. 'Stop!' he shouted from outside his house, when he saw us drifting dozily towards the front door. 'Let me take a picture, before you take her inside and your life changes forever.' It was a spontaneous act of kindness that I will always be grateful for. In an era of posed, premeditated photographs, it is an unguarded and infinitely precious memento. I stuck it to the fridge, so that we could see it every day: me, pale, exultant, damp-haired, gazing down at my sleeping daughter in her snowsuit; my husband, beside us, looking energised by his new role. Now a toddler, my daughter loves the fridge – like me, she sees it as a treasure trove of limitless epicurean opportunity – and we frequently find ourselves opening its shiny silver doors together. 'Dada!' she exclaims, every single time, jabbing at the image of my husband with a tiny finger. 'Yes', I always reply, 'and next to Dada is Mama, holding you.' '*Dada*,' she repeats firmly, returning to prodding her father. They say children possess an uncanny intuition. Perhaps my daughter does not recognise me in that photograph because I did not recognise myself.

I was extremely relieved to take to motherhood with less anxiety than I have taken to most other things in life – I instantly loved being a mother – but I rejected the social identity of motherhood. So keen was I to prove that having a baby didn't mean I had changed (of course I'd fucking changed!) that I gave myself no time to adapt to this new role, which I was both desperate to inhale and terrified of being overwhelmed by. I went back to work after the briefest whisper of a maternity leave and thus began a period of private agony: a push and pull between who I was and who I had been. Looking back, I think that in a subconscious attempt to 'have it all', I denied myself any of it. In the words of Rachel Cusk, 'I wanted to – I had to – remain "myself".' But in refusing to let go of a stagnant concept of who I was, I almost lost myself entirely.

I shared some pictures of my daughter on social media, but my narrative around her (the loaded topics of feeding and weaning and sleep routines), or of my experience of motherhood, has so far been scant. Perhaps this is unusual for someone whose work has such a strong personal element. It is not because I do not find my daughter fascinating – I do. I am endlessly charmed and undone by her. Her portly body, covered in peachy fuzz. The back of her petal-soft neck. Her tiny button nose. Her dimpled buttocks. Her delicately curled lashes. Her platypus-like toddler feet and her boldly rounded stomach. Rather, it is because this motherhood-shaped fragment of me feels too precious to articulate. Sharing this private, almost painful tenderness with strangers who could then pass comment on her, on me, on us, would feel like self-sabotage. I told myself that I did not want to alienate podcast listeners who do not want children; or to subject women who do not have but very much want children, to the agony of someone wittering on about her own bundle of love. But I wonder if I was, and still am, most terrified of alienating myself.

I am not the first and I will not be the last woman to agonise over whether you can have a child and work the way you used to. (Newsflash: you can't. At least not while they are tiny.) In the 1940s, Doris Lessing took the extreme route and left her two sons with their father in South Africa in order to return to the UK to write. 'No one can write with a child around,' she claimed. But to suggest that mothering and creative work, or any work, are incompatible feels pain-fully simplistic. A spectacular type of self-fragmentation. I was once chastised for using the term 'baby brain' because it conformed to a stereotype that giving birth made mothers less intellectual. Their mental fog becomes a way to fondly nudge them out of public and political discourse. *Off you go, sweetheart; you go sit over there, pet, with yer big leaky boobs.* At the time, I was frustrated at being told I wasn't allowed to describe how I felt. I've since changed my mind. Yes, like many women I know, I fumbled for words and thoughts and memories in the aftermath of my daughter's birth. I'd find myself in places, having no idea why I was there or what I was seeking. (Wholeness, probably.) Now, I know that this is not specifically baby brain. It's just what happens when you are extremely exhausted and have gone through a fairly traumatic, overwhelming and unfamiliar event like giving birth.

The contradictory providence of motherhood means that mothers are simultaneously elevated and sidelined: they are both the most and the least important women in the metaphorical room. 'There's a logical difficulty with treating mothers as an oppressed minority,' writes the novelist Tessa Hadley. 'Mothers are participants in their culture, all mixed up with men, woven with them inextricably into the flawed fabric of our societies, as different from one another and as multifarious as fathers are.' Flattening all mothers into one type of woman suggests that motherhood is a shared communal identity above that of the individual. I adore the sense of community that motherhood has brought to my life: the impromptu conversations with other parents in the park, doctor's surgery, local coffee shop. But sometimes the collectivism can be suffocating.

Motherhood does not 'legislate for complexity', writes Cusk. *Mothers* are seen as a single social group, with one set of political and social opinions. 'In motherhood the communal was permitted to prevail over the individual,' Cusk continues. Often this means being asked about your children and little else. This is especially true for stay-at-home mothers, whose *entire raison d'être* is assumed to be one of mashing, wiping and corralling. The flattening of motherhood excludes any type of 'other' mother. The sociologist Angela McRobbie describes this as 'the neo-liberal intensification of mothering' – a white, middle-class concept of 'pure parenting'. In her penetrating book *Hood Feminism*, Mikki Kendall says, 'I wasn't a single mother, but doctors would act like I was, unless my then-husband was physically in the room. Sometimes, even though we were very clear that I was the one staying home with our baby, they would start talking to him like he was the one qualified to make the decisions because he was white.' Forget the 'Mommy Wars', writes Kendall, what does it mean to be flattened on sight; for it to be assumed that 'to be poor and not white means you are less capable of being a good parent'?

One in five women at the age of forty-five do not have children, and yet 'we don't really have a way of talking about women's lives outside marriage or babies', writes Glynnis MacNicol. 'You disappear.' Child-free women are denied the legitimacy society gives to those who procreate. Instead, they are seen as flighty and formless, pitiable and self-indulgent, with buckets of free time. Writer and podcaster Elizabeth Day writes, 'There's vanishingly little attempt to think about how many things I might also be juggling, as if my childless status means I'm forever knocking back martinis and running off to nightclubs at a moment's notice.' It is a point of view enforced by my older sister, who found herself being asked to attend bath times in lieu of a proper catch-up with a friend, as if any company at all was better than being on her own – especially the restorative, nourishing, wholesome company of a *family*. And yet other women have told me that they yearn to be involved in this new dimension of their friend's life, but are excluded from family routine because their friend assumes they would find spending time with little children tedious. The only way to navigate the balance is for a woman – mother or not – to be asked what she wants, how she feels, what she needs.

Logically, we know that Freud's *madonna-whore* complex (whereby women are either maternal or promiscuous) is a fallacy, and yet women are still often flattened into either/ or – and even worse, pitted against each other. It's not just straight women, either – gay women are 'flattened into either butch or femme and naught in between', explains the journalist Sophie Wilkinson. 'We're either marginalised or sexualised.

With gay women, it's not about the madonna-whore complex; it's about women being seen as sexually useful, or useless. Lesbians do not fulfil sexual reproductivity (not without intervention), or sexual availability. It's a rotten feeling, knowing that femininity is still so narrowly defined.' In her upcoming memoir *The Panic Years: Dates, Deadlines, and the Mother of all Decisions*, Nell Frizzell looks at a woman's 'biological clock' from both perspectives. 'I wanted to halt this unnecessary and unpleasant division of women into apparently competitive camps,' she tells me. 'When I had my child, I became "niche", despite undertaking the third most universal human experience there is (after being born and dying) … I had given birth, I was now a parent, but somehow it felt like that was something I should only talk to other parents about. This, of course, is the problem.' A respite from the knotty intellectual interrogation surrounding motherhood can be found in the late, great Nora Ephron's response: 'Here's what a parent is. A parent is a person who has children.' I envy Ephron's pragmatism, but I do think that motherhood is more than just having children. That doesn't mean that children can alter your entire personality, mind. You can be the same shitty, self-obsessed person you were after kids as before them, and you can be a generous, nurturing person without ever being responsible for a child.

I left the NCT group chat as soon as it flashed up on my phone. To other mothers (or fathers), this may sound obnoxious or unwise. For many, a WhatsApp group with your fellow patrons of newbornhood is nothing short of essential – if only to find others going through the same midnight anguish as you. My reasoning for a digital French exit was simple enough: having foolishly decided to take the shortest maternity leave possible, I knew I would feel agonised by the updates of the group, who would likely take six months to a year off to muddle through this dreamworld, with its manic, fogged, park-walking pockets of love. This did not mean that I isolated myself from the wisdom of other new mothers. I was lucky enough to have a baby at the same time as a clutch of my best friends, none of whom felt the need for us to enter into collective, constant communication, but also never let a question or fear go unanswered. Being free from the whorl of baby-led cacophony at a time when my work/life balance already felt as fragile as a pulsing fontanelle was a relief: a lifeboat in a storm.

I now wonder if it helped me carve out my co-existing identities – however jagged that rupture was to negotiate at first. 'The problem with making new friends when you're all about to have a baby', sighed a friend recently, whilst juggling her dimpled seven-month-old daughter on her hip, 'is that all you then talk about is the baby. I want to talk about my baby. I want to talk about motherhood. And it's not like I'm ready to go back to work. But I want to talk about other things, within the same conversation, *with the same people*.' When my best friends had babies, we were lucky that our friendships pre-existed our new charges by decades. We never forgot who we once were to each other, whilst embracing who we had become. I may not have been able to see myself after my daughter's birth, but my best friends never lost sight of me.

Being a mother doesn't disappear from your consciousness (except perhaps when drunk – we all have friends who, having forgotten the existence of offspring while inebriated, loudly exclaim from the loo seat, 'Gosh I have a *childsh*, how *strangsh*!'). But it is a social identity that you can place carefully down, on a piece of velvet worn thin, when your children aren't physically with you (which, I've heard, becomes easier to do as they grow older). Frizzell offers me this beautiful vignette as an illustration. 'When my son was a few months old, I sat on the Overground, full of an irrepressible sense of excitement and fear and liberation and guilt. I looked up and down the carriage at people checking their phones, doing their make-up, staring out the window and one thought hit me with an absolute blow: *Nobody on this train even knows I'm a mother*. I couldn't believe that such a fundamental, all-consuming, defining feature of who I was could somehow also be invisible. This feeling brings me both relief and grief. I will never be "my old self" but I might look like it to a stranger on a train.'

IV.

The author of *Exposure*, Olivia Sudjic, writes that a self that allows for 'the acknowledgement of contradiction, the acceptance of self-doubt [and] the fragility of selfhood' is essential if we wish to keep our different parts represented. This is particularly challenging in a modern world desperate to package everything into digestible, easy-to-market 2D. There are tonics, of course. The writer Taffy Brodesser-Akner revels in her highly successful disorderly life. In the last year, she has published 90,000 words as a journalist for the *New York Times*, written a bestselling novel (with another on the way) and missed just two of her kid's sports games. *How does she do it?* people ask. *What's her secret? Her hack?* She must be so singular, so contained, streamlined like a whippet; a yogi of single thought; strained clear like a glass of celery juice. But Brodesser-Akner explains that she won't give them the answer they crave ('mindfulness' or 'doing one thing at a time'). She achieves what she achieves by being both mentally and physically fragmented. One leg on its way elsewhere, brain whirring on to the next thing. She rejects the idea that she can be made whole by being a Highly Regimented

Woman – today's ideal female, flattened and shaped by the strict routine and self-care demanded of her as a capable, tidy, modern working woman – a woman who fills Brodesser-Akner with 'dread'. 'My life is a mess. My mind is a mess. But nobody has been able to convince me that the value of a mind that isn't a mess is greater.' In her deliberate and bountiful haphazardness, Brodesser-Akner is a relief.

I think that's what Waller-Bridge is getting at with *Fleabag*. With her sparsely populated guinea pig café and her anecdote-worthy sexual adventures continuing into her thirties, there's an implication that we should feel like Fleabag has 'failed' at life. But Waller-Bridge shows that her protagonist's life is more truth than tragedy. Having broken the trophy at her sister Claire's work event, crashed off and attempted to seduce Kristin Scott Thomas's character, Belinda, Fleabag is shocked when Claire turns to her furiously, not, as she suspects, in order to shout at her for fucking up the evening, but to tell her, 'You just make me feel like I've failed.' Fleabag's operating system is chaotic, and her sense of self incoherent – her identity fragmented into who she thinks she is, who she escapes into, and who she thinks she should be. Yet it's clearly preferable to the life of her rich older sister, stuck in a miserable marriage and in brittle denial of her disparate fragments.

This does not mean that we should hold up Fleabag – straight, white and slim, with a financial safety net – as a poster-girl for the 'Young Millennial Woman', as writer Rebecca Liu puts it in a piece for *Another Gaze*, or as the voice of a generation. (This happened to Lena Dunham and, because of the limited narrative outlook of her TV series *Girls*, led to a backlash of epic proportions.) To do so would be to ignore the fact that female fragmentation differs according to race, class, sexuality, economic status and body type. I felt an immediate affinity with many of the struggles in *Fleabag*, but Fleabag herself is not and *cannot* be relatable to everyone. The idea that any woman – real or fictional – could speak for an entire generation is absurd – and yet it persists.

The idea of relatability is 'flattening and deceptively homogenising', writes Liu, because it ignores the fact that womanhood is a 'deeply variegated class'. And also because *relatable* is a coded word for *likeable*. Such is our obsession with on-screen female relatability that even murderers must be someone that other women can align with (perish the thought that we could absorb or enjoy women we cannot identify with). Take Villanelle, the anti-heroine of *Killing Eve*. 'There's something so relatable about Villanelle, something very curious about her and likeable,' insisted the actor Jodie Comer of her Waller-Bridgian character – *an assassin who breaks a young boy's neck*. Villanelle is charming and playful and pretty, even when she's killing someone. But while white women are free to subvert, both on screen and in life – remaining like-able and charming – the risk is so much higher for women from ethnic minorities. When *Queenie* was published, the protagonist, a twenty-something stumbling through life, was invariably dubbed a 'black Bridget Jones' – a shorthand which failed to take into account that as a black woman 'you can't mess up', says Carty-Williams. 'A lot of *Bridget Jones* is "Oh, poor me, silly me," and people being like, "Oh, Bridget, don't worry about it", but if you're a black woman, the reality is completely different.'

The woman who celebrates her splinters, or refuses to feel guilt for them, is often described as 'unruly'. Pop culture would have us believe that unruliness is something powerful – a radical resistance to the status quo. But the modern invocation of what this unruliness means is often self-fulfilling and banal:

the news coverage surrounding Brett Kavanaugh's election to the Supreme Court, for instance, focused more on how 'risqué' the pert-breasted model and actor Emily Ratajkowski was for not wearing a bra while talking about politics, than it did on the allegations of sexual assault. When actually, Ratajkowski is just a woman who doesn't like (or, let's be honest, doesn't need) to wear a bra, which in the light of the bra-burning feminists of the '70s isn't exactly new. Calling white women 'unruly' like it is a positive thing is further complicated because 'unruly' has historically played an instrumental role in the pejorative fragmentation and flattening of black women. In *Don't Touch My Hair*, Emma Dabiri explores how afro hair is considered unruly only in comparison to the hair of Caucasian people; the writer Roxane Gay, meanwhile, reclaimed the term 'unruly bodies' and used it as the name for her online magazine. Unruliness not only means different things for women who aren't white, but it also suggests a messiness that is sprawling. A chaos that extends beyond the constrictive parameters of acceptable femininity. But what even *are* the accepted parameters of femininity? How does one move beyond them in any real way? And why are there parameters at all?

In practice, the term 'unruly' has become about as radical (and as reductive) as the idea of women as flawless. In *Trick Mirror*, the essayist Jia Tolentino writes that 'womanhood has been denied depth and meaning for so long that every inch of it is now impossibly freighted'. We are left, instead, with a 'binary fatalism', where women in the public eye are flattened into polar opposites and must pick a side. Those who willingly and joyfully conform to the status quo – the 'basics': women who love mass-marketed trinkets of femininity like flowers and scented candles and fuck-me heels and date nights and empowered-motto T-shirts – are now as controversial as women who flout it. Flattening women into one or other category does not alleviate criticism; it exacerbates it. Take Meghan Markle. Discussion of the duchess does not centre on her as an actual person any more, but whether or not you think the critique of her is fair. She has become a canvas onto which people project their hopes, fears and dreams. Markle (too American, too Hollywood, too ambitious, too Black) is diminished, diminished and further diminished. She has been flattened into a paper doll. On one side, a victim. On the other, a hero. With nothing in between.

V.

'To create a single story,' says Chimamanda Ngozi Adichie, you show someone 'as only one thing, over and over again, and that is what they become.' In 1998, Monica Lewinsky, then a 22-year-old White House intern, became globally famous after her affair with President Clinton was made public. Almost twenty years later, she talked about the impact of this flattening in her TED Talk, 'The Price of Shame'. 'I ceased being a three-dimensional person,' she said. Instead Lewinsky became a stupid bimbo, a silly slut. The depressing truth is that to many – unwilling to acknowledge that a woman can be, and do, more than her worst mistake – she will forever and only be that. Cynics argue that her affair with Clinton did the opposite of erasing her: it put her on the map. *Look at her TED Talk. Her Netflix series. She's still talking about it.* But after everyone else spent so long talking about her, reducing her to a punchline, why the hell shouldn't she? Lewinsky may not have been erased from her own life, but her future political career – and, to be sure, being a White House intern at the age of twenty-two bodes well for your future – was taken from her before it could begin, flattened into dust with one blue Gap dress. In 2019, the psychologist Adam Grant posted a question on Twitter: 'What's the worst career advice you've ever received?' 'An internship at the White House will be amazing on your resume,' she flashed back.

In the last few years, two related trends have begun to dominate the internet. 'Call-out culture' is when the public holds to account an individual or corporation. At its most productive, call-out culture lends power to the disenfranchised. In 2019, Dolce & Gabbana were forced to cancel a runway show in Shanghai after the Instagram account @diet_prada flagged an offensive advert and revealed racist messages sent by one of the designers. But at its worst, call-out culture flattens. It erases nuance, so that there is little difference between the judgement delivered to a racist corporation and an influencer's foolish Instagram caption. 'Cancel culture' is the step after call-out culture – where holding someone to account is not enough and public opinion calls for their complete erasure. In the comments section, demand for someone's cancellation gathers momentum much like in *Lord of the Flies*. Unsurprisingly, this impacts women more profoundly than it does men. When a male celebrity screws up – Trevor Noah and his joke about Aboriginal Australian women being ugly but well-practised in oral sex thanks to their handling of the digeridoo; Matt Damon interrupting an African-American producer named Effie T. Brown to mansplain diversity to her – he is duly lambasted, before rising, a few weeks later, from the keyboard's ashes. But if a woman does it, her mistake is no peccadillo; it is proof of her worthlessness.

In February 2019, a peppy American fashion influencer named Dani Austin was called out by @diet_prada, after debuting her new line of Valentino-inspired fashion accessories – which were less of an homage than a blatant copy. 'Another day, another influencer launching a line full of knock offs,' hollered @diet_prada. Criticism was inevitable – the purpose of the post was arguably to invite it – and so began calls for Austin's deletion. In the comment section, she was called a 'bitch' and a 'cockroach'. 'For fucks sake can we just cancel ALLLL the Instahoes,' wrote another. Internet language is nothing if not flammable. The criticism quickly blew up beyond Austin's new designs into *who she was* and *what she stood for*: she was so basic. So thin. So *smiley*. In the same week, the British feminist writer and activist Chidera Eggerue, known by her alter-ego The Slumflower, dispatched a now-deleted tweet: 'If men are committing s*icide because they can't cry, how's it my concern?' The crass remark was quickly used as a reason to cancel her and her work – bold, original work, including the pioneering #SaggyBoobsMatter movement. 'Today is "Cancel Slumflower" day, huh? Lol. Took y'all long enough,' wrote one Twitter user. You don't have to agree with Eggerue's comment to find it troubling that instead of disagreeing with someone, we call for their elimination – as if we are in *The Hunger Games*.

Some say 'cancel culture' is merely empty rhetoric. That unless cancellation is enforced by legal or criminal sentencing or economic action – their job, earning capacity and power taken away, as with Bill Cosby and Harvey Weinstein – it does not actually exist. (Having said this, Weinstein was, at one point, making tentative steps back into public life. At a comedy night in October 2019, two performers were removed from an event they were performing at for heckling him. *Plus ça change*, and all that.) And it's true that although the toxic comments aimed at Austin and Eggerue went way beyond their errors, the two women don't appear to have suffered any long-term career impact. Rather, it has given them a new layer of personal truth. A few months after the bid for her cancellation, Eggerue shared a snapshot of her *Playboy* feature on Instagram, where she declared, 'I don't live my life according to a rigid set of ideas and theories that only apply perfectly on the internet. There's a real world where your own rules apply. I live my life according to prioritising my happy ending in a world where I'm statistically the least likely to witness that. And that's my feminism. You're welcome to define yours.' Austin, meanwhile, tried a new, revealing type of content about her alopecia – making the vulnerability imposed on her by public criticism her own. The impact of what undoubtedly felt like internet assassination is writ large upon their subsequent work. Eggerue and Austin are very different women, doing very different things – and undoubtedly, race plays a part in the critique of Eggerue, as it always does when a black woman is the subject of public commentary – but both have come out the other side of their attempted cancellations intact, and profitably so.

Celebrities exist under a spotlight – of money, fame and beauty – that warps as much as it informs. But however far removed cancel culture may be from the regular woman's life, it is based on a paradox that tracks back as long as history can recall: that one woman is responsible for an entire demographic. Austin may embrace having been flattened into a type – a bubbly, blonde, basic American influencer – but it isn't a trope, or a culture, of her own creation. It is a response to a culture that she has little control over. It's easier to direct this fear towards an individual – *Austin is selling us a lie! Her fake handbags are everything that is wrong in this world* – than to deconstruct the terrifying process by which women are flattened – sometimes voluntarily, but mostly without any clear alternative.

When Kim Kardashian West called Taylor Swift 'a snake on the internet' in 2016 after Swift fell out with her husband, Kanye West, it triggered what Swift called an 'apocalypse'. Swift stepped back from public view and built a life in London with her actor boyfriend. Three years later, she emerged with a much-lauded new album. Swift called it cancellation, but objectively it was not – she did not lose her manager, her record deal, her fan base. That she felt destabilised enough to disappear (as much as a pop star can) for three years shows that the impact of cancel culture can be enough to bring you to your knees. But in talking about her 'mass public shaming', Swift not only 'reclaimed the narrative' (as contemporary feminist discourse is wont to declare), she thrived within it. For Swift, now able to look into the eye of the storm after years of being sand-blasted, her stint as Unpopular Person on the Internet was merely confirmation that, 'I could survive it, and thrive in spite of it.'

VI.

In *Frantumaglia*, the bestselling author Elena Ferrante explores both her and her mother's fragmentation. 'She said that inside her she had a frantumaglia, a jumble of fragments … It was a word for disquiet not otherwise definable, it referred to a miscellaneous crowd of things in her head, debris in a muddy water of the brain.' For Ferrante, frantumaglia offers a resistance, a way to acknowledge – and display – her fragments, on her own terms: 'What I choose to put outside myself can't and shouldn't become a magnet that sucks me up entirely.' One of the greatest ironies of womanhood is that the more you resist your fragments, the more they turn into splinters and pierce you. The cruelty comes not from the fragments' existence, but from handing their arrangement over to someone else. 'Women need to be broken,' says Carty-Williams, simply. 'Because to be "together" is a fool's errand.' The dictionary would have you believe that to be *broken* is to be wrecked, crushed and damaged. But it also means *to be mutable and autonomous*; to have the chance to form into something better, something more valuable.

The Japanese art of kintsugi joins broken pieces of pottery back together with bright veins of gold lacquer. The fractures are transformed from unwelcome fault lines into something to be highlighted and celebrated. Beginning in the fifteenth century, kintsugi became so popular that people began deliberately smashing valuable ceramics for the pleasure of seeing the ornate repairs. Kintsugi suggests that when things are fragmented, they are altered but not irreversibly damaged. Rather, they are realigned to create something richer. It is entirely normal to seek wholeness. But what if wholeness is not our most valuable state? It is spectacularly freeing to think of our jostling parts as bound together by fortune rather than shame; to see that a frangible self can offer more than an unbroken whole. 'We can deal with an awful lot of rupture,' says the philosopher Alain de Botton, 'as long as there is the capacity to repair.' In trying to present a seamless version of myself to the outside world after my daughter was born, I almost razed myself to the ground. But as Lorde wrote, 'Only by learning to live in harmony with your contradictions can you keep it all afloat.'

To claim resolution at the end of this essay would be a flattening of the subject matter itself. The truth is that it is hard to imagine a world where women do not struggle to reconcile their fragments, where women do not feel paralysed as well as rewarded by choice, where women's fragments are not used as weapons against them. Our apparent choice can become a double-bind. It reminds me of Kristen Visbal's bronze statue *Fearless Girl*, erected in New York in March 2017. The defiant little girl facing the *Charging Bull* statue was commissioned by asset management firm State Street Global Advisors to celebrate International Women's Day. Only then it turned out that the very same company was paying women in senior positions much less than men. *Fearless Girl* began as a celebration, and morphed into a cautionary tale: that it is easy to aestheticise and immortalise the fearlessness of womanhood without really appreciating – or adequately remunerating – its compilation of selves. Millennial women are consistently told that they can be whoever they want, but in practice it's still complicated (not only because the same set of choices do not exist for everyone). In Anna Hope's blisteringly human novel *Expectation*, a mother snaps at her daughter in frustration, 'You've had everything. The fruits of our labour. The fruits of our activism ... And what have you done with it?' *We're trying*, I wanted to shout back. The flattening and fragmenting of women is so entrenched that even those of us who by dint of privilege and opportunity should have all the answers struggle to feel pride in who we are. If accommodating this flux in ourselves is a challenge, tolerating it in others is even more difficult. Our generosity needs to extend beyond our own fragmented pieces and towards those of others, too.

We should not mistake indecision for helplessness. The series of forks in the road can be overwhelming, but they are proof of our evolving selves. Even when sitting on my sofa in tracksuit bottoms, feeling simultaneously stressed and stagnant, I try to remind myself that I have agency. That my different social identities are a relief, rather than a bind. That however disparate I look to the world outside, I am still the same person inside. I love, and am loved, and that love cannot be fragmented by anyone unless I let it. Thinking about the fear and longing behind the splintering of ourselves – the truths, the clichés, the pressures – allows the light to shine through our shards. We are neither broken, nor whole, just creatures muddling through.

Work to Get Happy

A great deal of harm is being done in the modern world by belief in the virtuousness of work
Bertrand Russell, 'In Praise of Idleness'

I.

Hey, sorry I haven't got back to you. I've been TOTALLY slammed.

> God, don't worry at all. I'm com-pletely up against it. Literally Can.Not.Breathe. I haven't eaten a proper meal since last week.

Urgh, I know the feeling. Not one spare second. I haven't used a bathroom since last month.

> I actually haven't left the office this year. Gahhhhhh.

I mean, it's crazy – no, really. I've given up my house and sold my children, so that I can sleep under my desk and free up a bit more time to work. Let's catch up when things ease off a bit.

*

This conversation might be fictional, but you've likely had a similar one, albeit slightly (but only slightly) less dramatic. We are, we constantly lament, exhausted, frazzled, stressed, burnt out, *hanging on by a thread*. Most women I know feel like pressure cookers about to explode. In October 2019, we were able to visualise the toll this strain would take on our future selves, thanks to a life-size doll named Emma. Created by the furniture company Fellowes, Emma is what women in the workplace will supposedly look like in twenty years: she has a hunched back, varicose veins, red eyes, swollen joints, eczema, swollen sinuses and 'a rotund stomach caused by sedentary working'. She even has a hairy nose – the cherry on top of this depressing cupcake. To say that Emma made women feel even more fretful about work would be an understatement.

The modern pursuit of happiness and our determination to pin it down – as if it were something static that we could harness – takes myriad forms. But the one I find myself thinking about most often is how much this elusive concept of happiness centres on the idea of work; so that everything has become work, including the pursuit of happiness itself. Unsurprisingly, unemployment is cited as the biggest cause of unhappiness. But even those who are employed, and whose basic needs are met, wrestle with constant feelings of anxiety. This is partly because of how precarious work has become, with the rise of zero-hour contracts, self-employment and the 'gig' economy. For those of us fortunate enough to be in secure work, we live in an on-demand culture, a short-cut society, where we expect to *have* the best and *be* the best, and to value ourselves for our output rather than our motivation or conduct.

Almost every single creed on work culture begins with our lamentable failure to achieve what the economist John Maynard Keynes predicted in 1930: that, thanks to technological advances, we would work a fifteen-hour week. *But where is such a week?!* we cry. *This must be the reason we are not happy.* And so we work harder and harder to find this utopia, without realising that we are getting further and further away from what Maynard Keynes actually meant. We are on an everlasting quest to find 'the ideal work week', in the hope that the winning formula will bring endless happiness, fulfilment and satisfaction. Is the answer eight hours of work a week (apparently the optimum for our mental health)? Four hours (posited by bestselling educator Tim Ferriss – even more improbable)? Perhaps it's a four-*day* working week (as suggested in a Labour-commissioned report to combat overwork). Or is it, in fact, nothing to do with the hours, or days, but how we *are* at work? Are we overworked or undermotivated? Are we too immersed in our work or totally disengaged? Is it the government's fault that we feel like this or our own? Desperate to solve this ongoing conundrum, it is no surprise that there has been a renewed focus on 'happiness economics', with policymakers now looking to happiness indexes, like the UN's World Happiness Report, when considering a country's wellbeing. (The UK is currently ranked fifteenth in the world.) The grim irony is that, despite this quest, we have the longest average working week in Europe – with the average working day in the UK increasing from eight to almost nine core hours in the last twenty years.

The idea that if we work harder we will make more money and be happier is debatable. The Easterlin Paradox states that as a country becomes richer, the population becomes happier; but that if you look at the individual, personal income does not equate to happiness. There is a threshold (last put at around £50,000, in 2010), and anything earned above that threshold brings no additional happiness. But the Easterlin Paradox is controversial, and even amongst themselves, experts disagree. Indeed, to many the paradox may sound insulting. *If I earned more money, I could put a deposit down for a flat. Buy that sofa; go on holiday to Bora Bora; buy my kid a new pair of sodding shoes.* And yet it is common knowledge that plenty of rich people are very unhappy. Easterlin's theory, much-disputed though it may be, raises interesting questions about why (aside from to earn money) we work the way we work – if it's not to find happiness.

II.

Do you have a *leaky identity*? I know, the word 'leaky' is not a particularly pleasant one. I bet the theory, first introduced by the writer Derek Thompson in a piece for *The Atlantic*, hits a nerve, though. The office and home were once strictly separated by physical distance, but now – thanks to the internet and smartphones which mean you are always available, always *on* – the walls between work, home and our social identity have collapsed. In this way, the blending of public and private self is not something that only affects people like me, whose work centres on their personal beliefs and opinions, but anyone who is at work in the digital age. Our professional and personal selves have become indecipherable: work has moved from an occupation to a status, so that for many people, work is no longer just *a* form of self-representation, but *the* form. If your work becomes your identity – I *am* a doctor, I *am* a writer – versus your occupation – I work *at* a bank; I work *on* a magazine – then the parameters are harder to draw. As the *Vox* founder and podcaster Ezra Klein puts it, 'A job has boundaries. An identity has none.' I define myself through my work and feel unnerved when I spend a whole evening with a friend and work doesn't come up in conversation. But it wasn't something that I was wholly aware of until I read about what Thompson calls *workism*: 'the idea that work should be the nucleus of our lives, the centerpiece of our identity and the fundamental organising principle of our society'.

You can even be affected by someone else's leaky identity. My husband frequently emails from our bed, which is my Screen-Free Safe Place (capitals very much necessary). Because of his personal disposition, it doesn't affect his stress levels at all. But it affects mine. 'Put your phone away!' I mewl, from behind my book. 'Why do you care?' he retorts. 'Because I can see it in my periphery! It's *haunting* me. I keep catching glimpses of your inbox – which is precisely what I don't want to see right before I turn off my light.' A psychological study from 2013 vindicates me. 'One person's after-hours psychological detachment from work was associated with their partner's own detachment from their work,' conclude the German psychologists Verena C. Hahn and Christian Dormann. 'I *knew* you were making me feel leaky,' I tell him, smugly, as he looks at me slightly revolted.

The omnipresence of work in our lives can lead to burnout, a syndrome that exploded into public conversation this year after *Buzzfeed* writer Anne Helen Petersen's piece on millennial burnout went viral. Burnout is a condition related to chronic job stress, and it manifests as exhaustion, poor health (mental and/or physical) and feelings of incompetence and futility. Petersen describes millennial burnout as 'our base temperature. It's our background music', related to the pervasive 'idea that [you] should be working all the time' and any time that you are not working is bad. Burnout is not the same as stress (where you can work long, tiring hours but still be happy, still find meaning in your job, still think that you are *good* at your job) but it is a *type* of stress. 'The notion of stress at work has undergone an evolution,' agrees the epidemiologist Sir Michael Marmot, who cautions against the danger of meaningless work that 'touches no part of [you]' and is at 'the heart of poor health'.

Burnout is not necessarily linked to socio-economic difficulty. It consists of the same symptoms – exhaustion, anxiety and feelings of futility – but there is no recognisable pattern: it exists up and down the class register and across sectors. 'People patching together a retail job with unpredictable scheduling while driving Uber and arranging child care have burnout,' writes Petersen. But equally, she writes – and this may be infuriating to some – 'startup workers with fancy catered lunches, free laundry service, and 70-minute commutes [also] have burnout'. My teacher friends tell me that the blurriness of their role – with parents now texting and emailing them out of hours to ask them meaningless questions, or to offload their own parenting anxieties – makes it almost impossible for them to find time to prepare for lessons, or to have any time off in the evenings. Meanwhile, Leah Hazard, midwife and author of *Hard Pushed*, says the NHS exists but for the millions of healthcare workers who 'burn themselves out'. Adam Kay echoes this sentiment in his bestselling book about being a junior doctor, *This Is Going to Hurt*, which charts frustrating and meaningless bureaucracy that feels all the more galling when there is endless meaningful work to be done (like saving lives and delivering babies). It would be easy to assume that burnout happens more commonly for people who work in physically intensive roles, which can be relentless and repetitive and exhausting.

On the other hand, it could be (and indeed has been) argued that blue-collar jobs tend to have a sense of visible completion that most white-collar ones do not: a house is built, post is delivered, dirty crockery is cleaned. For many, burnout comes from feeling like your job is never-ending.

If you don't find your job fulfilling or meaningful – if you wonder why your job even exists – then you could have a bullshit job, says Dave Graeber, a professor at the London School of Economics and the author of *Bullsh*t Jobs*. 'Hell is a collection of individuals who are spending the bulk of their time working on a task they don't like and are not especially good at,' he writes. *Bullshit* jobs are different to *shit* jobs – after all, toilets and drains need to be unblocked. No one else can tell you if you have a bullshit job. 'I would not presume to tell someone who is convinced they are making a meaningful contribution to the world that, really, they are not,' cautions Graeber. But those are not the people Graeber is interested in. Instead, he is concerned with the 37% who, according to a poll in 2015, believe the work they do serves no purpose. Perhaps unsurprisingly, wellbeing is higher in employee-owned companies, where a democratic approach to decision-making leads to a sense of purpose and value.

Graeber divides bullshit jobs into five categories: flunkies (employed to make others look important), goons (employed to be aggressive or coercive), duct tapers (employed to paper over the cracks in a business), box-tickers (employed so that a company can pretend it is doing something that it is not doing), taskmasters (employed to get other people to do their jobs) and complex multiform bullshit jobs (it's complicated). I've identified as at least two of those in my time (though never, thankfully, as a goon). Perhaps we all have, at some point or another. Critics have pointed out the complexity of determining whether or not a job is bullshit. 'Who gets up each morning believing that they're about to make a meaningful contribution to the world? I've met doctors who question their purpose,' counters journalist Andrew Anthony. Graeber's theory may be provocatively named, but his argument – that we should find purpose in our work – is not a new one. It chimes with Czech psychologist Mihaly Csikszentmihalyi's theory of *flow*, or what computer scientist Cal Newport calls *deep work*: that pleasure can be found through concentration in a task that is challenging and achievable in equal parts. Such focus brings eudaimonic (purpose-based) happiness, rather than hedonic (pleasure-based), which has become the *Supermarket Sweep* of happiness. Grab that dopamine hit 'n' go! Don't stop at checkout!

Is it really appropriate to talk about burnout as a specifically millennial affliction? 'You think only millennials got sold a bill of goods about what to expect from life?' wrote one commentator under Petersen's piece. 'The most facile critique is that life has always been hard,' retorts Petersen. 'Your grandparents did World War II, like, buck up. But at the same time, the way that life is hard for millennials is that it's not necessarily more or less hard, it's hard in a different way.' Anna Codrea-Rado, the co-host of *Is This Working?*, a podcast about modern work practice, defines burnout as the accumulating expectation to do *more more more*. 'During the boom years of our parents' generation, when women first entered the workforce, it was a good thing to offer your whole self to work. We're coming to realise that giving your whole self to work is damaging – particularly for women.'

There is an argument to be made that burnout itself is not new, it's just new to people who haven't been historically oppressed. In a piece titled 'This Is What Black Burnout Feels Like', Tiana Clark explores the 'inherited burnout' of being a black woman: 'the [clenching] and [freezing] up every time I see a cop car driving behind me'. Clark wonders, 'if this zeitgeisty phenomenon – this attempt to define ourselves as the spent, frazzled generation – has become popular because white, upper-middle-class millennials aren't accustomed to being tired all the time? Aren't used to feeling bedraggled, as blacks and other marginalized groups have for a long time?' Neither is burnout limited to Western society. It is almost a national identity in Japan – depressingly, they even have a word for when burnout leads to death: *karoshi*.

It can't be long before burnout is recognised by the NHS as a type of work-related stress. But we should be wary of using it as a non-specific term. Almost every single zeitgeisty buzzword or phrase has suffered the fate of overextension, like 'gaslighting' (now applied to the mere act of criticising a woman) and 'toxic' (now applied to any kind of friendship or relationship that isn't goals-style perfect). I've heard people describing themselves as 'burnt out' when actually they're just really tired. We might also be combining paid work with many other activities, so that it is the *multiplicity* of work that is exhausting us. While working, you might also be a part of forty different WhatsApp conversations and guzzling down reams of internet news, making it impossible to focus a frazzled brain. We are not, whatever we may think, *always working* – although with their attendant sense of obligation, even tasks like replying to text messages and watching the news can feel like work.

III.

In their fascinating book *What We Really Do All Day*, sociologists Jonathan Gershuny and Oriel Sullivan gathered data from the Centre for Time Use Research (where they are co-directors) in order to determine how we spend time. The centre conducted a randomised study of 8,000 people, who were asked to keep time diaries over the course of 2014/2015, before meticulously measuring the data against diary entries from prior years. The conclusion, write Gershuny and Sullivan, is that the belief that we are all working harder and are more stressed and busy than ever is simply not true: it is – hold on to your eyebags – more of a "'folk narrative" about rapid changes in society than a real reflection of our daily lives'.

Rather, busyness has become about status. There is a *prestige* to the agony of busyness. If success was once measured by how much leisure time you had, it is now linked with how much of it you *lack*. It is 'a boast disguised as a complaint', writes Tim Kreider drily in 'The "Busy" Trap'. *Ouch*. Gershuny and Sullivan explain that 'when we think about our own lack of time, we are actually making a comparison with earlier stages of our own lives' – often young, footloose, fancy-free and, crucially, bored – 'while the true comparison would be with comparable stages of the life-course of older generations.' They note that leisure time has become more 'intensive' and overlaid with a 'cultural voraciousness': *Have you been? Have you seen? Have you read? Have you 'grammed?* This blurs the voluntary (free time) and the involuntary (work). Kreider adds that even this 'lamented busyness is [often] self-imposed: work and obligations [we've] taken on voluntarily'. The increase in workload has most affected those in high-status jobs, who are more 'likely to shape the terms of public discussion and debate,' argue Gershuny and Sullivan – meaning that it is not an 'objective phenomenon' but one that adversely affects privileged people. You could say that those lucky enough to be *able* to work long hours – lucky that our work is desired, recognised and remunerated – are also those who complain most about feeling busy. Could it be that the *truly* busy are the voiceless? Those juggling multiple low-income jobs – too, well, busy to self-define as being 'busy'?

To my total lack of surprise, Gershuny and Sullivan also find that there is a gender gap in busyness – with women much more likely to feel unhappily busy than men. I agree with them that this is likely due to an ongoing 'work-family' conflict, but I would go a step further and say that the female ability to multi-task (no, it really isn't a myth that women juggle tasks better than men) is short-changing us. I imagine this to be a common scenario for many women: while working at your desk, or on a conference call, you clear out your inbox and make a doctor's appointment for your child. All while putting on your sweater, writing a birthday card and eating a sandwich. I also find that women socialise – both in person and digitally – a *lot* more than men. (I can only measure myself against my husband, but sometimes I'm surprised he has any friends left.) And lastly, women – particularly women of colour – feel they are held to higher account for their work than men, and this makes the time spent doing it more loaded.

We like to think that the business of busyness is a contemporary problem of an anxious society, with the rise of FOMO (fear of missing out) an obvious symptom. But in fact, according to Adam Gopnik in the *New Yorker*, it's at least a century old. Seventeenth-century high-flyer Samuel Pepys, 'who had a Navy to refloat and a burned London to rebuild', might use the word 'busy', notes Gopnik, but never complains of busyness. He does not complain about having to fit someone in for coffee, or tight deadlines. 'Pepys works, makes love, and goes to bed, but he does not bump and he does not have to run.' Fast forward 200 years, Gopnik continues, 'and suddenly everybody is busy, and everybody is complaining about it. Virginia Woolf, mistress of motionless lull, is continually complaining about how she spends her days racing across London from square to square ... Proust is constantly rescheduling rendezvous and apologizing for being overstretched. Henry James, with nothing particular to do save live, complains of being too busy all the time.' I've noticed that I'm a bit like that too sometimes. When I moan about how busy I am, what I actually mean is that I have a lot that I *should* be doing – but I'm not actually doing it. At the moment of moaning, I could very well be doing nothing at all.

That being said, I am obsessively averse to wasting my time. I book conference calls instead of meetings. I put my phone on airplane mode (so much so that I made the extremely 1995 move of having a landline installed). I eat lunch at my desk, while typing away with one sticky paw. When I went freelance three years ago, I began to think of hours not spent earning money as time wasted. I considered the various ways in which I could outsource and offload to improve my output. I contemplated an email sorter, but was spooked out by the data collection. I thought about getting a virtual assistant, before realising that I'd find the bother of giving my admin to someone else more tiresome than just doing it myself. I tried out workflow systems like the Pomodoro Technique (whereby you segregate your work time into twenty-five-minute intervals using a timer). I realised I had fallen into a circular trap: I was spending more time seeking happiness in the *efficiency* of my work than I was in the work itself.

IV.

We are in the midst of a productivity crisis – in both an economic and personal sense. We have become obsessed with the idea that everything we produce should be *valuable and visible*, or else we're doing life wrong. Productivity has become something to be hacked and optimised. The productivity market is currently worth $82 billion with an array of apps such as Complice, which assembles a monthly report of your progress, based on goals that you input each day. The rather nasty-sounding tracking app Beeminder 'stings' you financially for missing a goal, while WOOP, which stands for 'Wish, Outcome, Obstacle, Plan', was described by life-hacker.com as 'the way to make your dreams a reality' (the exact type of statement that feeds this crisis). At the other end of the app-happy spectrum lie the New Luddites, who foster analogue-ish productivity habits that in themselves feel as unattainable as the high-tech apps. The novelist Jonathan Franzen portentously told *Time* in 2010 that he writes on an extremely old Dell laptop, stripped of WiFi access and even Solitaire; while the film director Quentin Tarantino hand-writes his scripts. 'I can't write poetry on a computer, man!'

In this febrile landscape of productivity and efficiency, the early bird itself becomes farcical. In 2016, the *Wall Street Journal* declared that 4 a.m. was 'the most productive hour of the day' (because everyone else is *quite rightly asleep*). After Apple's CEO Tim Cook revealed that he gets up every day at 3.45 a.m., a *Business Insider* journalist tried it for a week and reported that it made him 'shockingly productive' – but also that he was exhausted and snacking endlessly on crap. (I also find that 4 a.m. is 'shockingly productive' – but that as a result, lunchtime feels like the end of the day, if not the world.) There can be no greater example of how taut this tautology has become than the exhaustingly titled book *The Art of Doing Twice the Work in Half the Time*. The question is: when and where will this optimisation – of our time, of our happiness, of ourselves – end?

American website *The Cut*'s popular online column 'How I Get It Done' is one of many 'How I Do It'-type interviews fuelling the idea that learning the habits of successful women will osmotically transfer success (if not a sense of inferiority). The implication is that there is a right (productive) way, and a wrong (unproductive) way to do everything. I suffered a minor brain explosion on reading that women's club The Wing's co-founder Audrey Gelman uses a colour-coded email sorting system consisting of over sixty colours. Gelman concedes that 'it might sound crazy' (*might?*) but that it enables her to 'get people answers and responses most efficiently'. This is where millennial tech habits get truly meta: can sixty categories makes *anyone's* workflow more productive? Pity Gelman's assistant, Penelope, drowning in the opalescent treacle of her boss's inbox: there are only seven colours in the rainbow, meaning a minimum of eight shades per colour co-exist in one mail folder. Pray *who* can tell the difference, when staring squintily at a smartphone, between pistachio and mint? And thus the workflow system *itself* begins to generate the work.

When I was at university, one of my best friends nicknamed me Clipboard Pandy. It was, perhaps, inevitable: I am ruthlessly organised (anal) and have always loved keeping multiple to-do lists. As a nine-year-old (nineteen-year-old), these would include 'take shower' and 'brush teeth' so that I could *tick tick tick* the tasks off with a self-satisfied flourish. (In my defence, this is not unlike the approach of the polymath Benjamin Franklin, alleged inventor of the to-do list in the late eighteenth century, who wrote down a list of tasks like 'wash, work, read, work, put things in their places' in order to see what he had accomplished). But this level of efficiency was always something that I was hotly ashamed of: I was frequently teased for my five-pencil-case system at primary school. As I agonised my way through puberty, I yearned with every fibre of my being to be the fly-by cool girl, who didn't plan her day via intricate, time-stamped to-do lists – to be someone who just let it all *happen* upon her, like a leaf in an autumn breeze. This nickname was not something I was proud of. Yet now, in a time when our output has become our most valued attribute, the thing I spent my entire life apologising for has curiously become my trump card.

The to-do list has become a metaphor and a physical manifestation of our rabid, efficient quest for happiness. Bullet Journals, often abbreviated to the slightly-too-close-to-home BuJo, have repackaged the antiquated to-do list as an innovative product for optimised productivity. Any old notepad would surely be fit for purpose, and yet the Bullet Journal is a trademarked object: a Moleskine look-alike with an embossed BULLET JOURNAL across its chest, bifurcated by a lightning bolt of efficiency, and costing $24.95. Is the BuJo an anodyne method to cut through the chaos, or is it reflective of the fact that the to-do list has become an albatross around our necks? As Kate Walbert wonders in her short story 'To Do', 'Are we the sum of what we've crossed off? Or are we only what we still have left to do?'

I recently had the startling realisation that I had flattened my entire life into an infinite to-do list: work, leisure, motherhood and admin. Nothing was great, nothing was terrible, everything was just something to be ticked off. I wasn't depressed – rather, I was overwhelmed by *tickboxery*. With more choice than ever before in the way we live, travel and work comes endless opportunity, but also an insidious obligation to 'tick off' everything. Tickboxery is a way of skimming the water, clocking up as much as you can without ever delving too deep. You travel to a city for thirty-six hours; read a book while listening to a podcast. The act of getting things *done* – a sort of flimsy, surface-level productivity – has become more important than the *doing*. (Shout out to Shakespeare here, who reminds us: 'Things won are done; joy's soul lies in the doing.') My husband exhibits extreme tickboxery when it comes to travel. 'Haven't we "done" California?' he remarked, before our summer holiday this year. 'I'm riveted as to how you think one can even *do* California,' I retort. 'It's enormous. We've barely touched the sides. We haven't even come close to "doing" London, and we live here.'

This is the danger of *productivity as happiness*: it fosters the idea that you can lasso happiness itself, if you just do absolutely everything with enough efficiency. The quest for personal productivity has become 'a dominant motif of our age', writes the human behaviour expert Oliver Burkeman. 'It's easy to romanticise the task-oriented life,' he says. 'But the problem with "using time well" is that it risks transforming every moment into nothing but a means to future ends – which turns out to be a terrible approach.' Tickboxery and task-orientated productivity are offshoots of the on-demand life, where there is an expectation that everything can be faster or better. It is no wonder that people are turning to what sound like unspeakably dull yet calming sources of inspiration, which even in their banality, offer up insight into the *process* of others: videos on YouTube of people eating their dinner, doing their make-up, cleaning their house, or tidying their spice rack. The social media cleaning phenomenon Mrs Hinch, and Marie Kondo, the home-organising consultant who has made millions by popularising *danshari* (the Japanese art of decluttering), are living proof that streamlined efficiency – like the to-do list – can offer a semblance of happiness in a chaotic world.

I am far from resistant to workflow self-help. I have purloined Steven Covey's four-tier task system from the seminal '90s tome *The 7 Habits of Highly Effective People* (which has sold over 30 million copies to date), where you divide things into Urgent and Important, Urgent and Not Important, Not Urgent and Important, Not Urgent and Not Important. And after six months of book writing, I've whittled down my own crude and slightly obvious list of workflow tips, such as: don't listen to music with lyrics; turn off your notifications; drink lots of water, not coffee. But the best (and perhaps hardest to accept) workflow, nay, *life* advice is that no process will guarantee the production of good work, or – most importantly – bring you happiness. Instead, it is better to think of our work not so much as something we need to nail every single time, but something that we get merely good enough.

<h2 style="text-align:center">V.</h2>

In her book *How to Do Nothing*, the artist Jenny Odell ponders the commodification of free time. 'In a situation where every waking moment has become pertinent to our making a living, and when we submit even our leisure for numerical evaluation via likes on Facebook and Instagram, constantly checking on its performance like one checks a stock, monitoring the ongoing development of our personal brand, time becomes an economic resource that we can no longer justify spending on "nothing." It provides no return on investment; it is simply *too expensive*. It's a cruel confluence of time and space ... we also see all of our own time and our actions as potentially commercial.'

The fusion of work and (p)leisure has meant 'side-hustles' have become a way of life. Many people now work a usual 9–5, before beginning their 5–9. These millennials are known as 'slashies'. The snarks would say that the millennial woman's hustles tend to be homely 'hobbies' and not necessarily fiscally savvy: jewellery lines, cupcake businesses, personal blogs, pyjama design. (Insinuating that a woman's work is made up of her 'hobbies' is historic; particularly when that work is creative, which is often seen to be as arduous as farting rainbows.) But I have many friends who have grown a side-hustle into a bona fide business, taking the time to grow a company from within the security of a paid job: a dietician who set up an antique prints business; a teacher who set up her own tutoring agency. I grew my own side-hustles – a now-defunct blog, a podcast – into businesses by accident, alongside my full-time job as a website and newspaper writer.

Side-hustles are not just 'cute hobbies' for the privileged. They exist up and down the class register, says Petersen – the only people who *don't* have any, she continues, are the very rich. Slashies are both a reflection of increasing female ambition and an indication that for many women, the traditional workplace is *no longer working for them*. Maintaining multiple revenue streams is not about 'having fifteen jobs that you don't like', says Emma Gannon, author of *The Multi-Hyphen Method*. It's about 'future-proofing' yourself in a precarious work world – especially for a freelancer without the stability of an office. Ironically, now that side-hustles are a mainstream work practice, I have grown resistant to them. Last year, I began sharing my poetry via Instagram. The response was gratifying, but I quickly realised that I had turned something deeply personal – a creative act conceived during a difficult time – into something external and potentially profitable; work that could be validated, critiqued and shaped by the thoughts of others. It occurred to me that over the course of my career, there had been few creative pursuits that I did not mine for profit. And so even though it was an unfamiliar sensation, and perhaps counterproductive, I stopped sharing my poetry on any public platforms.

As a twenty-something freelancer, I was an enthusiastic member of Soho House (extremely elite – current membership approx. 57,000 people), until it dawned on me that I was paying an inordinate amount of money to not be able to work: I could never find a seat and when I did, I was told my laptop was not allowed in that part of the club. I realised that I had misunderstood the company M.O. It is not a place for work per se, but for socialising under the *pretence* of work. Co-work spaces are not the same as private members' clubs, but they also operate along the blurry line separating work and play. There are currently 1,300 co-work spaces in the UK, including the hydroponic work space Second Home – designed like a sort of in-work ecosystem with thousands of plants and trees – and the now ailing WeWork. Before its stock plummeted, the co-working giant's muddled promise to 'elevate the world's consciousness' included plans for a WeGrow elementary school, a WeSail, a WeSleep and a WeBank. As the world's most surprising introvert, I am deeply suspicious not only of networking (a friend of mine once summed it up as a 'series of nonversations', whereby there isn't necessarily any budget to pay anyone, but an abundance of compliments about shoes), but also of clubs that repurpose leisure time under the guise of work.

'Outside the walls of the Circle, all was noise and struggle, failure and filth. But here all had been perfected,' writes Dave Eggers in *The Circle* of his dystopian campus-style internet company where employees are strongly discouraged from leaving. There's a theatre, music, yoga, a nightclub, bicycles for hire, grocery stores, an organic garden, a clinic. A poster reads, 'LET'S DO THIS. LET'S DO ALL OF THIS.' Later, the character of Annie says, 'We want this to be a workplace, sure, but it should also be a *human*place.' It's enough to make you shudder – but is it really beyond the realm of possibility? Before its botched IPO valuation, WeWork was coming pretty close to creating a *human*place. And on Facebook's campus in Menlo Park, California, there is a pharmacy and a shopping centre. The billionaire media titan Michael Bloomberg pioneered the idea of in-office gyms, leisure spaces and canteens to encourage the idea that if their workspace served them well, employees would have no reason to leave.

In the last year alone, a spate of women's-only work/networking clubs have opened in London, garnering critique and desire in equal measure. Two high-profile ones stand out: AllBright – whose target membership is female entrepreneurs, a galling 157 times less likely to get start-up funding than their male counterparts; and The Wing – whose high-flying 'Winglets' in the States include Hillary Clinton and Alexandria Ocasio-Cortez. Whether they offer a correction to dribbly old boys' clubs or promote gender segregation in the workplace has been hotly debated. Regardless, in their different ways, both AllBright and The Wing operate to encourage and facilitate women's work – to offer what a traditional, male-skewed workplace often cannot provide – as well as connecting lonely freelancers, of which there were 3.3 million in 2017. That women could find other women inspiring within the confines of a plush-velveted, colour-coded-bookshelved, high-ceilinged townhouse in Fitzrovia like The Wing is not surprising. But I wonder how much the removal of discomfort (both physical and intellectual) plays in blurring our work/self identities. If the interior of your workspace is so much nicer than your home – Gelman says you should get a 'warm fuzzy feeling when you walk in' to The Wing – then surely this leads to the blurring of boundaries that workism thrives on?

A delightful work environment may well encourage workism, but it is also essential for those for whom work is a sanctuary. Not everyone who works remotely has a home that they can – or want – to work from. I am lucky enough to live in a family home where I have a study that is my own, but many millennial women live in house-shares with flatmates who they may not know, or like, particularly well. Communal spaces might be poky, or fraught with tension, and decorated in the landlord's very specific tonal taste of the 1980s – more conducive to migraines than freelance work. In this instance, you need your office to be nicer than your home in order to get anything done. Work can function as a refuge not just from the physical limitations of your home, but also the emotional. In *The Mother of All Jobs*, Christine Armstrong writes that for some working mothers 'released' from maternity leave, it is work, not home, that functions as their 'safe, happy place'.

VI.

I live my life on-demand. I buy my groceries, books and clothes online. The only thing I can think of that I don't buy from behind my desk is my morning flat white from the coffee shop at the end of the road, which signals the start of my working day. Being able to live an increasingly friction-free life, especially when my childcare hours are so precious, feels astoundingly gratifying. But there is something deeply concerning about the lack of discomfort in an on-demand life. 'The universe was not designed with the comfort of human beings in mind,' wrote Csikszentmihalyi. Yet we are doing all we can to make the opposite true. Though we may thrill at this ease – no need to queue! Or to interact with anyone unfamiliar/at all in order to make a purchase! – what happens when we *can't* demand what we want? Like success, or a particular job? Increasingly, the idea of success becomes not just something to dream about, but something to demand.

The idea that everything should come *to* you rather than be achieved *by* you is one that extends far beyond groceries and books. It reflects a collective aversion to delayed gratification. (The angriest people on Twitter are surely those whose ASOS parcels did not arrive on time.) There is no longer any pleasure in the seeking; merely (and even then, only briefly) in the acquisition. The influencer economy plays a significant role in perpetuating the myth among young people that careers are not progressing fast enough. Why bother to intern, or train, or work as an assistant, when you can get money, fame and fortune through a photographic grid? And it's only going to get worse: a whopping 75% of children aged between six and seventeen now want a career as a YouTuber. That may sound rich coming from me, with my sizeable social media following. But consider that I held three internships for a total of almost two years (all the while freelancing, secretarial temping *and* blogging) before I got my first decently paid job at twenty-five and started to build my reputation on social media, while forging a path as an editor at a national newspaper and styling clothes for brands. Social media was only ever the side-order to my main job – the thought that it could contain and control my entire employment is terrifying to me.

It's not unusual to feel unsure of your career trajectory in your early twenties – many of my friends, such as the property-agent-turned-teacher and my PR-turned-midwife sister, found contentment with their second career in their late twenties – but many younger millennials don't give themselves time to find out what they really want, and instead attempt to ape the ambitions of someone else – which more often than not leads to frustration and disappointment. 'The misguided idea that success is instant happens to a lot of women and becomes tangled up in this idea of female competitive jealousy,' says Codrea-Rado. It is the scourge of *comparisonitis*, whereby you cannot help but compare yourself to other women, 'rather than think critically about whether or not you really want that for yourself'. In the past few years, I have received an increasing amount of emails from women in their early- to mid-twenties, asking me for advice on how to reach their goals in the media industry. *It's just not happening*, they angst. *How do I get where I want to be?* I remember that feeling well – I almost quit journalism when I was twenty-four, as I wasn't sure I could afford to stay in the industry (which says a lot about the pitiful salaries for young people working in media). But what they say next is not something I remember feeling as a middling-aged millennial. *I feel like time is running out*, they write. These women are, at most, twenty-five years old. They want success within a certain timeframe. Now. And they want that because they see women like Kylie Jenner becoming a billionaire at twenty-one. To steal the wailings of Julius Caesar: 'Do you not think it is matter for sorrow that while Alexander, at my age, was already king of so many peoples, I have as yet achieved no brilliant success?'

Last year, the British model Leomie Anderson revealed that she was worried that she wouldn't be able to reach all of her milestones in time, one of which was earning a million by the age of twenty-five. The media coined it FOMOG (fear of missing out on goals) and Anderson was lightly pilloried for her precociousness. When I was growing up, 'goals' was a dry term used only by UCAS advisers. Now it is applied by a slang-adopting subsection of twenty-something women to anything that is attractive, covetable, charming, adorable and/or aspirational. You don't have to be a fan of zeitgeisty acronyms to acknowledge that FOMOG (like FOMO) is so much more than digital slang. It is symbolic of the pressures placed upon women, both by society and by themselves, in response to social conditioning.

'There is no inherent problem in our desire to escalate our goals, as long as we enjoy the struggle along the way. The problem arises when people are so fixated on what they want to achieve that they cease to derive pleasure from the present. When that happens they forfeit their chance of contentment,' writes Csikszentmihalyi. Not only does FOMOG leave no space or time for the struggle, but it also doesn't allow for recognition of the goals that *have* been achieved. Through the FOMOG lens, I was able to interrogate my own latent fear of thwarted ambition after having my daughter. I refused to count the home I had created and the child

I had birthed as goals actualised, instead feeling perpetually terrified about the imagined options that might slide out of my grasp. FOMOG can galvanise you, but it can also be a strange form of self-sabotage. When I was at a critically low mental ebb, which felt akin to burnout, I began to turn career achievement and fulfilment into a stick with which to beat myself. I thought my restlessness was a by-product of ambition and passion, when in fact, I realised, it came from a negative space. Rather than being driven by the desire to achieve, I was powered almost entirely by the fear of what I had *not*. My 'goals' were not those of an *autotelic self* – a self with self-contained goals – but a manifestation of tick-boxery driven by fear of invisibility. Now, I realise this is the *hedonic treadmill* (or the hedonic adaptation) live in action, whereby an improvement in circumstances – such as more money, a better job or, as in my case, having a child – provides no lasting happiness, and instead makes us thirsty for further accomplishment as we quickly adjust to our new situation. 'Desire hath no rest,' wrote St Augustine. 'Infinite in itself, endless, and as one calls it, a perpetual rack, or horse-mill.'

I have a horrible habit of not getting excited by success (however big or small). Instead, a feeling niggles at me: *What should I do next?* I am not the only one who undermines their every success by doing this. Named by the psychologist Tal Ben-Shahar, this concept is known as *arrival fallacy*: the idea that success is a finish line, and that once we've 'arrived' at the end of this yellow brick road, a rainbow will lead into a pot of golden happiness. This doesn't mean that happiness cannot be found through hard work, if the hard work makes you feel joyful. (And any success that alleviates economic hardship for you or your wider family is clearly only a good thing.) The issue is when that hard work does not, or *cannot*, bring you happiness, and instead becomes a means by which you attempt (and fail) to escape your own discontent – when we become 'addicted to busyness and dread', writes Kreider, because 'we fear what [we] might have to face in its absence'.

Curing myself of FOMOG is a work in progress. I was charmed and comforted by David Sedaris's 'Four Burners Theory'. In his essay, 'Laugh, Kookaburra', he lays out the four burners of life: family, friends, health and work. 'In order to be successful you have to cut off one of your burners,' he writes. 'And in order to be *really* successful you have to cut off two.' It's uncomfortable to think of sacrifice in such bald terms, as if switching off a burner quite literally means slamming a door in the face of something or someone we love. It's easier to think of being frazzled as a millennial inevitability – it's just the modern juggle! But I don't think it's about making absolute choices with no wiggle room. Monday to Friday your burners could be work and health. Weekends, your family and friends. (This doesn't really work with children; *that* burner inserts itself into every day.) But by toggling between burners, we can identify what is work, and what isn't – or shouldn't be. And, in doing so, we may find not a static form of happiness but a quiet sense of gently evolving contentment.

VII.

I recently started visiting an acupuncturist to alleviate my chronic back pain. As he wiggled the needles into my flesh, he commented, in an eerie echo of my mother, that he wished I worked less. His words were kind, but I wanted to weep in frustration. To suggest that the only way a woman can balance work and children is to work *less* is not only impractical (I am the primary earner, yet no one is telling my husband to work less), it is also counter-productive. The solution to the ongoing battle women with children face in managing their workload is not for them to work *less* (unless, of course, they want to), but for the system to support them *more*. Too often, a woman's work is discussed in isolation – can she go part-time? Can she get flexi-time? – but a woman doesn't have a child on her own. I find myself parroting the same line, constantly: *It takes two people to make a baby.* And yet men's flexible working requests are declined at twice the rate of women's. Only 1% of men who are eligible take Shared Parental Leave, because culturally it is still unacceptable for a man to absent himself from work for the sake of his family. Even if he wants to. Even if he earns less. *Even* if it makes sense for their family. For every man denied flexible working time, there is a woman who must either cut down her work or find a way (or another person) to pick up the slack. The refusal to allow a man flexible hours on days that he might need them *directly impacts women*. I am lucky that my husband can plug some of the childcare gaps by working from home. But the fact remains that for many women, it is not children who keep them at home: it is gendered work culture.

Many people like to believe that work is no longer gendered; that 'the fight has been won'. *Women can do anything men can!* We can, it's true – just for less money and typically with a lot more out-of-office work. The gap is closing in one sense – 75% of all British mothers are now in paid work, compared to 92% of fathers – but not in another: a woman earns only 81.6p to the man's pound, despite there being tangible proof that companies with women in board positions make more money. Even before they step foot in an office, we see a 'confidence gap' between men and women. Women will only apply for jobs they think they are 100% qualified for, whereas men will apply for a job they feel only 60% qualified for. This confidence gap directly impacts a woman's trajectory in the workplace, and makes her transition back after giving birth – a time when her confidence is inevitably dented – even more bastardly complicated.

Even the *idea* of work is much more loaded for a woman than a man. According to research conducted by Nobel Prize-winning psychologist Daniel Kahneman, a woman dreads *going* to work more than she dislikes actually *being* at work, with her positive emotions at their lowest during her commute. (I know how lucky I am that as a freelancer I do not have to commute.) Once at work, women are 53% more likely to get stressed than men. That isn't to say that the average woman hates her job; it isn't even to say that she hates the commute – she might actually value it as time to herself – but that she's stressed before she gets there, which could be due to a number of reasons. Perhaps she's worried about how her performance will be perceived, particularly if she works in a male-dominated office. Perhaps she feels flustered about what she chose to wear that day, knowing that as a woman she will be judged as much on what she looks like as on her work. Perhaps she's got period pains or she's pregnant and the commute is just the start of her day of discomfort. Perhaps she's worrying as to whether she packed her child's swim kit, or a spare change of clothes for a toddler with a gnarly record of potty-training. Because for many a woman, the commute is not the start or the end of her workday – it is merely the demarcation of one type of workload as it slips into another.

When we talk about 'work', we mean paid work. The unpaid work of the home has been historically thought of as 'hallowed' work, too holy to measure. (Sure.) But if unpaid work is not added to a country's GDP, then it remains largely invisible – and as women still take on the bulk of housework, then it means that much of what we do remains invisible. This is an obstacle to equality. Work is not just that which is done in an office; it is also the work of the home, the care work, the cognitive work. And what of that workload, known as the *second shift*, that we have only recently started considering as work?

A lot has changed on the homestead in the last few decades, but not as much as we might think. Gershuny and Sullivan note that while men's contribution to the home and childcare increased year-on-year from 1975 (before stalling, rather rivetingly, around 2000) and women's work has reduced by seventy minutes a day in this time, working women are still doing significantly more in the home than working men. (Famously progressive Finland is the only country in the world where men spend more time with their children than women do.) Working mothers today spend as much time with their children as stay-at-home mothers did in the 1970s, due to the fact that parenthood, and particularly motherhood, has become culturally 'more intensive'. I find this statistic surprising and comforting in equal measure. Earlier this year, behavioural scientist Paul Dolan hit the headlines after his talk at Hay Literary Festival, where he claimed that childfree women without a spouse were happier. I can certainly admit that life would be simpler.

My husband and I come as close as possible to co-parenting and 'keeping home' equally. He does the cooking, washing up, lightbulb changing, cat litter-tray emptying and bin disposal. I buy the groceries, tidy the house, do the laundry and pay the bills. But what of the unseen minutiae? Even if you manage to perfectly split the *physical* chores 50/50, evaluating the work of the home is a complex process. The psychologist Darby Saxbe found that women carry a much heavier *allostatic load* – the wear and tear on the body caused by stress – than men. According to Saxbe's research, it is more common for a woman's cortisol (the stress hormone) to stay elevated once she is home from work because, she tells me, the home environment is less relaxing for her if she is about to embark on the second shift of housework and childcare. The curious thing is that I feel like this even though my husband and I split childcare and housework 50/50. We have childcare on the days we work, and family who help out when I have to work on the weekends. I don't even have a commute. So why is my cortisol still elevated? Saxbe answers my question with a question. Why do I think I am more stressed 'after-hours'? Is it possible that I spend more time and energy ruminating over the details of what still needs to be done, or worrying about the future? I think about the fact that it is November, and I have bought all our joint Christmas presents already, in case I go into labour early. 'Women are often socialised to feel like the running the home and childcare is their domain,' Saxbe says, 'even if husbands contribute a lot of the work. They feel responsible for the "executive functioning" – planning, decision-making, anticipating consequences – that can carry a heavier cognitive burden.'

Saxbe identifies this stress – the invisible responsibility of *remembering*, rather than the visible one of *doing* – as the *cognitive load*. Cognitive labour is not something we think of as work, but it undoubtedly leaves us with less time to think about other things. In an incisive piece entitled 'Kids Don't Damage Women's Careers – Men Do', the author Jessica Valenti writes, 'It's easy to split, for example, who packs a school lunch or dresses a child in the morning. But how many dads do you know who could tell you their child's correct shoe size? This kind of invisible work almost always falls on women, and we rarely talk about the impact it has on our professional lives.' 'Do you know what size Z's feet are?' I asked my husband. '3G,' he replied, citing her shoe size from seven months ago. 'Do you know where your daughter's hair ties are kept?' I asked a friend's husband, a father of two young children (a couple who also split childcare

50/50), 'I do!' he said triumphantly. 'Would you replace the bow if you lost one?' 'No,' he said, decisively.

I was curious as to how this played out in same-sex parenthood. Saxbe says that there is no current research on the cognitive work in same-sex parenthood – which speaks to how little attention is given to the non-traditional family, in both research studies and cultural dialogue. The comedian Jen Brister, mother of twin boys, tells me that she thought she and her partner had a 50/50 breakdown of the childcare work. But one argument and one pair of earrings bought as a peace offering later, she is forced to conclude that while they split the physical tasks evenly, there is an imbalance on the cognitive responsibility. 'Our lesbian utopia is in fact *a sham*,' she admits. 'My partner almost certainly takes on the cognitive load in our relationship.' That said, she thinks it's less one-sided in a lesbian partnership than in heteronormative parenthood. Other women I spoke to in same-sex relationships echoed Brister's words. 'Things seem to fall far more squarely between us than they do with straight couples we know,' creative director Jess told me. Meanwhile, Ada – a company director based in West Yorkshire – described her parenting relationship as one where, despite being the same gender, she and her partner 'inadvertently followed traditional "gender" roles. So whilst my partner takes care of the more "physical" tasks, I take care of things that could be described as "female" tasks, which also includes the cognitive load.' For Ada, the idea of taking on the cognitive load as a feminine trait is ingrained, even in same-sex partnerships. 'I have noticed amongst gay friends where one could be described as "butch" and the other a "fem", that they appear to follow similar gender roles. And where both in the couple could be described as "fem", there appears to be more of an equilibrium and equality in relation to the cognitive load.'

It is not that my husband (who currently does more of the childcare than I do) is actively *against* remembering our daughter's shoe size. He just doesn't feel compelled to seek it out, or commit it to memory, because someone else (hi, hello) possesses that knowledge. Is it, as Valentini suggests, that women do the majority of this detail-orientated care work because they will be the ones judged if things go wrong? My child is not yet at school, or even pre-school. Who am I so scared of judging me? 'Women are doing more of the household organisation and domestic work not because her biological variation makes her better at it, but because of cultural influence,' says Pat Levitt, a professor of neuro-science at USC. 'She's bought into the message that she is better at it – and she believes it.'

The truth is that I do believe I am better at it. And I also believe that my work in the home is important. I don't just mean the essential work, but the adornments. The seemingly trivial finishing touches. I am a creative person, I like the way things look. Perhaps I do this kind of care work pre-emptively, giving scant opportunity for someone else to do it. Perhaps – and I think this is the least satisfying, but most truthful answer – it's a combination of both. My love of 'keeping home' might be because I grew up with a stay-at-home mother who knew all four of our shoe sizes and baked cakes and had bountiful supplies of hair ties at the tips of her fingers, but that does not mean that I have what Freud called 'household neurosis' (a tendency to clear up after everyone). It is not something that I do by default, but something I actively want. I want to be doing that work as much as I want to be doing profitable work. It's in-built by society, and it likely makes me more strung out than I need to be, but it's also a preference. This work is not always necessary economically – but it feels necessary to me.

VIII.

'It is no longer enough to like your job,' writes Erin Griffith. 'Workers should *love* what they do, and then promote that love on social media, thus fusing their identities to that of their employers.' A cornerstone of 'hustle culture' is that you should be narrating your career on social media – so that you are *doing* and *performing* your job at the same time. I am struck by this revelation every time I tweet about a new podcast episode, or an article I wrote. It is easy enough to make my work visible, but many jobs 'are about "thinking" and there's no *visible product* that comes from thinking', notes Derek Thompson. Making work out of the work can drain what you find fulfilling about your job in the first place. 'Having to externalise your whole life inherently takes away from the things that are scientifically made to make us happy,' as Thompson states.

Is finding happiness through work an individual mission or dependent on social change? Positive psychology dictates that 'the roots of the discontent are internal', in the words of Csikszentmihalyi, and that we all hold the key to our own unhappiness. It is a line of thinking that economists like William Davies actively dismiss. 'Disempowerment occurs as an effect of social, political and economic institutions and strategies, not of neural or behavioural errors,' he writes. Perhaps it is only achievable through radical corporate practice. Internet entrepreneur and CEO of Zappos, Tony Hsieh – famous for his outlandish work advice – proposes identifying and firing the unhappiest 10% of employees, supposedly leaving a relentlessly happy and committed 90%. Many left-leaning economists, thinkers and psychologists see Universal Basic Income (UBI) as the only way to alleviate burnout and depression among the unemployed. In theory, it would help shift the focus we place on work as well as ease financial anxiety, particularly for low-income households. UBI is unlikely to be introduced in the UK anytime soon – whilst Labour are keen to trial a basic income model, Boris Johnson's cabinet are unsurprisingly quiet on the matter. I think – and yes, I'm going to be equivocal here – that the solution is a bit of both (although Hsieh's advice sounds way too much like *The Circle* for my liking). Until social change shifts the balance for us, perhaps we are better off observing the evolving mottos of the tech industry – an industry fast transforming itself, at least superficially, from the epicentre of corporate burnout into an environment obsessed with balance. As a bright pink sign at the HQ of Slack – an intra-office messaging platform that melds social media and email – reads: 'Work Hard and Go Home'.

I came to realise I had not had burnout, but was simply exhausted and without focus. Certainly there are aspects of my work that I found, and still find, meaningless: endless emails about absolute guff that both the sender and I know will lead to nothing; having to debate and defend my work on social media in an endless feedback loop, as if I'm answerable to everyone and anyone; being asked to turn up ninety minutes before I am due to give a talk, only to sit there, twiddling my thumbs and eating biscuits; spending hours filling in paperwork in order for me just to get paid by organisations or publications. But I am not undervalued or made to do pointless, repetitive tasks in order to make someone else look good (although both of those things have been true in the past). I am extremely fortunate to find meaning and purpose in most of my work, the bulk of which I have created or sought out. And yet I cannot deny that even with that privilege, I have, at times, felt, trapped – subconsciously deciding to stay chronically stressed, rather than summoning the energy to implement any real change in my life. Clearly, not everyone has the luxury of 'navigating' a career – which is different from a job, which only pays the bills and may be divorced from your ambitions – but a vast bulk of us, in this ever-growing middle class, do have a semblance of control over how and into what we distil ourselves.

In almost every single interview with a Hollywood star, the celebrity is asked if they are happy. It always strikes me as a supremely odd question – as if happiness is a static state. And yet it is one we ask ourselves every single day. Happiness is transitory; it occurs at the peak of our experience. It is not something we should, or can, feel all the time. Especially not through work. In order to disentangle the various strands of work culture in this essay, I had to put aside the active pursuit of happiness. What I aim for now is contentment (the Ancient Greeks called it *ataraxia*). Negotiating a public/private work self might never be something I entirely manage, or even *want* to attain. I am most connected to my work, find it most meaningful, when it feels personal. Some of the most meaningful work I do is with one of my best friends, at my house, via a podcast, which has a three-fold blurring of the lines of friendship, work and home.

I don't think that re-nosing our identity is the answer – if anything, the need for constant verbal self-identification is what leads us to have these crises of the soul. Instead, I am moving from hustle to *flow*. Not through an app, or a work-hack method, but through a state of concentration. The truth is, we have the same amount of hours in the day whether we work our way through them in furious distraction or with methodical purpose – considering both the value of our work and the value of *ourselves* as we go.

Relentless Pleasure

*Do not bite at the bait of pleasure, till you know
there is no hook beneath it.*

Thomas Jefferson

I.

Let me begin with a familiar scene. It is Sunday night and you have three unwatched programmes lined up on Sky Planner. Squashed beside you is your laptop, where Netflix is vibrating with potential – two new series keyed up on its home screen. Waiting not so patiently behind is Amazon Prime (whose login you have borrowed from a friend, in exchange for your Netflix). Below one clammy palm is the book you've been trying to finish for three months which you *think* you like – at least Goodreads likes it and that colleague who always seems very engaged *raved* about it, and that's sort of the same, isn't it? Although you're finding it pretty hard to get through, truth be told. And under it all, lies you: a hapless bluebottle stuck to the flypaper of pleasure. That all of this culture is pleasurable, you are certain; with its physical and mental weight bearing down, you are equally sure that it is relentless.

The term 'infobesity' was coined in 2013 to describe the torrent of information clogging our arteries like cholesterol.

It turns us into 'pancake people', writes the playwright Richard Foreman. 'Spread wide and thin as we connect with that vast network of information accessed by the mere touch of a button.' In the middle of this information avalanche lies pop-culture saturation, where a new 'must see!' boxset drops weekly. We are struck again by the paradox of choice, making us feel like there is a right or wrong way to cut through the vast glut of entertainment. In a world motivated by tickboxery, not being able to touch the sides of this culture feels like a failure. We are endlessly consuming and yet seem to make no headway. And still, we persist – because take your foot off the boulder and you'll never make it back onto the climbing wall. But what are we trying to reach?

Squatting within that cultural overload is an epidemic of binge-watching, whereby boxsets are guzzled down whole, facilitated by the autoplay function. (You can even skip the opening credits, which I always do – like every other millennial whose impatience knows no bounds.) With 42% of millennials binge-watching boxsets on a weekly basis, this mode of consumption is not remotely radical. Guzzling is the new norm. My record Netflix binge stands at around five hours, before I felt the need to fumigate both myself and the sofa. But through a call-out to Twitter to discover the best binges, I soon discovered how pathetic my personal best is: thirteen hours of *Homeland*, sixteen hours of *Dexter* and fifteen hours of *Geordie Shore*. (That's a lot of WKDs.) Questions of practicality loom large: did these marathon viewers have loo and food breaks, or did they have a potty and an overly diligent Deliveroo driver delivering food straight to their sofa? Do they have children? (And if so, kudos.) Since 2014, as a result of the backlash (the implication being that we are mere servants to the screen, unable to break away), Netflix allows you to deactivate the autoplay function, so that one episode doesn't immediately skip on to the next. Of course, they don't publicise this. Most people I know don't realise that you *can* stymie autoplay, or they can't be bothered to find out how. That suits Netflix just fine. The content is *designed* to be consumed in epic form.

Binge-watching. Marathon viewing. Non-stop streaming. The activity is discussed as if it were a pathology. Which, in a way, it is. 'Weird stuff happens after eight hours of watching the same TV show,' writes Mary Choi for *Wired*. 'Your eyes feel crunchy. You get a headache that sits in your teeth, the kind that comes from hitching your free time to a runaway train of self-indulgence – too much booze, food or sleep.' In the episode of the sketch-comedy series *Portlandia* entitled 'One Moore Episode', a couple take binge-viewing to excess, losing their jobs, developing bladder infections and generally descending into decay, but still refuse to quit their binge. (That the four series of *Portlandia* themselves encourage binge-watching adds a deliciously meta element to the narrative.) 'Watching a fuckload of TV in a depressingly short amount of time' – as one Urban Dictionary contributor neatly puts it – requires *physical* and *mental* endurance, almost turning the experience into yet another form of work. In a world that demands completion, finishing a boxset is seen as a badge of honour. You are a warrior, who has made it through a treacherous journey, like Bear Grylls in the Arctic, roasting polar bear earlobes for your dinner. Except, of course, you are prone in front of a screen, one hand ferreting through a bowl of lurid-coloured snacks.

II.

'Binge-watching' as a term has been used in internet forums since the '90s, but the first cultural reference was in 2012, when the culture critic Mary McNamara described it as, 'any instance in which more than three episodes of an hourlong drama or six episodes of a half-hour comedy are consumed at one sitting.' TiVo, a digital recorder that launched in the States in 1998, became a meta motif in early-noughties television thanks to Miranda Hobbes' obsession with it on *Sex and the City*, but never took off in the UK. For the under-thirty-five Brit – who had merely dabbled in telly fests with the *Hollyoaks* omnibus on a Sunday morning – true bingeing began with Netflix. Born in 1997 as a mail-delivery video-rental service much like Lovefilm, Netflix introduced streaming in 2007. But it wasn't till 2013, when they launched their first piece of original content with *House of Cards*, that it caught the attention of the rest of the world. Watching this series was the first time I watched Netflix. It felt both familiar and strange, but I adjusted to on-demand entertainment so seamlessly that I barely even noticed the show was at my mercy. Or was it the other way round?

The first compulsive mass viewing happened much earlier, in 1952, with the TV show *I Love Lucy* attracting over 50 million viewers. (In comparison, the *Game of Thrones* finale in May 2019 had 19.3 million global viewers.) The 'migration' of the screen from public cinemas into private homes is of 'unparalleled significance in the history of the attention industries and their influence over people's lives', writes Tim Wu, author of *The Attention Merchants*. Wu calls these early years of television 'peak attention' – when 'regular attention was paid to the same set of messages at the same time' – in contrast to today's myriad attention merchants. Indeed, television became so seductive that in the '60s it was deemed a weapon of mass distraction and a danger to the precarious status quo of the home. What if stay-at-home mothers got addicted to the relentless pleasure of telly and were unable to complete their duties at home with maximum efficiency? (Guess what, they managed it.)

As a child of the '90s, I didn't watch TV other than *Blue Peter* – I preferred old VHS tapes of films such as *The Witches*, *The Lion, the Witch and the Wardrobe*, *Oliver* and *Annie*, with some *Pingu* mixed in. That was until the invention of the ultimate Saturday quartet: *Baywatch*, *Gladiators*, *Blind Date* and *Casualty*. (My brother put a sticker of Pamela Anderson in her groin-wateringly high-cut red swimsuit on the television control and it remained there until the television broke last year.) Watching all four programmes on the trot felt like a marathon and typically only one of us four siblings would be left by the end. The winner would melt into the corduroy beanbag, addled by three hours of television. But the highlight of the week was the Sunday morning trip to Blockbuster: running sticky fingers over frosted plastic and being told we were there for videos only, *no snacks*. (Every time I order popcorn, nachos and overpriced pick 'n' mix at the cinema now, I cannot help but think of my mother and feel rebellious.) In his book, *That Will Never Work*, the co-founder of Netflix, Marc Randolph, describes finding a note from two decades ago which read, 'In three years, we want to be one of the top 10 video stores.' 'How lame is that?' he later scoffed to the *Guardian*. 'I wanted to be as big as a single Blockbuster store.' Netflix surpassed Randolph's expectations and went on to become the behemoth behind the evisceration of Blockbuster. The world's single remaining Blockbuster is in Oregon and – being something of a tourist attraction – has no plans to close.

The televisual symbol for millennial teenagehood was *Friends*. In the US alone, 52.5 million people tuned in to the finale in May 2004, and 8.9 million in the UK. I can remember watching 'The Last One' like it was yesterday. I was in my penultimate year of boarding school and the television room was stuffed to capacity with adolescent bodies jostling for space on a sea of threadbare brown cushions (it was a Catholic boarding school – decor, if not term fees, emphasised frugality). Multiple tracksuit-bottom-clad bums squished onto each wooden chair, while a small but diligent crew in the corner churned out burnt peanut-butter toast. But with on-demand entertainment came the end of television as a collective activity. No longer are four siblings lying on dog-hairy bean-bags, watching the same shows; an entire year group at school is no longer watching the finale of a sitcom together. We may stream programmes as a couple, but the bulk of us do so solo. A group of friends might all devour *Game of Thrones*, *Top Boy* and *24* – but they watch it on different nights, perhaps different weeks, even different years. (I only recently discovered *Suits*, for example, while my husband started *Peaky Blinders*.) Our binge-language might (mostly) be shared, but it is jumbled and often lonesome, as if we are learning French on entirely different curriculums, in our own tiny sound-proofed booths.

To get briefly technical, the term 'streaming platform' includes both *content creators* like Netflix (who make and distribute their own shows, often with vast budgets, as well as streaming content produced by others) and *distributive hardware* like BritBox (who do not produce any original content). The largest of the subscription-only platforms is Netflix, with 150 million subscribers worldwide, but the next tier down is plentiful – there's Sky TV, BT Sport, Amazon Prime, Now TV, BritBox, Disney+, Apple TV+, HBO Max and NBCUniversal (in the States there's also Hulu and Roku). By the time this book comes out, there will undoubtedly be more, all vying for our time and money. The cumulative cost of these platforms is frankly exorbitant. If you were to subscribe to all of them, you would be forking out over £1,500 a year. Millennials are often described as the experiential generation (we love travelling and eating out) but we also *love* staying in. Is it really a surprise, when the monthly cost of all these forms of entertainment is more than a very fancy meal out? *With cocktails?* That going out may now be cheaper than staying in is the sort of insanity that feels somehow entirely normal to my generation: clothes have got cheaper – so we buy more; staying in should always be a cheaper alternative – yet we (with the help of Big Tech) have turned it into a privileged activity. The effort and expense of toggling between these platforms – cancelling your membership at one, in order to take out membership at another – becomes a strange sort of administrative burden. 'What we need is a one-stop shop,' notes the broadcaster Jamie East. 'One login, one bill, no strings.' Who knows – it might already be happening. 'The future Spotify of TV is merely a scribble on the back of a fag packet,' he writes – or more likely, on the USB of a vape.

As television becomes more and more lush – with shows like *Euphoria* filtering the banalities of high school through a technicolour unicorn paradise – it can lead to a sort of Stendhal syndrome. A psychosomatic condition causing rapid heartbeat, fainting, confusion and hallucinations that strikes after consuming too much beauty, the syndrome was named after the nineteenth-century French author Stendhal, who wrote of his visit to Florence, 'I was in a sort of ecstasy … Ah, if I could only forget. I had palpitations of the heart, what in Berlin they call "nerves". Life was drained from me.' It reminds me of the poppy field in California's Lake Elsinore, trodden to death over one weekend by 50,000 tourists. Or, of a laptop screen post-binge, still steaming-hot to the touch.

III.

Journalist Emil Steiner lists the following reasons for binge-watching: enhanced viewing experience; a sense of completion; cultural inclusion; convenience; catching up;

and relaxation/nostalgia. But something is missing from his list: duty. Like many pleasurable parts of modern life, the rapid consumption of popular culture has become 'cultural homework', which is when 'people start saying things like, "Do I HAVE to watch *Captain Marvel*?" and 'feeling a lot of pressure to read Sally Rooney!' writes culture editor Soraya Roberts for *Longreads*. It inspires a similar feeling to your friend's dad who everyone avoided because he was a vocal cheerleader of enforced fun ('Rounders in five minutes, champs!').

It used to be just newspapers and movie posters that implored us to watch something. 'Now members of the general public are saying it too,' notes the *Sunday Times* culture writer Jonathan Dean. 'The level of MUST SEE vs DON'T SEE has become a farrago, which wouldn't have happened in the past. And certainly not across so many platforms.' Journalist Samuel Fishwick calls it 'block capitals' television. 'It's the kind of IN YOUR FACE telly that – love it or HATE it – you just HAVE to talk about, non-stop. Or tweet about. Or INJECT STRAIGHT INTO YOUR VEINS.' This pressure can have the counter-effect of prompting an irrational dislike of a book, film or series without you having actually seen it, which Roberts calls 'reactance'. How many times have you thought, *This book has been hyped so much that I don't even want to read it any more*? This peculiar petulance – *I* won't *read it, you can't* make *me read it* – is especially directed at the creative work of young women (how unusual, that this affects young female creatives more than male), as if the creator herself is whinily imploring you to 'watch my art'. And if these everyday-critics *do* deign to read, or watch, this much-hyped piece of entertainment and they *don't* enjoy it, they feel like they have been sold a dud. There is a furious sense of entitlement – as if everything should speak to or for everyone, and if it doesn't then it's a fallacy that anyone is enjoying it at all – rather than the rational view that some things will do it for you, and some won't.

Roberts suggests that the pressure around zeitgeisty pop culture has led to a form of *essentialism*. This conservative movement emerged in the 1930s arguing for a standardised set of knowledge, and emphasising 'the larger culture over individual creativity'. 'Essentialist pop culture does the same thing, flattening our imaginations until we are all tied together by little more than the same vocabulary,' she writes. This sense of obligation – *You haven't read Zadie Smith? You didn't watch* Game of Thrones? – has led to a kind of curriculum of culture, and only by subscribing to it do you become an informed citizen. This form of cultural snobbery positions popular culture as something you can get either right or wrong. It turns popular culture into more than a hobby: it becomes a way to shape your identity. The idea that we might not like something that a lot of other people are calling 'smart' or 'radical' might make us feel stupid and boring. The enjoyment of whatever we're watching or reading is no more important than being able to *say* that we enjoyed it. 'Taste classifies the classifier,' writes Neta Alexander in *The Netflix Effect*. 'It is, rather, a way to position oneself in relation to others by acquiring and displaying cultural products.' It is a performative type of enjoyment, and in our culture of validation, it can be hard to resist.

'There are too many platforms and too many shows for one to take a firm grip,' insists Dean. 'Most Netflix shows are being watched by a very small pool of people.' It is misguided to suggest that pop culture has become one-note. *Eighth Grade* – a charming indie film about suburban adolescence – 'came out on the same weekend as *Avengers: Endgame*' – an extensively marketed and expensive Disney superhero film. While both were adored by their respective audiences, 'you'd struggle to find two more different offerings'. Essentialism is avoided by looking outside of echo chambers – whether IRL or online. I've begun to actively reach for books and boxsets that I haven't heard all my friends talking about; that don't feature people who look, and live, exactly like myself.

And then there are those of us who watch television purely for comfort. My husband watches *Friends* every evening while he cooks dinner; my personal safe-space telly is *The O.C.* The journalist Richard Godwin calls these 'non-event TV', great for when you're feeling 'dystopia'd out' and looking for something familiar and nostalgic. I groan when my daughter forces me to watch the same *Peppa Pig* episode I've seen five times already – but that's what my husband and I do on a regular basis. It's not just toddlers who seek solace in the familiar (think of the popularity of YouTube videos where someone spends twenty minutes in front of a mirror putting on their make-up, and we watch the whole thing, as if in a trance). There is also a very merry subsection of 'tripe TV', to steal Fishwick's term, that is rarely part of these highbrow debates about the golden age of telly, but loved (perhaps strangely) by many: *Takeshi's Castle*, *Homes Under the Hammer*, *Judge Rinder* (I won't say RIP to *Jeremy Kyle*). My sister's favourite programmes are *Police Interceptors* and *Motorway Cops*, for Pete's sake. When I was in the US recently, I became briefly obsessed with a programme about a couple who were no longer a couple, who sold houses together, called *Flipping Exes*. There is no end to what madness you can find – should you just let your remote wander far and wide.

The idea of essentialism becomes untenable when you consider that 'the universal spectator' doesn't exist. We are no more one type of viewer than we are one type of woman. We bring different motivations and interpretations to specific material. Take *Jailbirds*, a Netflix series set in Sacramento County Jail in California. I was completely absorbed by it. It was only with hindsight that I realised it was basically reality TV – except the inmates were incarcerated and unpaid, rather than frolicking around pools and being paid in lucrative swimwear sponsorships. The problematic hook of *Jailbirds* can be summed up by the fact that the bulk of the show's dialogue takes place around the toilet – as inmates fight, form friendships and fall in love via messages flushed down the pan, in an activity known as 'toilet talking' – which literally and metaphorically reduces the inmates to an apologetic squat, and aligns them with a receptacle of shit.

The idea of *narrative transportation* means that watching what are (somewhat distastefully) referred to as 'gritty' dramas, or documentaries, can increase our empathy for those who live lives different to our own. But prolonged exposure to harrowing material can also make us numb. The success of true-crime documentaries and podcasts – with stomach-churning real footage and sensationalist storylines – reveals the unpalatable truth that, for many, there is a glee to be found in grimness. That one person's difficult circumstances can be poured into pleasure for others is not a new idea. (Dickens, anyone?) But there is an argument to be made that the pleasure of watching a life less privileged than yours, as a form of entertainment, is a kind of exploitative tourism. That rather than amplifying vulnerable voices that are rarely heard, and often ignored by society, these voices are distorted and flat-screened into entertainment – and then relegated to background noise, as we half-listen while doing our laundry.

IV.

Free time has become our most precious commodity. A friend recently sent me a text bemoaning how flaky her friends were being. I don't mind people flaking on me, I admitted. I used to mind – but that was before I had a pile of books I was desperate to read and a boxset list as long as my arm. When someone cancels on me, I am *relieved*. It is a chance, to steal Sky's apt phrase, to Catch Up. The pressure from this relentless pleasure stems from the fact that everyone has different amounts of free time, says Dean. Someone with young children will have less disposable time for binge sessions than students. People who hold down multiple jobs, or work evenings, or have other care obligations, are less able to effortlessly guzzle down a twelve-part series on a weekly basis.

The tech gap of privilege shifts constantly. At first, the gap was between those who could and those who couldn't own an expensive smartphone or tablet. Now, these gadgets are still expensive but they have become classed as a necessity, even for many below the poverty line. As that gap closed, a new one opened up: between those who used their screens a lot and those who began limiting their screen time. You only need to look at how many Big Tech families ban or seriously limit screens in their home. In 2016, Steve Jobs, then CEO of Apple, revealed that his children had never used an iPad. And yet for some, screen time is essential. I recently read a *New York Times* article where a mother, sick of being asked how she juggled work without childcare, replied bluntly: 'Netflix is the babysitter.'

An aversion to boredom and a low tolerance for delayed gratification are at the root of binge culture. Soraya Roberts writes to me that we have become a 'bingey society' because 'our souls aren't being attended to, in the world that we live in – and so, we stuff them. With work, with food, with leisure. We're greedy. It comes from being given too much and at the same time too little.' Or as Oscar Wilde put it, 'Moderation is a fatal thing. Nothing succeeds like excess.' And what could be more excessive than a TV show which never (okay, eventually) ends? It is no surprise that the popularity of the boxset is soaring at the same time as films are in decline: between 2010 and 2018, Netflix tripled the number of their TV shows and sliced their film offering by a third. Why? Because films might be getting longer – but they just aren't long enough. They don't *ossify* in the same way twelve episodes of a series can. And what we seek right now is an incubator, protecting us from the outside world. We wish to be hermetically sealed into our TV shows like they are Tupperware. Turning us into bone.

When I was a child, my overriding emotion was one of boredom. Suffering through long mealtimes, I'd hang off my chair, wheedling, '*Please can I get dowwwwwn.*' 'Not until everyone's finished,' my mother would retort. She encouraged boredom. To her, it was less about specifically ensuring I was bored (although her favourite saying was always 'Only boring people are bored'), as it was a refusal to cater to my every whim, in every situation – a lesson for later life. She would take me fishing with her on a tiny boat for eight hours at a time and I would mutter darkly, knowing the vast, empty hours that lay ahead. The saving grace was that I was allowed to bring a book – typically a Roald Dahl. So while my mother meditatively fished for trout, I would guzzle down magical peaches and marvellous medicines, and then spend the other half of the boat trip daydreaming, writing stories in my head. My mother no longer has her fishing boat, but it lives on in my mind as a metaphor for the necessity of boredom.

At night, when I couldn't sleep, I wouldn't cry out. I would read books, colour co-ordinate my clothes and move the furniture around my bedroom. When my mother came to wake me in the morning, I would have rearranged everything, including the bed. Aged six. The first time I did this, she looked as confused as if I had stuck all my furniture to the ceiling like in *The Twits*. Boredom was so vital to my sense of autonomy and creative development that I cannot even imagine my life without it. As a result, I am never really bored as an adult. The absence of activity just means I can indulge in something solitary.

And yet boredom is being erased from our lives. We are no longer bored, we are 'homo distractus', writes Wu. Our aversion to boredom has become almost admirable. In 2014, the social psychologist Timothy Wilson asked participants to sit in a lab room and do nothing but think, for fifteen minutes. The room was empty except for a device that emitted a mild but painful electric shock. Despite all participants stating beforehand that they would pay to avoid an electric shock, 67% of male participants and 25% of women gave themselves electric shocks – in some cases, multiple times – simply because they were bored. Spending even fifteen minutes alone with their thoughts proved too much for many of them. I wonder what the results would have been if the study had been done fifty years ago. I suspect far lower. In his 1970 book, *The Joyless Economy*, the economist Tibor Scitovsky concluded that people were unhappy, even those who had plenty of money, because they were bored. Now, I wonder if the opposite is true: if people are unhappy – or *believe* they are unhappy – because they are never bored.

'I've already enjoyed too much,' says Samuel Johnson's character of Rasselas. 'Give me something to desire.' Rather than make time to ponder, we feast upon society's message that we should fill our days to capacity; focus on every goal; use our time wisely – and by wisely, I mean occupy any spare moment with streamed content. But it is the filling of what we see as 'vacancies of attention', says the psychoanalyst Adam Phillips in his book *Attention Seeking*, that often depletes us. We are spoilt and fatigued by pleasure, like Rasselas. In this situation, notes Phillips, satisfaction can sabotage desire. It is daydreaming, rather than 24/7 noise, that is essential to our happiness. I am so scared of losing my meandering mind that I don't listen to podcasts or music – except classical music – when I'm working or walking. My thoughts are so crowded, my focus so diluted by scrolling, surfing and viewing, that my attempt to hold on to rich and bountiful daydreams can often feel delicate.

The virtues of daydreaming have been extolled in literature for centuries. As Virginia Woolf writes of Lily in *To the Lighthouse*, 'Certainly she was losing consciousness of outer things. And as she lost consciousness of outer things … her mind kept throwing up from its depths, scenes, and names, and sayings, and memories and ideas, like a fountain spurting.' There are no barriers to entry: even the most 'modest, mouse-coloured people' can daydream. Daydreaming has long been associated with creativity, but I think it serves another purpose too. It allows us to construct our own narrative. 'The story that you are telling in your own head is not the same story that anyone else is telling,' said Zadie Smith to her fellow novelist Diana Evans. That can be dangerous if we expect the rest of the world to tell our story in the way we do. But as a private pleasure, it is essential. We may be stuck in our own 'flesh cages', as Smith puts it, but the mind wanders. It soars high and sets us free. In a world crowded with the white noise of other people's narratives – the collective narrative of social media; the multi-strand narratives of binge TV – having your own, singular, internal narrative is nothing short of essential.

And yet, can't the same feeling of singularity be achieved with a good TV binge? The social-health expert Julia Hobsbawm believes so. 'It seems to be that people want to reclaim time, to stretch and elongate it, and that sitting in one place watching one thing compulsively is a rather good way of slowing down.' Writing about the hypnotic effect of

TV on toddlers, the pop-science writer Stephen Johnson argues that their sustained stillness is 'not a [sign] of mental atrophy [but of] focus'. If the show is just the right amount of challenging, watching it could *perhaps* even qualify as a sense of purposeful *flow*. It's not daydreaming, but it's not work, either – perhaps it's a little of both.

V.

The general consensus when it comes to the internet is that it is the most mind-altering invention ever unleashed. 'The Net delivers precisely the kind of sensory and cognitive stimuli – repetitive, intensive, interactive, addictive – that have been shown to result in strong and rapid alteration in brain circuits and functions,' writes the tech and economics writer Nicholas Carr in *The Shallows*. But this kind of thinking – the idea that binge-watching is rapidly decreasing our neuroplasticity – ignores the fact that our brains are affected by *every single* external experience, cautions the neuroscientist Gina Rippon. Neuroplasticity – the brain's continual reshaping and re-forming – happens regardless of whether you are focused on thirty minutes of mindless television or thirteen hours of high-octane psychological drama. Rippon is the author of the acclaimed *The Gendered Brain*, which debunks the myth that male and female brains are different (known as neurosexism). Is this also the case with binge-watching, I ask her? Is the impact on the female brain no different to that on the male?

Rippon tells me that binge-watching does not affect the neuroplasticity of the male and female brain in objectively different ways. But if you look at the question through the lens of *social cognitive* neuroscience, then yes, women react differently. The impact is determined 'not by the sensory input of all the visual stimulation, but the social input', she notes. It is not about the time spent watching, but about the narrative itself, and how it relates to a gendered social experience. What kind of stereotypes are being perpetuated in the storyline? And how do they affect women? 'In the absence of pauses for reflection or fact-checking' – which we have when we are watching something incrementally – 'it is possible that a continuous stream of information could impact on self-identity (I am like this – or not), and self-esteem (would I ever look like this/be this heroic/clever/successful etc.) and a belief in some sort of "soap-opera" reality – either good or bad – which is unlikely to match up to normal day-to-day existence.' Put simply, women are affected more deeply by vast amounts of television in which women are abused or lack agency, than we are by, say, *Supermarket Sweep*.

That's not to say we shouldn't watch harrowing material. I think that we *should* actively expose ourselves to material that challenges, discomforts or upsets us (provided it is *constructive* – like a documentary made by a citizen journalist in a war zone – rather than *destructive* – the beheading of a prisoner by terrorists). It not only reminds us how lucky we are to be slumped on a sofa, but also helps us learn about the lives of those outside of our echo chambers. With that said, difficult material can distort when we consume it wholesale, and we need to be aware of that effect. For more sensitive viewers, relentless exposure to a narrative that is quite different from their own can start to seep into their reality. In 'The Cognitive Psychological Effects of Binge-Watching', literature professor Zachary Snider found himself in a vulnerable state after relentless exposure to Walter White and his crystal meth lab. 'I was noticeably more anxious and paranoid after binge-watching consecutive episodes of [*Breaking Bad*],' he admits.

When the DC Comics film *Joker*, starring Joaquin Phoenix, opened there was a deluge of commentary across the newspapers and radio, about how a film focusing on an angry man who commits violence against a society that continually rejects him could fuel incel culture. It was a reservation that I shared on *The High Low*. But in *Everybody Lies*, the data scientist Seth Stephens-Davidowitz uncovers a nationwide study by the economists Gordon Dahl and Stefano DellaVigna that merges three big data sets to prove that on weekends when a popular violent movie was showing in the US, crime actually *dropped*. The implication is that watching extreme content does not nullify our sense of right and wrong; rather, it increases our compassion.

Along with the (disproved) fear that we are curdling our brains with too much telly is the myth that we are unalterably diminishing our attention spans. Scaremongering pieces about how jittery and distracted we are – of which there are many – all cite a single 2015 study by Microsoft Canada that claims that our attention span has shrunk from twelve to eight seconds. *That's less than the span of a goldfish!* the world gasped. (Goldfish, it is said, can manage nine). 'The goldfish metaphor has yet to be tested in any soundly scientific way,' cautions Rippon. This blanket claim also fails to take into account that our attention span is 'task-dependent', notes the psychologist Gemma Briggs. It is not so much that binge-watching is culling our attention, but that watching television requires less attention than driving, for instance (and we all seem to still be doing fine with that). And anyway, retort scientists, that initial acquarian stat is rot: the much-maligned goldfish has a memory that can last for months, thank you very much.

The true scourge of our attention span is not tech itself, but multi-screening. Media professors Michael Z. Newman and Elana Levine split viewers into two categories: the hyper-distracted glancing viewer and the focused binge-viewer. It is perfectly possible to be both types of viewer, depending on the content (glancing distractedly at a subtitled Scandi noir series really, really doesn't work). I rarely watch a boxset without simultaneously doing an online groceries order, reading the newspapers, or reading on another screen *about* that same boxset I am watching. While watching *Unbelievable* on my laptop, I read on my iPhone the Pulitzer Prize-winning piece of journalism from ProPublica that inspired the Neflix series. I cast *Euphoria* from Netflix onto my television, while simultaneously Googling catwalk pictures of Hunter Schafer and reading Zendaya's Twitter timeline. The media theorist Dan Harries calls this *viewsing*: using other media while viewing a primary source. He argues that rather than distracting you, reading *around* the show while watching it can actually lead to heavier investment in the material you are consuming.

The truth is that I *views*, or glance, because I treat boxsets like something to just get through. I start a new show with excitement, but also with an inward groan. By the end, I have episodes on in the background while I have a bath, or tidy the kitchen, just so I can get the damn thing *done*. Roberts suggests this determination to finish is due to 'bland choice and a lot of dissatisfied people. That's where you get the impossibility of finding any real closure through choosing.' I think this compulsion to watch *more more more* has got to do with our obsession with completion rather than with dis-satisfaction; the feeling that our achievements must be finite, in order to count. I felt embarrassed to admit that I was not so much enthralled as fatigued when watching a boxset I enjoyed – one I loved, even. But it turns out that I am not alone: of the 726 people I asked on Twitter, only 66% reported that they were excited by the arrival of a much-hyped new boxset. The pressure is real.

VI.

Boxsets are a salve, as much as they are a stimulation. 'Netflix is like audio-visual diazepam. It numbs my senses and makes me forget about everything else,' writes Arwa Mahdawi. 'It does not even try to hide the fact that its ambition is to hook us all.' As Reed Hastings, Netflix's CEO, boasted in a statement last year, to the alarm of insomniacs like myself all over the world: 'We're competing with sleep.' (This year, Reed has announced that his competition is YouTube, which has seven times as many subscribers as Netflix.) So are we in the grip of an epidemic? One of the arguments against Netflix being an addiction is that there are just too many of us compulsively viewing for it to be classified as an addiction. But the idea that addiction cannot affect large groups of people is codswallop, writes Adam Alter in *Irresistible*. 'In 1918, a flu pandemic killed seventy-five million people [and] no one suggested that a flu diagnosis was meaningless. The issue demanded attention precisely because it affected so many people and the same is true of behavioural addiction.' Just because we haven't buried any tech addicts yet doesn't mean tech addiction is not a thing, notes culture writer and TV critic Paul Flynn.

In his divisive second book, *Indistractable*, the behavioural scientist Nir Eyal draws a distinction between dependency, distraction and diversion – terms that he believes we conflate when discussing tech and entertainment. 'Being dependent on something does not qualify as addiction. Some people overuse, some people are actually addicted, but the number of people that are actually addicted is way, *way* smaller than the people who *think* they are addicted.' When I call him in California to discuss further the idea that people really can't be addicted to Netflix, he responds, 'If people find over time that a product is not serving them, they will stop using it.' Isn't he overstating our agency here? Do we truly have the willpower to stop distracting ourselves, just because we aren't sure it's the healthiest use of our time? And if that was the case, wouldn't we be able to work ten hours straight without leaving our desk and ignore all the junk food that isn't good for us?

Eyal says that when we talk about the distraction of streaming platforms, what we actually mean is *diversion*. Distraction, Eyal continues, pulls you backwards; diversion reroutes your attention and is done with intent. 'And diversion can be very helpful.' As he talks about the benefits of diverting attention – he cites a study about children struggling with cancer treatment who, when given video games to play while receiving treatment, report much less pain and fewer side effects from the medication – I remember a *High Low* listener who wrote in to tell us how her podcast habit was a literal lifeline for her and one encouraged by her therapist, as the continual audio stream diverted her from suicidal thoughts. But those are specific and extreme life circumstances. What are the rest of us feeling the need to divert *from*? A common answer to this question is: the state of politics. (Truly, this is invoked for everything – and for very good reason right now.) Dean argues against the theory of diversion. How can this be true, he asks, when so many currently popular shows like *Succession*, *Top Boy* and *Unbelievable*, 'tackle societal issues and politics head on? You can't be diverted from something if what you are diverted *to* is about the thing you want to be diverted *from*.'

Eyal is the only person I have encountered who refutes that tech is inherently addictive. Instead, he argues for something called *learned helplessness*. If you tell people who aren't addicted that they are addicted, then they will begin to feel like they are. When actually, he says, they can just shut the laptop and go for a walk. It is a refreshing idea, but I am not convinced. Nor, it would seem, are many of his fellow Big Tech insiders. The whole argument of individual responsibility crumbles when you acknowledge 'that there's a thousand people on the other side of the screen whose job is to break down whatever responsibility [you] can maintain', insists former Google product designer Tristan Harris. Now a design ethicist (someone who looks at the ethical implications of tech design), he advocates for tech companies to sign a sort of Hippocratic Oath meant to protect rather than exploit 'people's psychological vulnerabilities' and restore agency to users. 'There needs to be new ratings, new criteria, new design standards, new certification standards,' he says. 'There is a way to design based not on addiction.' 'Really?' says Eyal to Ezra Klein. 'Are we really going to say to Netflix, *Hey, Netflix! Stop making your shows so good!*'

Along with the impact on our brain and attention span, the third popular fear associated with binge-watching is that it erodes our memory. Carr addresses the theory that our fear of memory loss is irrelevant, since we don't actually *need* a memory any more. We can just 'outsource' it all to the internet. 'It's no longer terribly efficient to use our brains to store information,' he quotes the writer Peter Suderman. Ah, *there* it is – that little word we all knew was coming: efficient. Well, it may not be *efficient* to use our brains to store memories, but outsourcing your brain to a hard drive is a terrifying idea – bringing us ever closer to the cyborg. Thankfully, Carr agrees. Outsourcing memories would serve little purpose, he writes, given that making memories strengthens our 'mental powers'. If identity is built on collective experience and what Carr calls 'cultural transmission' – the passing of cultural ideas and entertainment from one to another – then actually, an attachment to boxsets could be a positive thing. How many times a week do you text a friend with a link to an article you've read, or ask if they have seen a particular documentary? My conversations with my friends are now as much about the culture we are consuming – what we like, what we don't like, what we don't really understand – as much as they are about how we feel. What we consume helps construct us. And as long as we keep communicating through our consumption, we aren't in any danger of eroding our memories – or ourselves.

VII.

Perhaps we should just leave leisure time the hell alone. Does *everything* fun need to have a downside? We are wont to analyse every new development in modern life, until we leech all the fun out of it. Can't entertainment just be entertainment? If eight hours of television makes you feel good, helps you to relax, switch off from work or other problems in your life, then who am I – or anyone, in fact – to judge how you spend your time? Flynn cautions against the 'neuroticising' of entertainment, because it distracts (not diverts) from what we should be talking about: untenable work practices. Such distraction enables 'corporate culture to avoid addressing the pathological nature of twenty-first-century worktime – obviously a more pressing and genuine problem for most people. Associating mental health with our leisure diverts employers from responsibilities,' he says.

While writing this essay, I streamed considerably more shows than I usually do. It would seem that binge-watching is not just compulsive, it is also contagious. It appears through the power of osmosis. During this uptick of laptop time, I felt as if entire evenings were being eaten up by ... nothing. There was an opportunity cost to all this streaming: much less reading and much less sleeping. Neither made me feel good. As Eyal would say, this is not a behaviour that serves me. Or at least it served me just fine in the moment, but less so after, when I felt paradoxically heavy and empty. Some people are able to carry the weight of so much visual stimulus, but I have realised that I am not one of them. I like a colourful world, don't get me wrong – but to be calm and contented, I need to construct much of that colour for myself.

The twin ideas that binge-streaming affects how much we read, and that reading is morally superior to television, have a firm hold over how we view both activities. 'It is becoming a cliché of conversations between twentysomethings (especially to the right of 25) that if you talk about books or articles or strung-together words long enough, someone will eventually wail plaintively: "I just can't reeeeeaaad anymore",' writes Anna North for the *New York Times*. 'The person will explain that the Internet has shot her attention span. She will tell you about how, when she was small, she could lose herself in a novel for hours, and now, all she can do is watch the tweets swim by like glittery fish in the river of time-she-will-never-get-back.' There is a danger in deeming books as morally superior to other forms of popular culture, separating entertainment into warring factions as if we have to pledge ourselves to either one or the other.

People often ask me how I read as much as I do, and the truth is that I prioritise it – often to the detriment of most other things (like cooking). When I read for two hours without distraction, I don't feel marvellous because I am specifically shunning technology; I enjoy it because I am indulging in a single narrative, made of equal parts focus and imagination. As Laura Freeman, the arts journalist and author of *The Reading Cure*, puts it, rather beautifully: 'A book never bothers. A book doesn't wheedle. No one has asked you to subscribe, sign up, enter your card details, your username, your password. The battery never dies. The WiFi never cuts out. In an age when we are ever more targeted and profiled and mined for information, reading a book allows you to be, for so long as the covers hold you, truly quiet and undisturbed.' It is the only time when I feel that I am escaping the noise of the contemporary world. Not just the *actual* noise, but the anxious noise in my head. Reading is a crucial part of my mental health. I don't want to say that it's 'self-care', as that almost trivialises it and makes it sound temporary. Rather, it is and has always been, an essential part of me. It is probably my defining characteristic. Me without reading is like me without food. I would wilt and become silent. I don't read because it is 'better' than watching television. I read because I don't know what else to do.

We can attack pleasure relentlessly *and* sporadically. We can be both distracted couch potatoes and focused bookworms. As Steiner says, 'Binge-watching can be an addictive behaviour and a meditative one.' We tend to think of it as one or the other, but in Steiner's words, we might be 'seeing the forest *and* the trees'. There are many myths that we must debunk: binge-culture is obligatory. Binge-culture is essentialist. Binge-culture is destroying our attention and our memory and rewiring our brains. Instead of worrying (while continuing to binge-watch), it is important to remember how fortunate we are, to be able to pick between the adventures on screen, and those off – whilst acknowledging, hard as it sometimes is, that the former should never fully replace the latter. Except for on a Sunday night and then – well, you bring the snacks and I'll see you on the sofa.

The Authentic Lie

Do I contradict myself?
Very well then I contradict myself,
(I am large, I contain multitudes.)
　　　　Walt Whitman, 'Song of Myself'

I.

It all came to a head when a flyer fluttered through my letterbox. On one side, a drawing of a winged heart. On the other, a promise to 'gently wake up [my] authentic self' – presumed to be napping – through a twelve-lesson course. I didn't bite, but 'the teacher' rightly sensed a sympathetic soul lurking behind the front door. I am obsessed with what constitutes my authentic self and have been ever since I was little. I fixate on what I see as failings of my authenticity, from a piece of work that doesn't 'feel like me' to an evening where I behaved differently to the person I believe is my 'real' self. As a pretentious teenager, I went through a phase of writing down my favourite quotes in a leather-trimmed marbleised notebook, which I'd been given one Christmas and felt far too special to fill with my own flimsy words. An eclectic collection of bon mots from the likes of Milan Kundera, William Blake, Tony Blair and, er, Sharon Stone, many of the quotes dramatically interrogate the thorny concept of an authentic life. 'False face must hide what the false heart doth know,' from *Hamlet*. 'Most people are other people. Their thoughts are someone else's opinions, their lives a mimicry, their passions a quotation,' by Oscar Wilde.

Long before I took disposable Bic pen to earnest notebook, existential philosophers were gnawing at their quills over authenticity, which was associated with freedom, that most yearned-for state. Sartre believed people chose inauthentic lives over the anguish and impossibility of pure authenticity. Kierkegaard accused the media and church of 'levelling' our freedoms, meaning we all have the same experience rather than an individual, and therefore authentic, one. Nietzsche, that luxuriantly moustachioed belligerent, thought that in order to be authentic, we must reject conventional morality and determine for ourselves what is right or wrong. (I shudder to think what would happen if we adopted that mantra now, in the Outraged Era.) The very jolly Camus just thought life was absurd. (Note to self: Be More Camus.)

In this sense, the existential philosopher and millennial woman have much in common. I'm emblematic of a generation who, shaped by the siren call of social media and wolf cries of fake news, agonise over their life *purpose* or *truth*. Along with 'content' and 'curator', 'authentic' has become one of today's most overused buzzwords. Some people even bill themselves as all three, even though 'authentic content curation' could, let's be honest, be as prosaic as farting the alphabet. Where the existentialists thought authenticity could be established through the rejection of popular tastes, authenticity in the modern age has become something mainstream: something to expect in our selves, our food, our relationships and our brands. We see it as an essential part of living a better life; a fuller, more righteous life. By definition, *curation* and *authenticity* are opposites. And yet, as the means to curate ourselves – both on- and offline – increase, we become more and more obsessed with authenticity.

Our obsession has now reached its apex. Every week, I read a new piece about how to live an authentic life. To be true to yourself. To unzip the real you from the puffer jacket of fake you. Tips to achieve this run the gamut from ditching your phone to dancing like no one's watching. One of my favourite news stories on *The High Low* was about some doctors in Orkney who prescribed 'nature' to their patients with a leaflet suggesting activities such as making a bug hotel, appreciating a cloud, and the summoning of a worm out of the earth (without digging). It is undeniable that nature can be meditative and restorative, but nothing thrills me more than the image of a sentient adult lying prone on the grass, desperately imploring a worm to *make itself known*, dammit.

In *The Catcher in the Rye*, sixteen-year-old Holden Caulfield laments that he is surrounded by phonies (while ignoring any kind of self-analysis about his own phoniness). This is not a wholly unusual stance for a teenager, but it is also a reflection of a very modern preoccupation: the constant weighing up of who and what is real or fake. In his book of the same name, the writer Joe Kennedy coins the term *authentocrat* to describe those who, like Caulfield, are not simply obsessed with their own authenticity, but also with spotting lapses in that of others. The cynic in me wonders if the millennial pursuit of authenticity – including my own – speaks less of a desire to determine a sincere self, as it does an attempt to justify behaviour by placing it in the context of morality and originality. *So sue me, I'm making choices in order to live my authentic life.*

But what *is* an authentic self? Why do we feel so compelled to hook it, anchor it and find holes in it? As conversations about what makes a good life grow more clamorous and contradictory, we are taught to admire those who appear authentic and dismiss the inconsistent or insincere. But in our attempts to lasso and curate an authentic self, do we risk losing ourselves entirely?

II.

In the spring of 2017, the Saatchi Gallery in London held an exhibition called *From Selfie to Self-Expression*. The premise was to prove that selfies were nothing new and that to dismiss them as vapid and irrelevant was to brush aside a lot of influential (and, crucially, often female-created) art of the last century – which, the hotly contested theory argued, were 'selfies' of their time. Frida Kahlo's self-portraits; Francesca Woodman's black-and-white photographs of herself; Cindy Sherman's series of alter-egos, among others. Self-portraiture is of course not limited to female artists, but it has historically functioned as an important outlet for women, frustrated by how their identities were being flattened, fragmented and silenced by society. When the exhibition opened, I took part in a panel conversation about it. Because I'm young*ish* and carry a large digital footprint, everyone expected me to be the stalwart defender of selfies. But, as I told a rather disappointed audience, I'm ambivalent about the selfie. From a mental health perspective, we know to be cautious. Stories and studies are regularly published about sufferers of *selfitis*: mainly young women, and occasionally young men, who spend up to nine hours a day taking six hundred or so selfies. But what I find most interesting about the debate is how strongly some people react to selfies. Most critics claim it is the constructed authenticity of the selfie that makes them roll their eyes in distaste; a faux-candid, narcissistic, *desperate* bid for attention indicating low self-esteem. But I don't believe selfies nauseate spectators because they are inauthentic. Rather, it is the attempt to capture an authentic self that makes people wince. Their vulnerability feels similar to seeing a cold toddler, shivering on a British beach in winter. You want to wrap it up and pull it into warmth and safety. This is the impossible fly in the ointment in the age of authenticity: we demand the preservation of an authentic self, but we recoil at attempts to pin one down.

The dialogue around selfies feels almost old now: for a Gen Z reader, this essay probably comes across like a historical text. The generation after me have moved on to TikTok, an app that quite frankly feels too tragic for an early-thirty-something woman to download. Instagram self-portraiture has progressed beyond selfies into something more collective, with women commonly enlisting another person to take their picture – often their partner, giving rise to the 'Instagram husband' hovering nearby, documenting his paramour's every move. (For some highly prolific Instagrammers, there will be social media managers and personal photographers.) We are able to be not just subject of our images, but subject *and* spectator. This cognitive dissonance is crucial; it allows for a detached assessment of our own authenticity, which the psychoanalyst Louis Ormont calls, 'the observing ego'. It is now entirely possible to scroll through our social media accounts and 'read' ourselves like a stranger.

'Having two identities for yourself is an example of a lack of integrity,' said Mark Zuckerburg in 2010. Though not best placed to lecture on integrity, Zuckerburg's point exemplifies our demands for a uniform digital self. In real life, we're constantly *code-switching* – adjusting our tone, inflection, personality, and even perhaps our appearance and views – depending on who we are talking to. The psychological theory of *The Looking-Glass Self*, coined by sociologist Charles Horton Cooley in the early twentieth century, suggests we base our behaviour on the perceptions of others, or on what we *think* others expect from us. The self, Cooley argues, is not so much shaped by us, as it is crafted and reinforced through social experience. It is not fake to shape-shift according to feedback – it is human instinct. We naturally present a rotating roster of selves to our best friend, parent, boss, child, pet hamster and so on. (Greet your boss like you would your best friend, and you might get sacked.) We use white lies and softeners multiple times a day to ease conversation, often without even realising it. Cooley's looking glass is not so much a single reflection as it is a hall of mirrors, through which we're always spinning.

And yet online, we expect seamless consistency – *one true self*. A white lie on the internet becomes a confusing aberration. A betrayal. A woman who professes to hate make-up and then suddenly starts wearing boat-loads isn't being herself, in all her contradictory glory – she's an inauthentic hypocrite. *Don't trust her, she changed her mind!* warn the authentocrats. But an authentic self is not one which is set in stone – although we have come to think of consistency as authenticity. Rather, it is a self made of many, in a constant and necessary state of flux.

In the 1970s, the literary critic Lionel Trilling mused that the authentic self, though best left undefined, was most likely the 'distinction between an inner true self and an outer false self'. The internet has created a strict line between these selves, where we understand our *extrinsic* self to be one crouching inside our smartphone and our *intrinsic* self to be hiding at home on the sofa. But it is not enough to have these separate selves; it is inauthentic to present one self online and another at home. And so we attempt to break down these boundaries through endless sharing, turning ourselves inside out for the consumption of others. Sharing has become how we socialise. *This is me*, says our every tweet or Instagram post. This is the *real* me. We're often told the internet makes us less authentic – the angles, the filters, the artfully artless captions – but I think there's an argument to be made that it's making us more authentic too, if only by drawing attention to this attempt to lay bare an interior self.

There are benefits, of course, to sharing. It means we tell stories about ourselves through social media platforms that 'reflect and construct expectations for honest and authentic communication between equals,' writes Nicholas John in *The Age of Sharing*. As a writer, I find this storytelling invaluable: Twitter is a treasure trove of news and personal stories I might otherwise miss, from voices I might otherwise not know. I am less sure about John's claim that sharing on the internet is non-hierarchical. While it's true that it has changed the face of public conversation, and to enormous benefit, sharing is still weighted in favour of the privileged – 72% of followers are held by 1% of Twitter accounts, notes Christian Rudder in *Dataclysm*. We might all have *access* to the same tools, but that doesn't mean everyone's sharing is valued at the same level.

The downside to our non-stop sharing is that it has started to feel essential rather than voluntary: a stream-of-consciousness babble about who we think we are. 'Sharing your life is the opposite of living your life in isolation,' writes John. 'I must share my life because it is distinct from your life, and the assumption is that you cannot know about my life unless I share it with you.' That's true, of course. We can't know about someone's life unless they tell us. But this compulsion to share has become incessant. *Knowing someone's authentic self* now means knowing when they go to the doctor or when they eat a particularly delicious bagel. Pink Floyd's Roger Waters may have once written that we are amusing ourselves to death, but I wonder if we are expressing ourselves to death. Extinguished by our own self-expression.

III.

Radical transparency is a business term made famous by Ray Dalio to encourage honesty in government and politics, which has since seeped into the environs of online womanhood. Forget not washing your dirty laundry in public – it is now entirely normal to offer up our grubby gussets for public consumption. As Zuckerburg also said, 'Privacy is no longer a social norm.' It is hard to believe that until recently, it was considered distasteful to ask someone their political views. Nowadays, you are as, if not *more*, likely to write about your most intimate personal issues online for strangers to stumble upon, as you are to tell your loved ones. Numerous times, I have found out something exciting, profound or deeply sad about a close friend through her social media accounts.

In my early twenties, I went through a series of shiny new jobs and created an environment – or rather, an Instagram following – where it was assumed I would share my life. A few years ago, I grew uncomfortable with this kind of visibility and yanked the brakes. I still used social media, but I began to share much less personal information, far fewer pictures of myself (to my reluctant Instagram husband's relief) and stopped posting in real time. This careful folding in on myself felt like essential self-protection. The era of the sharing self dictates that 'the more we share [note: no object] the better the world will be', writes John. But self-disclosure is not always cathartic. 'Online sharing expands the public at the expense of the private.' Anything you share online becomes the property of others to distort and comment upon as they wish.

When I had my first child, someone remarked that I was making mothering look 'easy'. My Instagram grid lacked any shitty nappies, laundry messes and crying faces (mine included). The implication was that I was betraying the mumhood by not 'sharenting' (sharing your parenting) how utterly exhausting and sticky the whole affair is. But I think people are smart enough to assume there is plenty going on in people's lives that we do not see on Instagram. Do I need to show you my episiotomy for you to know I had one? Do you even need to know that a woman you have never met has had an incision between her vagina and her anus? (Cat's out the bag, now.) Speaking is no more an indication of profundity than silence a mark of inauthenticity. And yet the suggestion that you are lying about anything unseen or unspoken is an inevitable by-product of our shareable world. That is not to say that women who do share(nt) the warts 'n' all of motherhood aren't doing something worthwhile; they provide comfort, encouragement and education to me and many others. But I rail against the idea that to be sincere, it is mandatory to spill your psychological guts. That if you share *some* things, you must share *all* things. That to be authentic, you must lay bare a personal chaos. A woman choosing not to share parts of her life should not be seen as inauthentic.

Tavi Gevinson, a former teenage blogger, was one of the first women to profit from self-documentation on the internet. At thirteen years old, @tavitulle, as she was known then, could be seen sandwiched between glossy, grave *Vogue* editors on the front row at fashion shows; a diminutive figure sporting a grey bob, plastic glasses and a pair of neat cotton socks. At fifteen, she was editor-in-chief of a now-defunct popular online teen zine called *Rookie*. In her early twenties, she was given a year's free rent in Manhattan by a property developer in exchange for extensive social media coverage of the building. Now twenty-three, she is a poised writer and actor with a quirky-chic style. Recently, she interrogated the effect that 'honing [her] shareability lens' has had on her attempts to present an authentic self on the internet for *The Cut*.

'Somewhere along the line, I think I came to see my share-able self as the authentic one and buried any tendencies that might threaten her likability so deep down I forgot they even existed.' This doesn't mean everything Gevinson posted was artificial; rather that it became impossible, as it so often does, for her to disentangle her thoughts from the thoughts of others.

This is a risk for anyone who offloads even a single part of their self to the internet, but is particularly true for those who publish their work online. Writers who publish online, writes Allegra Hobbs (online), are *all* presenting an optimal self; even if their shtick is a 'self-consciously unadorned authenticity' that rejects the polished world of social media. I wonder at length about the effect being my own salesperson has on my work. As a freelancer, promoting my writing on social media – including this book – is a necessary ingredient to its success. But how much does the sharing taint what Gevinson calls 'the purity of intention'? And if we count social media as work – which most creative people now do – then even as I strenuously resist it, how much of what I share on Instagram is subconsciously shaped by my followers?

The problem with mining yourself for content is that it is impossible, given our lack of objectivity when it comes to ourselves, to know the full depth of what we are mining. And because the internet lives 'in the moment', who knows how what I share now will affect my future or the future of my children, whose pictures I post from time to time (the average parent, rather terrifyingly, displays almost 1,000 pictures of their child online before they reach the age of five). I tie myself up in knots, trying to figure it out. It feels disingenuous to delete my social media accounts, even as I worry about their effect. I decided to stop partaking in profitable brand partnerships a year ago (though this isn't to say I never will again), but I'm not naive about the impact that social media – something that once seemed inconsequential and is now stitched to me like a shadow – has had on my career. I know *The High Low* might not be what it is without mine and my co-host's Instagram followings. I know how vital my social media accounts are to the pollination of my work. And yet I feel nauseous every time I think about their existence.

'The woman who does not require validation from anyone is the most feared individual on the planet,' writes the social scientist Mohadesa Najumi. Our desire for validation is far older than the internet – what is 'Does my bum look big in this?' if not a bid for validation? (The only response: 'No, it is perfect, like a peach, plucked fresh from Tesco.') People-pleasing adversely affects women, who contort themselves into strange shapes and seek reassurance in places they often shouldn't. With 74% of women feeling pressure to please everyone, it is perhaps no surprise that posting, liking and commenting has such a large effect on our confidence. 'It's like that conundrum of the tree falling in the empty forest,' muses Jenny, the 35-year-old protagonist of Emma Jane Unsworth's novel *Adults*. 'Does it make a sound if there's no one there? If you put something on social media and no one likes it, do you even exist?'

Never have we had more tools for validation – and yet never have we been more insecure (the two are not unconnected). An episode of Charlie Brooker's dystopian drama series *Black Mirror* called 'Nosedive' features a terrifying probe into social media as self-worth. Set in a saccharine future-present, where social media and status have fused into one, citizens are given a mark out of five which then hovers above their head. Every single act is given a rating, so that even the tiniest, most insignificant interactions require false cheer. It is not so much an internal worth made external, but the erosion of an inner self entirely. The only thing that matters is your visible, digitally shaped self. Validation is more than a perk: it is a tool for survival. Of *course*, it's voluntary. Of *course*, there is an alternative. The counter to the status-addicted Lacie Pound who boasts a 4.2 rating is her mutinous brother, Ryan Pound, and his paltry 3.7. But Ryan is a black sheep, well below the waterline of social validation. He is also, crucially, a man, and so the conditions for his social and aesthetic validation are vastly different to those of his sister. Just because something is voluntary doesn't mean it's easy, or even always possible, to resist. Under these conditions, the possibility of making an 'authentic choice' becomes hard to see.

The appeal of *living your best Insta-life* – also known as *doing it for the 'gram* – has seen people take farcical measures to capture beautiful content, while pretending they 'just happened' to be there. A turquoise lake in Russia was nicknamed the 'Siberian Maldives' after swarms of Novosibirsk residents frolicked in its waters, inflatables in tow – despite the fact that the brilliant colour is the result of toxic ash from a local power station and can cause chemical burns. 'WE ASK YOU VERY MUCH THAT IN YOUR QUEST FOR A SELFIE YOU DON'T FALL INTO THE ASH DUMP!' desperately warned Russia's largest coal producer (no doubt fearing the lawsuits) via the social network VKontakte. And yet blow-up unicorns continue to carry their stubborn human cargo over this pond of metal oxides.

Social media hot-spots swiftly rise to fame and are discarded at even greater speed once they become so popular as to be deemed inauthentic: Norway's Trolltunga mountain where a sliver of cliff juts out dramatically, like a long finger; Portobello Road's candy-coloured houses in London; New York's Pepto-Bismol pink Pietro NoLita café (currently on the outs, thanks to the recent millennial-pink overkill), and the painted houses of Rue Crémieux in Paris. I thought I was exempt from this (I've never Instagrammed an avocado or a coffee, cross my heart and hope to die), until I found myself on the cusp of ordering a multicoloured latte at a cafe in LA last summer, after the barista made me laugh with his pitch: 'It's the drink to make everyone else's Instagram content look shit.' I stopped myself, a 32-year-old woman, mere moments before I could taste the rainbow.

IV.

In *Why Social Media Is Ruining Your Life*, journalist Katherine Ormerod debunks the myth that social media should or *could* offer a behind-the-scenes look at the authentic person beneath. To Ormerod, it's a no-brainer that there's a disconnect between who you are online and offline. Social media is calculated, contrived and curated – but then so is a photograph album, which is what Instagram was originally designed to be when it went mass in 2012. It is a natural impulse to share the best bits of life and leave the cat's furball, slick on the kitchen floor, to the mop. We all know that social media is a highlights reel, yet we constantly lament that it doesn't show an accurate picture. (My favourite example of this filtered existence was when Kanye West admitted to spending four entire days of his honeymoon editing a single picture of himself and Kim Kardashian.) But recently, there has been a shift in how we use Instagram. It has acquired an ethical dimension. Some enthusiastic early adopters have since completely shut down their profiles, while others have sought some kind of 'social responsibility', writes Ormerod. It may be impossible to show 'the authentic person beneath', but for some people 'there's a renewed drive to make sure there's an authentic intention behind what we are doing'.

And so Instagram grew tunnels of possibility, becoming more than just a platform to show off your mini-breaks (though to be sure, it is still that) into an exploration of human fallibility. Nowhere is that clearer than in the *Instagram vs reality* trend, which functions to remind people that, *duh*, social media is not real life. The trend was a response to the widespread feeling that what we were posting online no longer provided genuine insight into our lives, but rather had become too pretty, too polished and gave us raging FOMO (again, it is still that). In response to #goals-style perfection, a trend was born where you posted a picture of your *Instagram* – looking lovely swimming in the sea, say – followed by one of *reality* – you again, but this time with your bikini skew-whiff, hiccoughing sea water. It was the perfect solution for the woman who wanted to post a buff picture of herself, but felt under pressure to show her less glamorous angles in order to prove her feminist substance. (That women feel compelled to 'prove their feminism' on Instagram – often with a branded charity T-shirt – says a lot about how loaded and surface-skimming the conversation around modern feminism has become.) Instagram vs reality fleshed the woman out beyond mere flesh: she became a woman who wanted to share a good picture, yes, but was also willing to poke fun at herself; a woman self-aware enough to show that social media perfection is a shared hallucination. The trend did little to eradicate the compulsion for women to post pictures of themselves looking their best (if not better than in real life). The fabulous pictures were, crucially, still the *first* shared in the twosome. Instead, Instagram vs reality merely puts further pressure on women, writes Jia Tolentino, to look 'very perfect and [be] very honest' at the same time.

When Ormerod published her book, she dug through her Instagram archive and re-captioned a slew of glamorous photos for her almost 60,000 followers in order to reveal the often painful context in which they were taken (poor health, work strife, a traumatic divorce). This was not a one-off. After a devastating miscarriage at five months pregnant, Ormerod posted a series of photographs in which she was concealing her pregnancy, with multi-part, long-form captions. In doing so, she went beyond personal catharsis and hit pressing talking points: the fashion industry's poor maternity-wear offering; the lack of conversation around late-stage miscarriage; why so many women feel forced to hide their pregnancy. The delicate balance between glamorous and heartfelt does not always hit the mark, mind. I tittered at the sass of Goop employee Marissa Casey Grossman, who, when criticised for tagging the brand of her swimsuit in a picture dedicated to deceased friends and family, retorted: 'If they are looking down on me, they want to know what I'm wearing.'

In 2015, an eighteen-year-old Australian fashion influencer named Essena O'Neill – known for her bikini selfies and sunny, smoothie-filled updates from the Gold Coast – broadcast her social media breakdown to over 600,000 followers. After deleting more than 2,000 pictures, she edited the captions on the ninety-six remaining posts, in a sort of pre-emptive Instagram vs reality binge. 'NOT REAL LIFE,' she wrote under a picture of herself in a long white dress. 'I didn't pay for this dress, took countless pictures trying to look hot for Instagram, the formal made me feel incredibly alone. MORE COMING SOON,' she concluded, with a hyperlink to a website called letsbegamechangers.com. O'Neill described it as a site for 'veganism, creative imagery with purpose, poems, writing, interviews with people that inspire me, and of course the finical [sic] reality behind deluding people off Instagram.' The website never launched. Followers were left wondering if her digital self-destruction had been a marketing ploy that hadn't paid off.

In late 2019, O'Neill reappeared – a world-weary Insta-veteran returning to the battlefield of constructed self-promotion – with a 'community project' called Authority Within. This time, things would be different, she told the *Guardian Australia*. She was no longer interested in earning 'insane' money via her body or the promotion of 'a cute vegan product'. The clunkily named platform is arguably too weird to have gained any kind of mass traction, but is far more interesting than the pictures she sensationally decimated. (Categories are named things like 'Ideological Cesspool', 'Neoliberalism 101' and 'Woke Witches'.) Stamped at the top of the homepage is a quote by the French philosopher Gilles Deleuze: 'If you're trapped in the dream of the Other, you're fucked.' O'Neill's looping, furious, stream-of-consciousness screeds remind me of the long Instagram captions sage social media marketing managers now recommend as the way to achieve authenticity on the internet. 'Trust me, I know how to pull those capitalist strings. Style your soul, bare your flesh, pose for perfection, we all know she pays the best,' O'Neill writes in one blog post. But she no longer has the platform to send her messages mass. Her current Instagram profile (if it is even hers) has 3,000 followers and features just two macro images: a Banksy-lite piece of graffiti with a man writing, 'I like the real you more than the Instagram you'; and a simple manifesto in black typewriter script on a white background: SOCIAL MEDIA IS MY PLATFORM NOT MY LIFE.

The *New Yorker*'s Carrie Battan dubs the shucking off of a former digital self, the *getting real moment*. Personal revelation makes you feel better and others less alone – and makes *others* feel better and *you* less alone – and 'combines digital culture with therapy culture with an attractive mode of economics,' writes John. The getting real moment offers catharsis and often features what I call the *raw 'n' flawed* revelation, where a woman 'lays bare' her own imperfections or insecurities.

(The irony, of course, is that these insecurities are typically broadcast on the very same platform that likely exacerbated them.) Last year, the supermodel Kendall Jenner revealed her battle with acne as part of a partnership with the American dermatology brand Proactiv. Jenner's 'confession' had been so hyped up that the tabloids had thought she was about to announce she was gay. Instead, she exposed she'd once been plagued by pimples and was congratulated by Kris Jenner, her momager, for being 'brave and vulnerable' and sharing her 'raw story'.

The writer Richard Seymour calls this a *superficial subversion*, which helps rather than hinders the personal brand. With the acne safely hidden away in her past, Jenner's revelation makes her *more* attractive to fans (and brands), while also posing zero aesthetic risk. And yet part of me wonders if this isn't also the best use of sponcon. As someone with a mild case of acne in her early twenties, I think I'd have been comforted to know that a famous, seemingly flawless woman had had it too. Isn't this the transparency we yearn for from reality stars, who typically hoodwink us with their tummy-flattening teas and hair-growth gummies? But Jenner was being disingenuous, wrote Rebecca Liu for *gal-dem*, in suggesting her acne had been cleared up solely with a face wash. 'True authenticity,' writes Liu, 'would see the heiress-supermodel acknowledge that her attractiveness is due, in part, to her access to excellent surgeons, beauticians, and pricey skincare.' (I can only speak for myself, but my own acne cleared up with prescribed medication – not a face wash.)

So quickly did it become obvious that personal revelation on social media could be remunerated – if not with cash, then with followers – that a term emerged for those who used personal problems or natural disasters to hook in the likes: *sadfishing*. A close-up of your badass eye make-up might come with a wistful note about how it's okay not to be okay;

a self-portrait illustrated with a long caption about the Australian bushfires. It *is* okay not to be okay, and the bushfires *were* catastrophic. But Instagram has entrenched, to a worrying degree, the idea that everything a woman wants to say must be funnelled through her self-image. In that sense, Instagram is not remotely modern: it is positively ancient.

When the pop star Demi Lovato posted a picture of her cellulite on Instagram, she received more likes on it than on any other post. 'Demi Lovato faces "biggest fear",' screamed one headline dramatically. Our desire for authenticity has led to a fetishisation of flaws: the idea that imperfections must be proudly bared or, at the extreme end, invented. That was the charge levied at Missguided in 2017, when shoppers accused the faster-fashion brand of photoshopping stretch marks onto models' bodies. Rather than booking a model with stretch marks, Missguided decided to paint on their own, so they could ensure the striae were placed *just so*. This creative manipulation of a woman's flaws is no more authentic than photoshopping them into oblivion, so that she is smooth like an egg. (The brand vehemently denies any photoshopping took place.)

Even without such a cynical approach, suggesting that we should love our marks, scars and cellulite can feel like a new kind of bind. Like if you don't loudly declare undying love for your flaws, then you're doing the sisterhood wrong. Yet most women I know, particularly those who have given birth, do not love their stretch marks. Accept them as inevitable? Sure. *Adore* them? Hmmm. I'm deeply sceptical about the idea that a stretch mark is a mother's *proof of her love for her child*. The proof of my love is the child herself — standing in front of me, making herself loudly known. Most women I've seen claim their stretch marks as their favourite part of their body (because they are 'real' and 'imperfect' memories from 'the battlefield of life') are on Instagram. And frequently, it comes from women who are incredibly beautiful: a flaw contained within perfection.

This was the accusation hurled at actor and activist Jameela Jamil when she criticised Kim Kardashian for advertising body make-up. 'I have such severe eczema all over that my legs are covered in huge patches of pigment loss from scratching. I have a tonne of stretch marks, and because I have Ehlers Danlos Syndrome, *every* time I cut, I scar. I *refuse* to have these normal human marks weaponised against me,' she wrote on Twitter. *But hold on*, responded her followers. *What of women who* like *wearing body make-up?* Who don't feel confident leaving the house without it? Jamil later apologised for her 'preachy' tone, but the backlash she received raised an interesting point about who is allowed to celebrate their flaws. If you are otherwise gorgeous and slim – as Jamil is – it is easier, suggested some, to see your 'raw' self as your authentic one.

In 2018, the year before it folded, Mothercare unveiled a campaign featuring new mothers in their underwear, holding their tiny babies. The women had big smiles and soft tummies, with clearly defined caesarean scars and linea nigras. 'Beautiful, isn't she?' read the slogan. My heart bloomed seeing these women, with babies and lines like mine. But I also winced when I saw the advert, and still now I feel conflicted. Certainly, the campaign was an improvement on their 2017 offering, featuring a little girl dolled up as a 1950s housewife pushing a toy vacuum cleaner and playing with replica homeware. Mothercare's attempt to represent a raw version of motherhood is a salve to new mothers who saw their own bodies reflected, rather than the childless women peddling medically unapproved 'new mommy' girdles elsewhere on the internet. But it also frames a post-partum woman in the context of how she looks, rather than of what she has achieved (birthing a bowling ball and then staying up all night with it, for months on end). In that sense, heart-warming though it was, the advert is not in the least bit radical: it still adheres to the idea that beauty is currency for women. Rather than shift that narrative, the advert merely attempts to shift the definition of what is beautiful.

Expanding the parameters of female beauty into something more inclusive is essential. But to relate everything a woman does – even giving birth – to her appearance, does not so much 'free' the 'authentic woman' from her aesthetic confines, as re-order her within the same, limited framework. The raw 'n' flawed movement is as restrictive as that of the 'real woman'. The myth of the real woman was created by Dove in the early noughties, in order to represent different types of female bodies. It was a noble goal (and a highly successful marketing campaign), but merely flipped the narrative: so that real bodies became those with lumps and bumps, and model bodies – the small swathe of women deemed too toned, or too smooth – became *un*real. They might be rare – but they are not unreal. In much the same way, the positive intention of the raw 'n' flawed movement risks turning imperfection into a new consumer commodity. A stretch mark is not a market value. And there is no such thing as a real woman. All women are real, *by dint of being women.*

V.

The MTV series *Catfish* investigates the use of fake internet profiles in the murky world of online dating. The series came out of a 2010 documentary by Yaniv Schulman, a honey-tongued young filmmaker from New York who fell in love with a budding pop star named Megan. But Megan did not exist. Rather, she was one of fifteen digital aliases created by

Angela Wesselman-Pierce, a middle-aged woman whose fictional identities provided a reprieve from her stressful life as primary care-giver to two severely disabled stepsons. The title for the series came from Vince, Wesselman-Pierce's husband. Surprisingly sanguine when informed of his wife's online escapades, Vince told a folksy story about the catfish. At the turn of the century, cod was in high demand on the east coast of America. Sending it across the country from Alaska via train was logistically simple – but the cod were arriving mushy, tasteless and often dead. The fishermen deduced that this was due to inactivity, and so they put the cod's enemy, the catfish, into the tanks. The cod zipped around to avoid the catfish, and arrived alive, energised and full of flavour. His wife, Vince suggested, was the catfish in a tank of cod: she kept everyone's lives interesting.

Over the last few years, catfishing has become an accepted part of a fake-news world. We lap up tales of scammers, grifters and con-artists – from the small-fry pettifoggery of Instagram influencer Caroline Calloway's $165 'creativity workshops', to the Bernie Madoff-sized fraud of Elizabeth Holmes, whose blood-testing start-up, Theranos, was once valued at $9 billion and based on a technological impossibility. We are mesmerised by millennials who attempt to trick the system. 'Full disclosure I have been mildly obsessed with caroline calloway and what a trainwreck she is,' wrote @emehfr on Twitter. 'I can't look away from a good train wreck!' wrote @aswangakira. A 27-year-old Cambridge graduate, Caroline Calloway's 700,000-strong follower count was built on long Instagram captions about college heartbreak and a deep love for flower crowns. But Calloway truly went viral when attendees started revealing that her five-hour workshop had involved the eating of a salad ('Delicious,' said one fan; 'Too salty,' said another), the donning of a solitary flower for photo ops (they had to return the flower at the end of the workshop) and a small care package containing a thermal blanket – a wink and a nod, said Calloway, to Fyre Festival. (Calloway is no dummy; she pre-empted the scam before it had even become one.) In 2019, Calloway went viral once again when her 'ex-best friend' Natalie Beach revealed she had been the ghost-writer for Calloway's captions. (True, says Calloway, but not on the posts that actually made her big.) A brand that had been built on authenticity – heartbreak, an addiction to Adderall, a cancelled memoir she felt she could no longer write honestly – was suddenly flimsier than a photoshopped stretch mark. As the internet is wont to do, it piled on Calloway with calls for her deletion. Calloway responded with a tornado of never-ending Instagram stories, a perverse sense of delight and a new marketing hook. In the spring of 2020, Calloway published her first book: *Scammer*.

The strange but seductive tale of Russian-born Anna Sorokin, aka Anna Delvey, aka 'the Soho Grifter', is less easy to laugh off but no less intriguing. In 2019, she was charged with five counts of grand larceny in Manhattan for swindling $275,000 out of acquaintances, hotels, banks and boutiques with a series of bounced cheques over a two-year period. The story is even more exceptional for the fact that she was paying via cheque (who settles a large bill nowadays by whipping out their chequebook?). Allowances were made for Sorokin because she carried herself with the air of someone exceptionally rich, meaning that no one doubted she would eventually pay, or questioned the stranger aspects of her personality, living situation (exclusively in hotels) and origin story. Perhaps the most brazen part of it all is that Sorokin did not operate quietly. She hung out with famous actors like Macaulay Culkin, employed the celebrity trainer who had sculpted Dakota Johnson's buttocks for *Fifty Shades of Grey*, and fooled a high-net-worth, artsy circle of New Yorkers into thinking she was setting up a private members' club with an arts foundation.

The daughter of a former truck driver, Sorokin was merely following the New Yorker's mantra 'fake it until you make it', insisted her lawyer Todd Spodek. In the age of social media, he said, could she really be blamed for her 'delusions of grandeur'? Her 'chutzpah' and 'moxie' are by-products of our time. This was the first instance that social media had been invoked as a defence by a criminal attorney – and unsurprisingly, it didn't work. Sorokin was sentenced to four to twelve years in prison. She regretted nothing, she told the *New York Times*. She'd do it all again – just differently. This time it was not the scammer who scored the book deal, but the scammed. Rachel DeLoache Williams, a former *Vanity Fair* photo editor and conned friend of Sorokin, was paid a $600,000 advance by Simon & Schuster to write *My Friend Anna*, proving that being scammed can pay dividends – especially when you tell an authentic story about it.

Of all the authenticity grifters on the internet, the most unnerving – and certainly the most dystopian – are the robot-influencers. These AI fashion plates include the nineteen-year-old Brazilian model Miquela Sousa, known as Lil Miquela, the blonde Trumpian self-proclaimed 'robot supremacist' Bermuda, and the face-tattooed Blawko – all created by the LA-based tech start-up Brud; and Shudu, a Grace Jones-lookalike created, not without controversy, by a white male photographer named Cameron-James Wilson. (Wilson responded to criticism by revealing that Shudu only collaborates with brands that have a woman or a person of colour at the helm.) Lil Miquela, who has almost two million followers on Instagram, lives the life of teen dreams. She wears Prada and Chanel, has released four songs on Spotify and 'made out' with the supermodel Bella Hadid for Calvin Klein. She attends Pride marches, is pro-choice and supports

Black Lives Matter. She has a boyfriend. A reflection. Even a shadow.

That Miquela is digital fiction does not seem to concern the Miquelites, or the brands she partners with – who are probably relieved she will never turn up with a pimple or a hangover (or turn up at all). She even had her own getting real moment, after her account was 'hacked' by Bermuda in 2018, in a meta PR stunt by Brud. 'Here's the hard part,' Miquela wrote on Instagram. 'My hands are literally shaking. I'm not a human being.' (You'd think the comment section would be filled with *well, duh!* Instead, it was brimming with heartfelt messages of support about how Miquela was *real to them*.) Miquela's unwavering perfection is, unsurprisingly, deeply profitable. Brud scored $6 million in venture capitalist funding in 2019. Before we wring our hands in despair, we need to ask ourselves: are these avatars so different to many young women on Instagram? As much as social media might be drenched in a new authentic rawness, notes Emilia Petrarca, it is also weighed down with 'fake-looking real humans … [who] alter their bodies and edit images of themselves so heavily that CGI characters somehow blend naturally into our feeds'. As Lil Miquela put it: 'Can you name one person on Instagram who doesn't edit their photos?'

It may seem strange, given our obsession with authenticity, that a 2D robot could prove so popular. 'Honestly, the fact that she's not "real" doesn't bother me at all,' Matty from Florida told *NME*. 'Who's to say what's real, right?' (Yes, we are all existentialists now.) Miquela's lack of flesh and blood is *precisely* the key to her popularity. Authenticity in the digital age calls for an impossible consistency no human can provide – and so Miquela's simulated moods and computer-generated smattering of mocha freckles stepped up to fill the void. She is an Insta-cyborg of ethnically ambiguous, woke, idealised young womanhood: a puppet whose strings are pulled to respond to the demands of the market, creating maximum appeal and profit. In a world where we agonise over what is real and what is fake, there's no ambiguity over who or *what* Miquela is. She is authentically fake. Lil Miquela's superficiality is comforting to her audience – largely at the intersection of young millennials and Gen Z – who no longer trust humans (unless those humans are Greta Thunberg).

There is infinitely more outrage over Calloway's continued online existence than Lil Miquela's. To be clear, Calloway's content is navel-gazey rather than social-rights-orientated; she demanded money from people for her workshops, which Miquela never has; and to many, she functions as an example of what white women can get away with on the internet. (It is no coincidence that Sorokin is also white. Had she been a woman of colour, noted a friend of mine, the hotels would have never accepted so many empty cheques in the first place.) These differences are important, but I still find it excruciating to think that a company-controlled avatar is considered more authentic than a real young woman like Calloway, with her batty tea parties and chaotic Instagram content and grief over her father's death. Instead of being seen as, perhaps, a rare example of a truly authentic woman on the internet – this cringey, ugly, contradictory and *human* behaviour being the very thing that social media papers over – Calloway is held up as a cautionary tale of our times: how social media created the worst kind of person.

Like many tales on the internet, Vince's story about the catfish cannot be scientifically proven. Chatroom sceptics doubt the veracity of *Catfish* itself; rumours abound that the documentary and long-running series are more scripted than spontaneous. It seems only fitting that a show about authenticity online should have both an origin story *and* a filmmaker deemed more slippery than a catfish in a tank of cod.

VI.

Demanding authenticity from celebrities is a very modern requirement. Once upon a time, when gowns were boned satin and hair was whipped up into frosted peaks, celebrities were iconic in their mystery. There was a gulf between the Hollywood screen siren and her audience. Certainly, the private lives of the super-famous were fascinating: Charlie Chaplin's slew of teenage brides (three of his four marriages were to women under the age of eighteen) scandalised 1920s Hollywood – without, of course, having any impact on his career; while Elizabeth Taylor's seven marriages define her, even now. But there was no sense of entitlement or owner-ship. You got what you were given and, more often than not, that was a glamorous red carpet picture or a glossy magazine shoot before the drawbridge went back up for six months. Now, inscrutability is seen as suspicious and trans-parency is proof not only of substance, but of goodness. (The only type of celebrity we permit a loose relationship with authenticity is the structured reality TV star – ironic, given the name. Perhaps it is a mark of our own moral flux: no need to be authentic, so long as your fabrications entertain us.)

We have developed a 'fear of the fake' writes Seymour in *The Twittering Machine*. 'On social media, this desire for authen-ticity has become much more urgent', manifesting as a 'fas-cination with catching celebrities in real, "unfiltered", moments of intimate disorganisation, with plastic surgery gone wrong, make-up melting in the heat, tantrums, rows and bad deeds [which has] its roots in the urge to tear away layers of illusion and expose the horror beneath'. Social media has given us direct access to these celebrities, so that we may constantly gauge their authenticity like the good little authen-tocrats that we are. When a famous woman refuses to share something about her life – whether it is meaningless (where her dress is from), or meaningful (her sexual orientation, or who fathered her child) – her social channels are filled with the fury of a thousand fans.

In his book *Popular*, the psychologist Mitch Prinstein details the seven-stage quest for status. Stage five, *splitting*, is the point at which the 'the high-status individual realizes that his personality is not based on his or her actual character at all'. In her biopic *Miss Americana*, Taylor Swift describes having constructed her celebrity identity through the register of 'praise and punishment', which ensured that she 'became the person everybody wanted [her] to be'. It is the hinge on which authenticity squeaks. If you are a celebrity in the public eye, there comes a point at which you realise your fans don't know, or don't care about, who you deem your authentic self – they are merely fans of the self they constructed for you. (In his book *Celebrity*, Sean Redmond goes as far as to suggest that this relationship is now so reciprocal that fan and celebrity have merged into one hybrid beast.) We construct. And then we consume. The only difference is that it's no longer just celebrities who must navigate the split between private and public self. Now, with social media, it is us too.

Held to increasingly impossible standards (talk too much, like Jameela Jamil, and you're considered annoying; talk too little, like Anne Hathaway, and you're boring), can we blame those celebrities who blatantly style their own authenticity? I get in touch with Tina Brown, former editor of *Tatler*, *Vanity Fair* and the *New Yorker* and expert in all things celebrity culture, who is cynical about the notion of celebrity authenticity – believing it to be just another tool celebrities use to manipulate a thirsty public, baying for truth. 'Authenticity has become a new brand of fakery in today's celebrity marketplace,' she says. 'Social media posts of styled "candid" instances; TED Talks revealing rosebud moments of turnaround in life's journey. "Authenticity" is just another commodified approach in making yourself interesting to your audience.' It is true that performative or contrived authenticity, where people drip-feed 'naked' revelations to bolster their reputation, has become a crucial part of celebrity culture. In a 2018 interview with Lena Dunham for *New York Magazine*, Allison P. Davis writes that Dunham sent her an endless stream of raw, unfiltered text messages, fully knowing (perhaps even intending) they would be included in the piece. Dunham went as far as showing Davis a picture of her self-described 'diseased' uterus, removed from her body and exposed 'like a bloody, swollen, crimson orb'. Through 'therapeutic authenticity', Dunham's art has become so intertwined with her self that it is no longer possible for Davis to tell them apart. 'At first it felt overwhelming, but then I got used to the intimate snippets of her life. She became like a TV show I was binge-watching,' said Davis.

Lower down the celebrity food chain are those celebrities whose ascent to fame is Warholian (instant, overnight, built on flimsy foundations: reality TV stars, a now-defunct pop band, or the ex-girlfriends-of). For them, calculated candour typically manifests in a tell-all about their diet 'battle'. Staged pap shots – in which they guiltily down a full-fat Pepsi, while wearing deliberately unflattering leggings, pulled taut and sheeny over the groin – tactically set the scene for the inevitable weight-loss video. (It is not unheard of for a 'D-list' celebrity to gain weight in order to land a video through which she may make money losing it.) But I think it is misleading to suggest every famous person – as if they are one homogenous body – manipulates authenticity. 'So, too persuasive a performance of authenticity will be taken as a sign of inauthenticity. The authenticity-obsessed want something to be real, but they're on a hair trigger to cry foul if it seems too real to be true,' notes journalist Steven Poole.

When Keira Knightley opened up about suffering from a mental breakdown at twenty-two, she was applauded for her honesty. Knightley had hypnotherapy just to be able to stand on the red carpet (a contractual obligation to promote her films). Given her previous disinterest in pandering to her fans, it seems unlikely that her disclosure was a ploy for popularity. And yet, there was benefit beyond catharsis in sharing her story: it centred Knightley in the authentic gaze. *So she isn't just that irritating woman who told us she 'looks quite pretty' in* Love Actually, was the subtext. *She's vulnerable, messy, fucked-up like the rest of us.* If even a famous, beautiful actress – with all the supposed trappings of wealth and fame – can feel like that, then it makes us, the hoi polloi, feel like less of an emotional failure. But talking about her mental breakdown doesn't make Knightley any more authentic a woman/ celebrity/mother than had she stayed schtum. And yet, popularity still comes with disclosure. When a leaked security tape from 2014 showed her husband Jay Z and her sister Solange brawling in a lift, Beyoncé refused to talk about what happened. Her popularity nosedived. She was accused of being cold and robotic. When in 2016 she dropped her confessional album *Lemonade*, which included multiple references to cheating, she was suddenly beloved again – because she bared if not all, then some. She gave answers.

There is a certain myth that women can only do so well before they lose their truth. Authenticity is admirable only until it becomes too obviously status-seeking or profitable. 'The middle-class admiration for authenticity is predicated on the patronising condition that the little man shouldn't get too big for his boots,' writes Poole. Now imagine we're talking about women and double that statement. Then double it *again* for famous women. 'Who gets to be fully human in public?' tweeted the writer Rebecca Traister in 2019. 'Who gets to have their soft underbellies exposed without getting flayed and gutted?' Not only who *gets* to be – who would *want* to be?

VII.

If authenticity is threatened by self-consciousness, then how do you live an authentic life? Perhaps it is living a life free not of peer pressure, but of peer *awareness* – which would make my friend Lara the most authentic woman I know. When we were seventeen and everyone I knew took the bus, Lara rode a third-hand Pashley bicycle. When the rest of us were in Pizza Express doling out dough balls, Lara would be foraging for nuts in health food shops (still pretty woo-woo in the early noughties) that she would store in Kilner jars in her kitchen. While we splurged every week on Primark babydoll dresses that weren't even our size, but were infinitely more attractive because of their £5 price tag (I know, I'm sorry – it was 2008), Lara saved up for a year in order to buy a purple cocoon coat from a shop that only our mothers would go into, and that would have looked hideous on anyone but her, with her flaming red hair. At the pub, while I desperately sought out the eyes of some dubious boy, she played backgammon with old duffers she'd befriended at the bar. *Nothing* Lara did then, and does now, is designed to be fashionable. But because her choices are so clearly made by an independent and contented mind, to me she is the definition of authentic. And growing up, everyone agreed on this – even if we weren't self-aware enough to realise we were all capable of making decisions based on instinct rather than social expectation. Now that we are in a wellness epidemic, Lara's choices are no longer quirky talking points. Lots of people eat nuts, ride bicycles, practise yoga. But Lara hasn't moved on to new things just because everyone else has caught up. Neither is she less authentic because her activities and choices are now mainstream. Her authenticity was never dependent upon her activities being unusual.

'Authenticity is like charisma,' writes Andrew Potter in *The Authenticity Hoax*. 'If you have to tell people you have it, then you probably don't.' It is hard even now for me to distinguish between my authentic tastes and those I absorb from my peers. The question is further complicated by the internet: how do you remain authentic when you're constantly internalising compliments and criticism not only of yourself but of your peers – privy, as you are, to their mutating digital selves – in equal measure? For me, this has meant digital disassociation. Not so much to regularly log off my digital self, as to irregularly log on. Friends are always surprised to hear that I don't keep Instagram on my phone and only check it roughly once a week. I wouldn't go so far as to say that I'm summoning worms out of the ground (without digging), but I'm not against, say, plucking a few blades of grass and watching them wave in the breeze. Now that I'm sharing so much less of myself on social media and checking the sharing of others less frequently, I feel more like myself. But I also accept that I may never really *know* what makes my authentic self. As Zadie Smith writes in the *New York Review of Books*, 'a self can never be known perfectly or in its entirety'. Even when it's your own.

Beach's essay about Calloway went viral across both sides of the Atlantic, which baffled me. (Why did a story about a mildly toxic but not uncommon female friendship warrant such a tell-all?) But I was struck by one line: 'Caroline was caught between who she was and who she believed herself to be.' Does it take a scam of epic proportions to feel like that? Aren't we *all* caught between who we are and who we believe ourselves to be? Our identity, in eternal process and progress, so that it is only ever – as cultural theorist Stuart Hall puts it – 'a matter of becoming'? By that token, if Calloway is a scammer, then we are all scammers.

The postmodern philosopher Jean Baudrillard argues there is no way to tell – nor any *value* to be found in – the difference between an original and its copy. Consider our modern craze for memes: images, videos or symbols snappily re-captioned and unrolled in their thousands across the internet. What if the meme has more meaning in its tenth reinterpretation than it did in its original form? Who even knows what the original *is*? And isn't a meme, with its layers upon layers of meanings, more authentic than a single intention?

As I type this conclusion, an Instagram post by Dolly Parton is making meme history. The post is a collage of four photographs featuring Parton in various guises with the name of a social network written over each one. A picture of her in a dapper gingham jacket and pussybow blouse belongs to LinkedIn; Facebook is a geeky school yearbook-esque picture; Instagram, with its love of black-and-white archive shots, features a photograph of a young Parton in double denim; while the fourth and final digital identity, Tinder, shows Parton in a bustier, wearing bunny ears and a bob tail. Dozens of celebrities enthusiastically follow suit and now my friends are joining in. Parton's meme shows that we *do*, in fact, alter ourselves on different digital platforms. I like to think this meme is a watershed moment for the new decade: an acknowledgement that Cooley's hall of mirrors is something that we might allow ourselves to dance through on the internet – without fearing accusations of inauthenticity. It shows how the only way to be a truly authentic self is to be porous and polyvocal. To rewrite and rewrite and rewrite ourselves out of the frame.

Looking Forward to
Hearing Back

We text, text, text
Our significant words.

I re-read your first,
your second, your third,

look for your small xx,
feeling absurd.

Carol Ann Duffy, 'Text'

I.

On my thirteenth birthday, I got my first mobile phone: a
Nokia 3310, which I immediately sheathed in a faux Burberry
cover I'd found in a Colchester pawnbroker. My mother had
taken some persuading. She was convinced that spending
any longer than two minutes on a mobile phone call would
fry your brain. (In her defence, it was the year 2000. Everyone
was still unsure we'd actually survived the turn of the millennium.) She needn't have worried. Aside from prank calling
boys I'd never met – their numbers passed among my friend
group like bags of Wotsits: 'Here, take Dan, I met him last
summer, he seemed all right'; 'Try this number, it's my
cousin's friend, he's called Alex' – I didn't actually want to

call anyone. I had just two ambitions for my tiny new friend: I wanted to beat Snake, and I wanted to send six-part text messages.

You only need to whisper 'six-part text message' to a middling millennial woman for her to clutch herself in exquisite nostalgia (if you said it to a man of the same age, I suspect he would either remain blank or groan). On the original Nokia models, texts had a limit of 160 characters and were capped at a string of six messages, which would typically arrive in the wrong order. Text gaps could remain for hours. Sometimes, forever. The appeal lay as much in what was hidden as in what was read. 'I've got 2/6 and 5/6!' you'd shriek. 'Can someone help me fill in the gaps?' These messages became our version of the Socratic problem: with a scholar's zeal, we constructed meaning from half-sentences and nonsensical narratives. Petty mysteries lay within these broken texts: were you forgiven by a moody friend, or dashed to hell?

This delectable yet maddening puzzle was the baseline of our teenage texting. The waiting, the confusion, the unreliability. But it was also exactly what allowed us to nurture comforting delusions. At seventeen, I was almost able to fool myself into believing that my then-boyfriend was not *necessarily* ghosting me when he didn't reply for three weeks – just that maybe parts 1, 2 … 3, 4, 5 and 6 (though boys never got to number 6) hadn't turned up yet. At the same time, texting and emailing as a teen were strangely straightforward. You would text one person with concentration, rather than thirty-three different people at the same time, as you might very well do now. You felt no obligation to reply, because there was never any doubt that you would. Texts were exciting. You only texted people you liked – not people you 'liked'. Texts were my first encounter of *operant conditioning*, a way of learning through reward and punishment for certain behaviour. Coined by the American psychologist Burrhus Skinner in the 1930s, it is more commonly known as 'the rat and the lever method', after the famous experiment showing rats were more likely to pull a lever for a treat when they did not get one every time. The six-part text message was a perfect reflection of this variable reinforcement: a digital roulette where you were never quite sure what would come next.

Nostalgia, when misdirected, can be a dangerous thing. But when it comes to this subject I can't help agreeing with Grace Dent, who writes that 'life back in the days when we had one shit Nokia and a landline between five friends seems blissful. One was permitted lost weekends and periods of secret skulduggery or just to lie about reading a paperback without the sense six people were owed a text message.' The sad truth is that no form of communication will ever be as exciting as multi-part text messages were in 2000. That is as much to do with the fact that social media did not yet exist, as it is because I was thirteen years old and my texts came from my best friends – and boys I would never meet. My emails (sent from my extremely chic first ever email address, sugarcandy27@yahoo.co.uk) consisted solely of PowerPoint presentations created with the limited artistic medium of ClipArt. The advent of Bebo, MySpace, MSN Messenger and WAYN (I favoured the last two) could not have predicted how I would eventually feel about digital communication. Even the opening of a Facebook profile once I hit university – back when you needed a '.edu' email address to activate an account rather than just a scan to prove you were a foetus – didn't cause me undue strife. But somewhere along the journey from multi-part text messages to a never-ending cycle of constant communication, there was a psychological rupture. My phone morphed from a thrilling roulette – into a Tamagotchi of anxiety and dread.

II.

The buzzwords we hear most often when it comes to phones are *nomophobia* (fear of being without your phone) and *phubbing* (when you ignore someone right in front of you, in order to answer your phone). Forget the generational divide – even my parents are obsessed with their smartphones. My dad virtually lives on email and will answer calls during mealtimes, while my mum is so attached to her iPhone that she invested in a little cross-body leather bag for it, complete with a delicate diamante apple on the front. But why is there no word for the fear of being *with* your phone? (There is only *telephobia*, but that refers to the specific fear of making phone calls.) Am I the only one hurtling *away* from the operant conditioning and dopamine hit of my smartphone?

My fear and dread are due to a two-fold sense of obligation: the expectation to maintain conversations across, at the very minimum, a triumvirate of digital communication – phone, email and social media – until you expire; and the assumption that you are always *on* and answerable to everyone. The endless email cycle for anyone whose job is not manual is now accompanied with the cheery, passive-aggressive sign-offs of global internet language (which feel much more American, I might add, than British). Popular pass-ag platitudes include 'Looking forward to hearing back!', 'Reaching out again!', 'Circling back!', 'Let me know!' (or even 'LMK!'), demanding reciprocation that was never actually established nor consented to. Meanwhile, instant messaging apps, particularly those with group chat functions, essentially enable dialogue to continue ad infinitum. I am struck fairly regularly with the thought that I could die without ever having 'completed' certain digital conversations. Text messages end with the promise to 'speak later', leaving me more often bewildered than comforted. Didn't we just *finish* speaking? What could I possibly conjure up to titillate with later? I worry I will never be free of the demand to reach out, around and upside down.

We call it 'speaking' but of course it's not – millennials are terrified of phone calls. Absolutely bleeding terrified. (And Gen Z aren't much better.) We are, as Hannah Jane Parkinson writes for the *Guardian*, Generation Mute. An unannounced call is answered – *if* it is answered (mostly, we screen calls from a safe distance) – with suspicion. *What have I done wrong? Who has died?* (And if no one has died, *Why the fuck are you calling?*) An unanswered call is never followed up with a voicemail (no one listens to those any more) but an immediate text of reassurance. *Don't worry, nothing wrong! Just calling for a chat.* Calls are scheduled in advance and, as the appointed time draws closer, the instinct to wriggle out becomes overwhelming. If you want to make calls even worse for someone who already loathes them, I strongly advise you schedule them. It makes even a smear test feel like a better option. Me, I *like* phone calls (although I don't like scheduling them). Much more time-efficient. But they only work if the other person picks up the phone. And they don't. Not really. Not ever. Instead, we are *scripturient*, observes the writer Richard Seymour, 'possessed by a violent desire to write' or, rather, type 'incessantly'. Much of the writing now is done *around* the original writing so that we are positively 'swimming in writing'. The follow-ups, the chasers, the furtherings and looking-aheads.

It takes an average of 200 milliseconds for someone to respond in spoken conversation. In the past decade, technology has aimed to match this, writes Julie Beck, and has now come as close as it can, 'until they implant thought-to-text microchips in our brains'. (In Russell T. Davies' dystopian drama *Years and Years*, a teenage girl has a smartphone implanted into her hand so that her on and offline selves are fully fused.) Instant messaging apps like WhatsApp create a scenario where the expectation is that you should reply within seconds. But because it's impossible to do that, at all times, for everyone, the result is a breeding ground of anxiety, sending people spiralling in one of two ways: a cycle of neediness and chasing, or complete avoidance. Instant messaging may mimic the speed of an IRL conversation, but it doesn't give you the opportunity to gauge how a message has landed. You don't get the chance to correct your words. You don't get to see the nuance of the body language of whoever you're writing to. Or, as the psychologist Sherry Turkle puts it, you don't 'get to see the shadow of your words across someone's face'. Instead, you indulge in *metamessaging* – where you read between the lines.

It is the absence of shadow that causes me grief. I frantically flit between having my phone on and off airplane mode, simultaneously keen to avoid the messages coming in – and equally nervous about missing them. I am 'suspended between a compulsion to do too much and a wish to do nothing', as Josh Cohen puts it (a feeling not necessarily limited to our digital communications). More often than not, this failure to find a middle ground means I opt out entirely. I turn my phone off for an entire weekend, put an out of office on my email, and use my husband's phone (no angst there) or the landline. Friends and family tell me they admire my clear boundaries. I know how to turn *off*, they say, as though I were a Buddhist thinker. The truth is not so much that I have actively chosen to 'turn off' – myself as much as my phone – as it is that I no longer feel able to navigate the white noise looming ever larger in my life. I deleted social media apps from my phone not for a 'digital detox', or because I am 'above' social media (such snoots are tiresome), but because I feel besieged by seeing and hearing what everyone is doing, all the time: it began to feel like madness, indulging in the cacophony of fifty people's lives, before I had even eaten breakfast. How do we expect to live present and clear, if our minds are addled by other people's holidays, hangovers and new shoes first thing in the morning? The constant flow of communication (if it can even be called that) has eroded linear dialogue, and it can feel like we are no longer listening, just lobbing a series of non-sequiturs at each other like darts forever missing the bullseye. '*Rapport*, I need *rapport*,' I screeched to someone the other day. Sometimes I feel as though I have transmogrified into a collection of googly emoji eyeballs: nothing but pupils, constantly skimming and observing. Clearing, deleting, replying, dispatching.

In October 2019, I conducted a Twitter poll that revealed I was not alone in my angst. Of 1,580 respondents, 45% said they felt exhausted by the arrival of a new text message – only fractionally more than the 43% who felt excited. 12% just felt annoyed. When asked the same question – supplanting 'new text' with 'new email' – 67% of 743 people reported they felt exhausted, and 22% were excited. Given it's normally linked to work, its unsurprising that email is the more tiring medium. But the fact that almost half of us also dread texts, which are primarily used for personal reasons, makes me think that the sense of obligation around digital communication makes work out of play, even when it's with someone you adore.

The agitation comes not only from the fact that conversations are unending and that you will forever be held to a response, but that there are also so many ways to tell if someone is ignoring you. WhatsApp has an admirable arsenal of tools to make you feel paranoid: ticks that go blue when someone has read your message; the 'last seen' status update; and knowing when someone is online – a fertile field of anxiety, I have been told, when you are dating. A friend recently spent an entire weekend with her eyes trained on the online status of a man she was seeing, taunting herself with the knowledge that he was writing near-constantly – just not to her. Even the dreaded ellipsis on iMessage (which serves as a cue for tension in many a contemporary boxset) tells you when someone is typing. Known as the 'typing awareness indicator', it serves little function except making you vibrate with unease when the three tiny dots suddenly disappear. But why do we need to know when someone is typing? What purpose does it serve, except to amp up the urgency of exchange? I fear that *that* is its designed purpose: intentionally creating anxiety to keep you hooked to your device. *Oooh look, my reply is on its merry way, I had better stay here to read it – hold on, they've stopped typing … Wait, have they gone? As in, just left halfway through a message? Why would anyone do that? They hate me. I knew it. Christ, maybe they've* died? *I don't wish death upon anyone but … Oh thank fuck, the dots are back.* And so on and so forth. Abandoning a message is rarely a deliberate act of cruelty – people abort to rescue a toddler on top of a sofa, or because the kettle has finished boiling – but it is the not knowing that makes silence seem even more deafening than the din you may wish to escape from.

III.

It is sometimes hard to believe that Nora Ephron did not direct the 1998 rom-com *You've Got Mail* as a horror film. Since the seminal 'email movie' came out, there has been a tonal shift, writes Adrienne LaFrance. We've gone from a time 'when AOL would gleefully announce, "You've Got Mail!"' – where the very worst that could happen via email was falling in love with the owner of a rival bookshop – to an age where 'Gmail celebrates the opposite: "No new mail!"' At a cultural moment when we are more sensitive than ever about our time – how we spend it, how we value it, what visible product we have to show for it – email has become a 'reservoir of your own time managed by other people'. This sense of obligation has spawned an almost intolerable efficiency, where the average office email goes unread for just six seconds. It used to be that only a few professions – doctors, plumbers, taxi drivers – 'required this kind of state of being constantly on call. Now almost all of us live this way,' writes Freeman in *The Tyranny of E-Mail: The Four-Thousand-Year Journey to Your Inbox*. We have become so absorbed in reading and replying and re-immersing back into whatever we were doing outside of our inbox (which can take up to twenty-five minutes every time) that we have little to give the rest of our day. Our inability to 'finish' a digital conversation becomes as much a concern – if not *more* of a concern – than the conversation itself. This is known as the *Zeigarnik Effect*: a psychological term that describes how we are more preoccupied with incomplete experiences than complete ones. Caught in this endless feedback loop – as impossible to complete as Snake was when I was thirteen – it is no wonder we're feeling fraught.

In this heightened state, the out-of-office has thrived. When the comedian Steve Coogan resurrected his douchey journalistic alter ego Alan Partridge in 2019, 'Partridge' emailed his 'colleagues' at the BBC to announce his return. When one journalist replied to his spoof email, she got an automated response: 'I'm not in the office so both cannot and will not respond to your email. If your email is urgent, perhaps you should have tried calling instead. The very fact you were content to type out your query long hand and settle back to wait for a reply suggests you can wait, even if you've put a red exclamation next to your email to make it stand out in my inbox. Won't wash with me, that.' The recipient posted the message on Twitter, where it quickly went viral, not just because of its on-the-nose humour, but also because it inspired envy. Sure, there's nothing *stopping* you from crafting an arcane out-of-office (OOO) like this – except for the fact that it would forever mark you out as an outlier or oddball. (Only the sturdiest among us can risk becoming water-cooler gossip.) To resist email culture, especially as a young*ish* freelancing woman still building a network, would feel not unlike adopting the mantle of Bartleby the Scrivener – Herman Melville's fictional clerk who stagnates to death after refusing to capitulate to the endless correspondence of his job.

The OOO has become an art form; the funniest and most outlandish frequently turned into memes. 'Dear person who has sent me a yet-unanswered e-mail, I apologize, but I am declaring e-mail bankruptcy,' reads one from Harvard law professor Lawrence Lessig. I recently learned of a man who was so fed up with email culture that his OOO simply read: 'Nope.' (I spend an inordinate amount of time wondering if he is an absolute hoot in real life, or just a doomsayer.) We festoon the OOO with detail, garnishing it with geo-tags: 'I'm in New York'; 'I'm in Asia'; 'I'm in Cornwall' (massive time delay, that last one). The simple 'I am not in the office' has largely been replaced by the American expression 'I'm on annual leave' (which makes it sound like you're on a tour in the Falklands, rather than enjoying a week in Formentera, noted *British GQ*, acidly). Some add a punny gif, or a black-and-white archive picture, in the body of the text in the vain hope that a decorative plea will encourage people to respect their unavailability. (That's not to say that we aren't *working* on the re*working* of the *work*/life balance. Just that it doesn't include going off email for any significant stretch of time – and certainly not off texts.) And yet, humour aside, we've killed the OOO through sheer over-use. The level of obligation on almost everyone who uses email at work means that even your daily constitutional warrants an auto-response ('I won't be able to answer your email for the next 3–15 minutes depending on the speed of evacuation'). On the surface, the OOO might seem like an assertive statement of unavailability.

But listen closely and you'll hear a plaintive moan from deep within the abyss of Outlook. *Please just leave me aloooone.*

The truth is that you can trim it with raffia, tie it up with a dinky bow, even throw a handful of digital glitter over it and still the OOO can feel like using a cardboard box to stop a flood. I find myself tinkering with my OOO *while* OOO, to give it more impact – bolding-up a word, adding an underline here or there for emphasis. We all know that, despite writing 'I will not be checking my email **at all** during this time', we are definitely still checking our email during this time. (This goes hand in hand with people assuming that if you're a freelancer, you must *always* want to work, and that if you don't instantly respond to an email, then you must have moved to Cabo and retired.) There's this idea that you can just ignore email – indeed, many do – but it takes a lot of moxie to do so without an OOO.

If I find digital communication so stressful, then why do I keep sending messages? Well, clearly I would have few friends and little work if I opted out entirely. But also, *sending* messages actually feels good, writes the informatics professor Gloria Mack – it is receiving them that's the problem. I notice this when I fire off twenty emails, or clear my WhatsApp inbox and feel efficient and clear-headed and satisfied. To be the recipient, to be called upon, is entirely different. And yet I am not sure I entirely agree with Mack's theory that receiving a message feels necessarily bad. As much as receiving messages makes me anxious, *not* receiving them can be worse. Rationally, I know that a delayed response does not always mean the sender has spontaneously decided they loathe me with the fire of a thousand suns. Certainly, my own delay in responding is rarely loaded. And yet it is all too easy to slide from angst-er to angst-ee. The damn truth is that it feels both good *and* bad to receive a message – the first instinct quickly swallowed by the second.

IV.

'It should cost £100 to start a WhatsApp group,' declared the comedian Ivo Graham. The exhaustive nature of group communication is well documented, with people falling into one of two camps. 'Yay! Constant comms with my besties,' says the person maintaining seventeen different WhatsApp groups. And, 'Oh dear God, please save me from this sinkhole of chatter,' groans the person who is reluctantly dragged into one. The racket of a WhatsApp group – glancing at your phone and seeing you have 103 notifications – can feel like being stone-cold sober at a party, five friends drunkenly pressing you against the wall, hollering nonsensically at you with tequila-tinged breath. As I write this, I'm part of just three WhatsApp groups: one with my family, one with my godson's other godparents, and one with my podcast colleagues. As a keen Wexiteer, I remain sane only through muting them and nudging WhatsApp off my home screen, so that I have to swipe three times to reach the app. It's not that I don't enjoy texting (I do actually get a kick out of the ping-ping nature of instant chat – just not every day and not on someone else's terms), but the unscheduled drip-feed of messages makes me feel like I am drowning. How the hell do the rest of you cope?

Some WhatsApp groups are sacred – you're an ass if you 'ever question the content of the family WhatsApp group', warns the writer Nikesh Shukla. Some are dangerous – in 2018, university students at both Warwick and Exeter were found to be having vile misogynistic, racist and anti-Semitic group chats. Some are about recovery and survival – peer support groups like Safe Link for victims of sexual assault. But for the most part, the WhatsApp group is a tyranny of triviality: a mindless, maddening, enriching, life-enhancing, unrelenting chunter of chatter. It is largely accepted that the worst type of group is the event-specific, banter-heavy one, which continues long after the jolly itself 'to keep the memories going'. For example, 'Hey guys, anyone around Soho for beers?' Response: 'Neil, we went on a ski trip together four years ago and none of us have seen each other since. I know you saw the whole "fondue dick-dunking thing" as a team-bonding exercise "that has worked really well in the past", but some of us are still scarred – quite literally – by it. We've all left the company since then – perhaps it's time we shut down the group, too?'

The WhatsApp group is a natural evolution of the group email, which first came into my life as a 'chain mail' of superstition in the early noughties: REPLY TO THIS AND SEND IT ON TO TEN PEOPLE, OR YOUR LIFE WILL BE OVER. Although WhatsApp has primarily taken over as the intra-friendship tool – you can even open it on your desktop so your boss is none-the-wiser – for large-scale events, the slightly retro group email still dominates (and always with the sign-off '**Please do *****!!!NOT!!!***** Reply All**'. You can put 487 asterisks on that entreaty, Beth – we all know someone will). For the millennial woman, the emotional stakes are never higher than with a hen do: the ultimate expression of heteronormative female friendship (closely followed by the baby shower and/or the thirtieth birthday). The group email for a hen do – which often bloats into an event with multiple stages, made up of every single woman the bride has ever met, so that it becomes not so much a hen do, but a hen *tour* – is ripe for satire. The maid of honour is cast in the full-time role of project manager: if you don't get back to her, rest assured you *will* be responsible for her nervous breakdown.

In *Everything I Know About Love*, my podcast co-host Dolly Alderton includes an only mildly exaggerated group email template for the middle-class millennial hen do, which focuses on a penis-straw-heavy brand of forced fun. (I won't deny that my own hen do included penis straws.) 'Hello any woman Emily has known for the past 28 years!' the email begins merrily, before descending into a militant, time-stamped schedule of activities – including a game of 'dildo football' and a 'tampon tree' (to keep Emily rooted in wom-anhood) – and concluding with the *nota bene* that 'an invitation to the hen do does not guarantee an invitation to the wedding'. The agony of the hen do itself is matched only by the exhausting obligation to reply to every costly update.

Caroline Moss and Michelle Markowitz's hilarious book *Hey Ladies!* lampoons the passive aggression of a collective digital conversation between eight twenty-something women with similar gusto. The year-long group email chain is unrelenting, demanding instant replies even at 8 a.m. on New Year's Day. It frequently descends into petty feuds and metamessage splin-ter groups whose only function is to analyse the *tone* of the original group chat. The message sign-offs neatly reflect the dichotomy of female friendship in the digital age. In real life, it's affable, convivial, affectionate. On screen, it's underscored with a high-octane subtext: unless a friend replies to you, they do not care about you. 'In the future, please always respond to my emails within 5 minutes, just so I know that you're alive, lol!' implores one. 'Can everyone please text me when they're PMS-ing and I'll add into our shared google calendar?' reads an attempt to regulate these bouts of anxiety. And then there are the desperate pleas to be excused from the din. 'Can you please take me off this thread!!!!!!' writes the future bride of the group. 'It's seriously annoying.' Yet, by the end of the book, they're all still on the email chain. Even the defector has returned. The wheels keep on turning; the random mes-sages and anxious quarrels continue. Because another one of the ladies has just got engaged and she needs them to organise her hen do, and – well. What's the alternative?

There is a ribbon of affection running through the cheery snark of *Hey Ladies!* but the title cuts close to the bone. Men do not send group emails like this. Men do not, largely, seem to care when a friend does not text them back, or does not 'let them know!' if they would like to go to the cinema. This is not my way of saying, 'I just get on better with boys!' (the opposite is true), but having observed many of my husband's group WhatsApps and emails, I am forced to glumly conclude that when men organise something via group message, it comes with less tension and obligation. This is also not to say all women are uptight about communication (and it is especially not to say that we are *born* like this), for I know plenty who don't give a jot. Texting or emailing your female friends is often fun; I feel lighter and brighter after a silly, crass twenty-minute exchange with a best friend. But the particularly female fear about how you 'come across' is a significant part of many friendships between women – so that even in your most solid, enduring relationships, it can be hard not to infer acceptance or rejection in your digital exchanges, with nothing in between.

'Women use the word "tomorrow" far more than men do, perhaps because men aren't so great at thinking ahead,' writes Seth Stephens-Davidowitz in his book *Everybody Lies*. Women are culturally conditioned to be efficient and empathetic friends. These attributes are not unrelated. Part of Being A Good Friend is promising up your future self. In looking ahead to tomorrow, the email or WhatsApp message becomes a way to protect our friendships from insecurity. Perhaps this is why I have become so terrified of digital communication: if navigating the conversation on behalf of my current self leaves me feeling sapped, to offer up my future self for the taking is terrifying.

V.

The internet linguist and author of *Because Internet*, Gretchen McCulloch, calls 'looking forward to hearing back' and its merry gang of little enforcers, *phatic expressions*. Other examples include 'How are you?' and 'What's up?': social niceties that pad out a conversation rather than carrying any actual weight. She tells me, in not quite these words, to chill out. '"Speak later" is just idiomatic. Expressing the wish to resume your communication is quite a friendly thing to do.' Surely, she suggests, it is better than the alternative – 'Fuck you, go to hell!' Well, when you put it like that. People who follow up, even the most ingratiating, are not trying to chase me into an early grave, she tries to reassure me. They're just whacking in a load of *conventionalisms* – words that become rote through usage. David Shariatmadari, the author of *Don't Believe a Word: The Surprising Truth About Language*, says phatic phrases are part of a 'linguistic perpetual motion machine'. The sheer number of messages we send and receive means that 'we have to employ ever more creative strategies so that we aren't left in limbo'. As these phrases get used more and more, they blend into the background, 'so we have to invent new, more insistent ones to make sure we're getting people's attention'. He compares it to hyperbole – we no longer say 'it's freezing', but 'I'm absolutely freezing'. We are not tired, we are 'unbelievably exhausted' and so on and so forth. Phatic expressions are a way to 'engage in a little emotive persuasion'. Like the exclamation mark, they become another way to stand out.

Feeling overwhelmed by the pressure of written communication is – and I suspect you know what's coming next – not remotely new. We've been angsting over it since before the quill was invented. 'The merchant goes home, perhaps, after a day of hard work and excitement, to a late dinner, trying amid the family circle to forget business,' writes the harried Victorian businessman W. E. Dodge, 'when he is interrupted by a telegram from London … directing, perhaps, the purchase in San Francisco of 20,000 barrels of flour … and the poor man must dispatch his dinner as hurriedly as possible in order to send off his message to California.' Or in the words of Samuel Morse, who sent the first telegram transmission in 1844: 'What hath God wrought?'

While we're on the phone, McCulloch digs through her stash of old postcards, which she uses to trace how language has shifted throughout history. Fishing one out from 1909, bought from a used bookshop in Montreal, she translates it from French. '*Sir, I am sending you six more postcards today. I hope that you received the six last cards that I sent to you on the fourth of this month.* Is this not the "Did you get my text?" of postcards?' laughs McCulloch. Except this is not a tale of unreciprocated postal harassment. Digging deeper through the bookstore, McCulloch finds another postcard written in the same handwriting, from a woman named JB to the same male recipient, dated one month later. '*Sir,*' she reads to me with a triumphant flourish. '*Thank you very much for the beautiful cards that you sent me.*' JB, it turns out, was not overwhelming her penpal with tens of postcards and then demanding that he reply. They were merely corresponding. It was normal etiquette for her to ask him if he had received her letters, rather than a chivvy. So what if it isn't a chivvy now? What if 'I hope that you received' was the phatic equivalent of 'Looking forward to hearing back' – just common exchange?

In *Because Internet*, McCulloch writes that the fractured format of modern communication predates recent technology. It was the invention of the landline telephone in the 1870s that prompted 'the first major technological rupture' in conversation. Okay, I say, but it still allowed back-and-forth dialogue. It didn't feel like you were just *lobbing* bits of information at one another and seeing what stuck. When I have a phone conversation with someone, I know that unless they are very distracted they will respond to what I say. That might have been the case when people actually *spoke*, parries McCulloch, but studies show that they rarely actually managed to. 'Recall the phenomenon, telephone tag,' she says. 'You try and call someone, they are not home, you leave a message with someone's spouse, they call you back, they get your voicemail and then you call them back ... No one enjoyed this! Email liberated us,' says McCulloch.

I concede that there has always been anxiety in communicating, but I remain unconvinced that the expectation of constant replies has not intensified in the last five years. 'Following up' is not a modern problem, it just becomes harder to execute because in the '80s you could blame not getting back to someone as the fault of telephone tag. ('I left a message with your secretary/mother/cat!') But 'I didn't get your email' is a risky move, and thanks to the itemised log, pretending you didn't get someone's WhatsApp is completely impossible. I see phatic expressions not as harmless little adornments, but as electronic distress flares. We need to remind someone to circle back, follow up, let us know or shoot to the top of their inbox because, stretched by our attempts to 'finish' a digital conversation, we have written ourselves into a kind of lunacy. Paradoxically, our level of communication has never been higher – and our level of human connection never lower. As our social groups open up to encompass anyone able to contact us, we start to see everyone as owing us a response and, in turn, we are drained by the boundless demands of others. 'We stop seeing people as individuals and instead as obligations,' writes

Turkle. And with that comes a frenetic, resentful and increasingly insincere digital relationship.

'Far too often in the name of inclusion and generosity – two values I care about deeply – we fail to draw boundaries about who belongs and why,' writes Priya Parker in *The Art of Gathering*. She quotes Barack Obama's aunt, who once told him, 'If everyone is family, no one is family.' The same is true of a gathering, she writes. 'If everyone is invited, no one is invited.' I'd extend that to our digital circles: if everyone is obligated to connect, then that connection means nothing. According to the anthropologist Robin Dunbar, we can have a maximum of 150 connections at once. That sounds like a lot, until you factor in the extraordinary number of people we come into contact with, both tangentially – neighbourhood acquaintances, children's friends' parents and teachers – and digitally – your entire social media network. Parker cautions against gathering just for the hell of it. Instead, she says, to hold truly purposeful meetings, you should ask yourself: why are you gathering, who are you gathering with, and what do you want to achieve?

Applying this to our digital communication would be freeing, I think. At a time when it is normal for texts and emails to lack purpose and intent, let us ask ourselves: why are we saying what we are saying, who are we saying it to, and what do we want to achieve? This feels especially important now that we uphold so many of our relationships over digital platforms, 'where we navigate intimacy by skirting it' writes Turkle in *Alone Together*. Maintaining friendships without having to leave your home can be liberating for those with physical or mental disabilities, but for many of us, it can foster a false intimacy. 'Previously, you would text to arrange to meet a friend and the text itself would be purely functional,' explains author and journalist Victoria

Turk to me. 'Now the text *is* the meeting.' If you don't speak the same text language – think of it as a love language, but via a keyboard – that friendship could be at risk over something that in real life might not be an issue at all.

The Harvard law professor Jonathan Zittrain calls the lack of accepted techniquette 'a shared hallucination' that works only as long as you and your correspondent(s) share the same delusions. 'Hallucination' is an apt word: you have no idea what's intended and what you're imagining through meta-messaging. The very well-adjusted McCulloch thinks that conventions provide a rudimentary etiquette for digital dialogue (and that 'looking forward to hearing back' is part of it). Turk, meanwhile, wrote her book *Digital Etiquette* for those of us drowning in this chaotic, digital minefield, for whom 'just following up' are 'the three ugliest words in the English language'. (In case you're wondering about which three words Turk deems the most beautiful – they're 'unsubscribe from list'.)

When I feel unable to give what is demanded of me, my reaction – like that of many other women when they feel threatened or sensitive – is to go in hard with the platitudes in case I look deliberately unhelpful. Turk agrees that women modify their written communication in a way men do not, but she and I are on opposing ends of the spectrum in the way we do so. I double-check every email before sending, scatter-gunning softeners – 'so sorrys' and 'thank you so muches' – all over it to ensure I come across as clear, but not too demanding, and apologetic when I cannot help. Meanwhile, Turk scans her emails in order to remove any modifiers she has been conditioned to add as a woman. For those of you who revert too often to the 'soooo sorry' (Stephens-Davidowitz notes that women are much more in favour of the elongated 'o' than men) there's a tool for that. In 2015, Tami Reiss invented a Gmail plugin called

Just Not Sorry, which highlights doubtful and apologetic statements – like 'I think' or 'I'm not sure' or 'would you mind' – so you can easily eliminate your qualifiers.

Turk may remove her modifiers, but she admits a fondness for exclamation marks. 'I can hopefully be as helpful as possible!' she writes to me. Several studies have found that women use exclamation marks more than men. Indeed, the *New Statesman* writer Amelia Tait found that when women *didn't* use exclamation marks in an email, they were perceived as rude or cold. What if it's not that women should be moving away from the exclamation mark, but rather that men should be moving *towards* it? We could all do with a few more 'non-verbal cues', Turk writes in a piece for *Vice*. 'Exclamation points, emoji, or slightly more florid vocabulary' can help replace body language, tone and facial signifiers and 'can all help to communicate our meaning and avoid awkward misunderstandings. Shouldn't that be the "professional" thing to do?' Possibly, yes. As Freeman writes, the most exhausting part of written communication is having to 'translate all your different moods, tones, personalities, and styles into some kind of textual equivalent' – and then interpret anything incoming. In creative writing classes, you are encouraged to ditch the exclamation mark. It is hammy and didactic. But in digital communication, particularly among women, it becomes a plea, a latent bid for validation. A way to be reassured that we are worthy of affection and attention.

VI.

The Giving Tree by Shel Silverstein has divided people since its publication in 1964. A parable on the joy of giving, the children's book tells the story of a child who strikes up a life-long friendship with a female apple tree. As a young boy, he sits and talks to the tree, eats her apples, swings from her branches and carves sweet notes into her bark. But as he grows older, Boy loses interest in Tree and so she gives more and more of herself to entice him back, offering up her wood for him to make a boat. Eventually, Tree is nothing but a stump. She tells the now old man that she has nothing left to give. He responds that all he wants is a quiet place to rest. Tree, depleted and weak, is happy to give him this – despite the fact that he has taken everything from her. Is Tree providing Boy with shelter and food in return for his company? Or is Boy wringing Tree, a symbol of nature, dry for his own selfish gains?

I thought a lot about Tree's story while writing this essay. Is digital communication something reciprocal, giving as much as it takes, or are we tethered to a medium that takes and takes and takes, until we are a stump of vulnerability? Where we become so absorbed in reading and replying that our relationships become a flattened archive of written exchanges, rather than a treasure trove of meaningful correspondence? According to Seymour, we write not so much to each other as to a machine that builds a 'hive mind' of content (and offers boundless opportunities for surveillance). 'We write to it, and it passes on the messages for us, after keeping a record of the data. The machine benefits from the "network effect": the more people write to it, the more benefits it can offer, until it becomes a disadvantage not to be part of it.' Part of what? 'The world's first-ever public, live, collective, open-ended writing project. A virtual laboratory.' In an episode of *Friends* called 'The One Where No One's Ready', Rachel sits down at her kitchen table and tells Ross she's going to catch up on her correspondence. I find seeing her open a neat box of notecards almost too painful to watch. Oh to sit down every other week, rather than every second of every day, to catch up on my correspondence! (I love writing and receiving thank-you letters – but it is a dying art and I am a dying breed. Now you're lucky if you receive a text message after having someone for dinner, or giving them a birthday present.) From a distance, it reminds us that once upon a time correspondence was occasional and pleasurable, a single pathway between you and your recipient.

There are ways of dealing with the hum of the machine. Many of these I am already an expert in: muting groups, for example. Nomophobes may boggle reading this essay. *What the hell is she complaining about? She's hardly tied to her device.* Indeed, I've found multiple ways of *un*tethering myself. But this sense of obligation has seeped deep into my bones. It covers me with its tender film, so that even if I am not actively engaged in this digital communication, I know that I soon *will* be, know that I soon *should* be. Of course, we can just ignore messages – unwelcome or otherwise – or entreaties where we cannot offer help. I know and admire women who ignore almost everything that comes into their inbox (except when they don't reply to me and then it's just annoying). 'Sometimes I go missing. It is my right as a human being, and those close to me have grown tolerant of it,' Dent writes in the *Guardian*. McCulloch says she feels no obligation to get back to someone who is asking something she cannot give. My best friend replies only to messages that interest her and ignores those that don't. But I am not so brazen. I nervily reply to all communications as if they were fleas: contorting myself into desperate positions to flick them off my back.

The messages we flick away first are very often those that mean the *least*. 'No,' I tap-tap away tiredly, I am not able to 'cover the launch of a new cruise' (never written about travel; am not eighty years old), nor am I the right person to 'herald the return of the persimmon to the fruit and veg market' (never written about food; could barely identify a persimmon). Emails like these are the easiest to dispatch, because they take up the least amount of emotional bandwidth. The idea is that once you answer the 'dreadmail' or the 'procrastigrams', you can get to the real *meat* of your inbox, writes Katy Waldman for *Slate*. But our time is finite. And so the meaningful correspondence suffers. 'You put off responding to [a message] because you want to give it your full attention – and thus never answer, giving the sender the impression you don't care, when in fact it is the most important thing in your inbox.' This is not confined to email, she writes. 'Anecdata suggest that voicemails, particularly from parents or grandparents, inspire similar behaviour in friends and colleagues. (Furthermore, I tend to mark meaningful texts as perpetually "unread" in lieu of answering them, but that could be my own private pathology.)' The most maddening thing about the looking-forward-to-hearing-backs is that they usurp the rightful place of important messages. We spend so long replying to the chaff, that we ignore the damn wheat.

In his book *Walden*, the nineteenth-century philosopher Henry David Thoreau cautions against living 'thick' with no space between our interactions. How, he writes, can we respect each other, if we 'stumble over one other'? We persuade ourselves into meeting regularly because of etiquette; but 'society is commonly too cheap'. We have not 'had time to acquire any new value for each other … [to] give each other a new taste of that musty old cheese that we are.' How to find our way out of the abyss? I'm a believer in voice-notes, which can be sent any time but have a warmth and tonal quality that written messages don't. 'Texting "hahaha" is no match for hearing a friend laugh,' notes Parkinson. We need to bring the phone call back – not despite people being terrified of it, but *because* they are terrified of it. A phone call may now seem exotic, but I think that communicating less often and more robustly is our only way back to one another. It's true of work correspondence, too. Imagine how many one-question emails you could save in a week if you just had a regular twenty-minute phone call. We can never get rid of all interruptions. And nor should we want to. Trying to regiment and regulate our time is a smokescreen. But I believe that we can begin to repair some of the ruptures in the fabric of communication. We do not need to be available to everyone, always. There is only one person I need be in continual contact with: the musty old cheese. Me.

The Raw Nerve

It would appear that emotions are the curse, not death.
Annie Dillard, *Pilgrim at Tinker Creek*

I.

There are twenty-three statements on the 'Are you a highly sensitive person?' self-test, devised by the psychologist Elaine N. Aron in 1996. They include:

- I have a rich, complex inner life.
- I am conscientious.
- I get rattled when I have a lot to do in a short amount of time.
- I am annoyed when people try to get me to do too many things at once.
- Changes in my life shake me up.

I score twelve on the test, putting me, by Aron's metric, on the HSP threshold. I am not remotely surprised – I'd have been more shocked if I didn't qualify. (Around 15–20% of people do, apparently.) I am ridiculously sensitive. Some would say laughably so. Not just about anything happening to those I love, or animals being tortured, or global tragedies – all standard fare for even the moderately sensitive person – but about entirely nonsensical things. I ache when I see a picture of a pensioner, even if they are in the news for something horrible, because I imagine them standing pathetically in their underwear with flesh like a melted candle. I ache when I read a blind-date column and one person is like an enthusiastic puppy, excited for date number two, while the other drily notes, 'I was relieved he didn't ask for my number.' (The *Guardian* 'Blind Date' column, February 2019 – still thinking about it.) I even once felt the ache at Cancun airport, after my husband said it was his least favourite airport and I felt sorry for the airport, as though it had ears. I am, in short, extraordinarily and irrationally soft.

We all are now. And in ways that go far beyond a mere personality trait, leaving us stymied and stultified, incapable of moving through the world without an emotional-support peacock. The millennial 'snowflake' has become a narrative myth for my generation, leaned upon by conservative thinkers. (Never mind that *Fight Club* author Chuck Palahniuk, who invented the term, didn't actually intend it as a pejorative description.) Famously dubbed 'Generation Wuss' by the provocative writer Bret Easton Ellis, snowflakes demand safe spaces and trigger warnings and echo chambers hooked up to 5G, to lie inside of and suck our thumbs while listening to a lullaby of our own opinions. We need our botties wiped and our minds soothed. We are furious, coddled, traumatised, triggered – sometimes all at the same time.

There are real issues behind these clichés, which the conservative brouhaha and clarion calls for 'free speech' frequently distract from. If women need trigger warnings before rape scenes on television, perhaps we should look at why so few rapists are convicted? If women, particularly women of colour and trans women, need safe spaces, maybe we ought to consider why they feel so unsafe in public places? If, like me, you are privileged enough to not require safe spaces or trigger warnings, it does not mean that you should dismiss them, like a man who will never need an abortion but is nevertheless vehemently against them. And yet, leaving tiresome stereotypes aside, I have always wondered about how my generation's sensitivity compares to that of previous generations – if only because I am so much more sensitive than my stoical mother, whom I have never even seen cry. But when I conduct a poll via Twitter – which, to be clear, is not a scientifically accurate study – and 4,600 millennial women reply, the result is extremely close: 51.1% say they are more sensitive than their mother, compared to the 48.9% who say they are less. On seeing this result and reading the hundreds of responses, each perceiving sensitivity in a slightly different way, I realise there is a clear difference between sensitivity and emotional expression – and it is confusion over the two that has seen our generation clubbed with this unfounded myth. We are *outwardly* more sensitive to perceived injustice, to unwoke language, to disparity – and we certainly aren't afraid to express our emotions in public. But we are *inwardly* resilient. The facts speak for themselves. We take fewer sick days, we work longer hours and, despite this, millennial parents spend more time with their children than their parents did. Fragile, you say? Okay, boomer.

The truth is that we became adults as the fabric of civilised society, of civilised *conversation*, began to tear. For the past decade, we have been surrounded by disorientating social-media platforms, a flammable political climate, soaring house prices and job precarity. The result is a sense of unbearable insecurity – which has changed not only the way we live and value our lives, but also how we talk about them. A *naive realism* has flourished, where we believe our choices and opinions are objective truth, and those who disagree with us are biased, untruthful and irrational – even cruel. With over

264 million people globally now suffering from some sort of anxiety disorder (and it is a significantly higher proportion of women), our collective sentiment is like a giant *raw nerve*. A raw nerve is when damaged nerves transmit the wrong signal to the brain: it feels like being stung by a hundred bees, pricked by a thousand needles or slashed with shards of glass. It is not just something that manifests in the individual (although having recently birthed the child I spent the previous essays incubating, I certainly feel like I have been flayed raw). Rather, the raw nerve has become a cultural psychosis.

II.

The phrase *all the feels* is short-hand for being overcome with feelings (often contradictory ones). Like many internet-born colloquialisms, all the feels has an unnerving subtext: we are suffused in feelings that obliterate our rational judgement. In his book *Nervous States: How Feeling Took Over The World*, the economist William Davies dissects when and how we became one great big feeling. Short answer: technology. Digital platforms not only encourage us to emote, they depend on it for revenue. (A shift in the emotional tone of social media can actually correlate with a shift in the stock market – the study of which is called *sentiment analysis*.) Davies draws attention to a leaked Facebook memo from 2017, which boasted of being able to identify vulnerable teenagers who felt 'insecure' and 'worthless' and 'would therefore be more receptive to certain types of advertising'. The digital titans of Big Tech need access to our every emotion not just for ad revenue, writes Davies, but also to improve artificial intelligence. 'Our rage, glee, sorrow and horror provide tutorials for machines learning to behave like a human.'

Our ability to glean knowledge in real time has had a direct impact on how we make everyday decisions. We haven't changed internally – it would be impossible to psychologically rewrite the human species in one generation – but we feel a need to mirror the rapidity of a search engine. A 2017 study revealed that people were more likely to trust a search engine than a human expert – because the search engine could deliver the information more quickly. There is no longer any scope to pause and take a breath. Evidence takes too long; emotion is instant. The way we talk online has filtered down to the way we talk offline, so that internet rhetoric colours all of our dialogue and has spread like a contagion. We have become, writes Davies, 'a vast neural network through which sentiment travels from body to body, at ultra-high speed.' We no longer experience feelings. We *are* our feelings.

Most of us only started to use social media around 2010, but feelings began to replace reason more than a decade earlier. Princess Diana's death in 1997 was a huge turning point. Her passing unleashed an unprecedented torrent of public grief (and politicians took note). People sobbed in the streets in their thousands. 'It would be idle to attribute this cultural shift entirely to the influence of a single, deceased member of the royal family,' writes Matthew d'Ancona, 'but the impassioned aftermath of her death was a bold punctuation mark in a new national narrative that favoured disinhibition, empathy and personal candour.' Diana herself was a woman governed by her emotions. She 'legitimised the role of feeling in the public space', writes d'Ancona: speaking about her bulimia; shaking the hand of an AIDS patient in 1989; *that* 'there were three of us in this marriage' *Panorama* interview with Martin Bashir. Diana traded in feelings – they were her legacy.

The general consensus is that if we could all be a bit more empathetic, the world would be a happier, fairer place. (And to echo d'Ancona here: 'God forbid that we should return to the stiff upper lip' that I think is actually still pretty prevalent.)

Barack Obama famously said in 2015, 'The biggest deficit that we have in our society and in the world right now is an empathy deficit.' But I don't think that's quite correct. Empathy means *putting yourself in someone else's shoes* – and isn't that exactly the problem? We are constantly putting ourselves in each other's shoes, claustrophobically inhabiting one another's every opinion and experience and weighing them to determine their validity, jostling together like sardines as we choke on everyone else's feelings. We are so absorbed in one another's intimacies that we have become incapable of rational thought.

In his provocatively titled and persuasive book, *Against Empathy*, the psychologist Paul Bloom argues that empathy has become a misused buzzword. It has transformed into a catch-all term for 'everything good, as a synonym for morality and kindness and compassion', he writes. It is frequently mistaken for sympathy, which means aligning yourself with someone's suffering (not inhabiting it). While empathy is an important part of our emotional catalogue, as a decision-making tool it is short-sighted, corrosive and insensitive. I am convinced that an overemphasis on empathy, especially when it is to the detriment of other emotional philosophies, is a root cause of the raw nerve. There are three reasons why. Firstly, empathy is tribalistic. It is infinitely easier to put yourself in the shoes of someone similar to you – which often means, given the balance of power, that those who are already privileged benefit. Bloom uses the example of the Sandy Hook massacre of 2012, where the affluent town of Newtown in Connecticut was inundated by so many toys that town officials, forced to recruit volunteers to help manage the flow, begged people to stop donating. A greater number of schoolchildren were killed in Chicago that year, but it was easier for middle-class white families – with the capacity to donate money and gifts – to empathise with those families who had lifestyles like their own.

Secondly, empathy on any kind of large scale is impossible. You can 'intellectually value' multiple people, writes Bloom, but you cannot emotionally be in more than one pair of shoes at once. Go on, try it. As Annie Dillard puts it, 'There are 1,198,500,000 people alive now in China. To get a feel for what this means, simply take yourself – in all your singularity, importance, complexity and love – and multiply by 1,198,500,000. See? Nothing to it.' Thirdly, and I think most importantly, empathy is irrational. This is particularly dangerous in medicine, where putting yourself in the shoes of a patient or their family could mean making an unethical decision that goes against medical advice. I often think of the doctors who treated Charlie Gard, the baby with mitochondrial DNA depletion syndrome. Charlie died in 2017 after a fierce battle between Great Ormond Street – who said treatment would only prolong his suffering – and his parents, who still had hope. The doctors were accused of lacking empathy and were verbally abused by protestors, who lobbied outside the hospital. And it's true – the doctors *weren't* being empathetic, because as a doctor the one thing you can't do is put yourself in a patient's shoes – but that's not to say they weren't sympathetic. Bloom uses therapists as an example. If you visited a therapist in a complete tizz, would you want them mirroring your anxiety – or would you want them to sympathise while remaining calm and dispensing rational advice? Empathy can compel us to act, but not always in rational ways. Instead of empathy, Bloom calls for *radical compassion*. Compassion is objective and allows decisions to be made with a level of remove, rather than from within the eye of the storm. I can think of nothing the raw nerve needs more right now.

It is our preoccupation with empathy that has seen us trying to centre ourselves in every narrative and every conversation: to be in the *right* pair of shoes and on the *right* side of debate. It's absolutely exhausting, and has resulted in what James Mumford, in his book *Vexed*, calls 'package-deal' opinions. It has split us into political and cultural tribes, where you must stay in your lane or risk rejection. To dissent is terrifying. To disagree is *to be morally wrong* and risk cancellation. It has got to the point where many people are scared to express their point of view in case they are publically shamed for not staying within the 'package' of ideas ascribed to them. This is deeply restrictive and blocks progress. (Nor is it something that affects just one political side – for all the open-mindedness of the left, some of the most furious refusals to entertain another opinion and outraged bids for cancellation come from the 'liberal'-minded.) If we are all encouraged to stay in our wheelhouses, then how on earth will we ever meet in the middle? Under these conditions, it is less about being right and more about *not appearing wrong*. This has resulted in a sort of virtue-signalling, where you share to 'signal something about yourself', as Nesrine Malik, author of the polemical *Why We Need New Stories*, puts it to me.

It used to just be your tedious Uncle Bernard who offered unsolicited opinions on every single subject – nowadays everyone appears to care deeply about absolutely everything. It's positively *exhausting*, both to take part in and to bear witness to. I'm always surprised by how certain so many people seem about so many things. Information flies at us from all corners, all the time, so we think we know about an issue we've read one sentence on, five minutes earlier. Believing we know more than we do is called *the Dunning-Kruger effect*. We have begun to fill the gaps in our knowledge with the opinions of those *who seem like us* – or even those of the *person we want to be like*. It sounds callow and you may scoff, but it is incredibly difficult to resist because it is incredibly hard to *realise* that you are doing it when we are exposed to the opinions of so many others. Isn't it just easier to take the pre-wrapped package? When the raw nerve collides with the Dunning-Kruger effect, you end up with a dual hag-beast who thinks they know everything about everything and sees someone else's personal choices as an indictment of their own opinion or experience. I observed the beast recently, when a woman tweeted that she had given birth to her daughter without any pain relief. It was very painful, she wrote, and she was proud of herself. Immediately, another woman leapt in to tell her that the tweet shamed women who'd had epidurals. As if this woman's birth story existed solely to offend someone else.

Anger can be productive and galvanising – particularly when it is a collective, social anger that incites change. But all too often it is a petty aggression, or a performative rage. 'Outrage was once reserved for the truly unjust,' writes the DJ Ashley 'Dotty' Charles for the *Guardian*. 'It was for civil rights activists and suffragettes. It has fought against police brutality, institutional racism, unequal pay, segregation and voting rights.' Now it's about woke-scolding those who aren't offended by *Peppa Pig* or the negligent mummy elephant in *Five Minutes' Peace*, or – at the conservative end of the spectrum – spluttering in revolted outrage that the actor Jodie Turner-Smith chose to bare her taut, heavily pregnant tummy in a crop top on *The Graham Norton Show*. This is the raw nerve as distraction. 'Outrage doesn't sit on its sofa complaining about how Kim Kardashian culturally appropriated braids,' writes Charles. 'It refuses to give up its seat on the bus in 1950s Alabama.' Not everyone will agree with Charles (or me) – and *that's okay*. We don't have to agree. But it shouldn't mean we see ourselves as being on opposing sides.

Distilling ourselves into every cause and every conversation renders them meaningless. You can be annoyed by someone or something without feeling duty-bound to express it. It sounds obvious and yet it seems like we've forgotten it's possible. Those of you without Twitter might think you're exempt from this hellscape. My friend, you are wrong. The beast has made its way into all forms of culture, so that we see it on television, in the pub, in our politics. We don't pause or reflect. We listen in order to respond – not to learn. The most radical answer, says Davies, would be to slow down. I think the most revolutionary thing we could do is to say: *I don't have an opinion. But I'd love to hear yours.*

III.

In his book *Humankind: A Hopeful History*, the Dutch historian Rutger Bregman reflects on a parable of unknown origin:

> An old man says to his grandson: 'There's a fight going on inside me. It's a terrible fight between two wolves. One is evil – angry, greedy, jealous, arrogant, and cowardly. The other is good – peaceful, loving, modest, generous, honest, and trustworthy. These two wolves are also fighting within you, and inside every other person too.'
>
> After a moment, the boy asks, 'Which wolf will win?'
> The old man smiles.
> 'The one you feed.'

It's a charming, folksy story – easily digestible, kid-friendly – but it's also a powerful reminder of how easy it is to feed your wolf. The term *online disinhibition effect* describes the loosening of social restrictions and inhibitions normally present in face-to-face conversation. It comes in two forms: benign (reactive) and toxic (aggressive). It means even the sanest of us can get wolfed-up by the internet. A troll is not born of the internet, but the internet amplifies the wolf within. The uncomfortable truth is that trolls are not *lonely people with mean little lives*, as we used to think, but normal people who don't exercise self-awareness on the internet. (Which is most of us at one time or another: technological evolution is considerably faster than cognitive.) As the web-comic Penny Arcade succinctly sums up in the *Greater Internet Fuckwad Theory*: 'Normal Person + Anonymity + Audience = Total Fuckwad'.

The writer and podcaster Ezra Klein calls social media a 'polarization accelerant' because the internet is an attention economy, running on fury and rewarding outrage with eye-balls. There is an enormous sliding scale for what constitutes an internet troll. Trolling is not one-size-fits-all: there is a dictionary's-worth of trollish behaviours. *Sea-lioning* is the seemingly harmless but persistent request for information which can be found elsewhere, with the aim to exhaust and undermine. *Doxing* is where you share private information about someone online. The *gotcha moment* is an attempt to disprove someone else's claim by triumphantly providing information that contradicts them. Call-out and cancel culture can quickly descend into straightforward harassment.

It is especially rife in politics, where it has become 'part of the job description' for female MPs to receive reams of online abuse. Toxic disinhibition is what allowed people to call Tracy Brabin a slut when she wore an off-the-shoulder dress to work (unnervingly proving that anyone – even while being abused – can be an influencer, the £35 ASOS dress then sold out). It's why Luciana Berger receives tweets telling her she is going to 'get it like Jo Cox did'. And it's even worse for black and Asian female MPs, who receive 35% more abusive tweets than their white colleagues – one in twenty tweets received by Shadow Home Secretary Diane Abbott are classified as abusive by Amnesty International. After Cox was murdered in 2016, David Lammy wrote, 'We can't carry on like this, where disagreements over political issues become so visceral that those on the other side of a debate are not only mistaken but are evil, pernicious and wicked.' But we *have* carried on like this. It is baffling that social media networks still refuse to expose the identities of trolls even as online hate leaks offline, sometimes to tragic consequence (because they are non-interventionist, they say). 'The actual problem with the Internet isn't us hastily tweeting off about foolish people,' Choire Sicha once wrote for the *New York Times*. 'The actual problem is that none of the men running those bazillion-dollar Internet companies can think of one single thing to do about all the men who send women death threats.'

While super-trolls proudly display in their bios the number of times they've had their Twitter accounts shut down, there are still some people – typically those who don't use social media and don't read newspapers – who maintain that *words do not carry physical weight*. It is an attitude which 'flatly ignores copious evidence for how emotional and physical being are unified, quite apart from the practical ways in which threatening speech is implicated in violence,' writes Davies. I wonder how many of those who dismissed Boris Johnson's comments for the *Daily Telegraph* about women in burqas looking like letterboxes, as *just some stupid thing he said*, know that Islamophobic incidents rose by 375% the following week. That it was the biggest spike in anti-Muslim hatred in the whole of 2018. How's this for a new saying: sticks and stones will break your bones, but words spread damage faster.

During my time as a fashion columnist at the *Sunday Times Style*, my absolute least favourite activity was the 'Wardrobe Mistress Q&A', conducted on Facebook Live. People would bring me their sartorial quandaries and I would be filmed replying to them. In one session, I was told my eyebrows were horrible and I didn't know how to wear my face – a comment as pointlessly harsh as it was hilariously nonsensical. Not being able to wear my face is the least of my problems. I have since learned that I'm also dishonest, unkind, stupid, a bad writer, a bad speaker, a bad friend, a bad mother. I should shut up, go away, fuck off. I have to resist the temptation to write these comments on my body so that when I'm feeling crap, I can simply lift up my shirt and trace over the words to remind myself I am worthless. And yet, I am one of the fortunate ones – because I have never been told to kill myself, nor received rape threats. The bar is *that low*. 'Because I choose to [write online] as a career,' writes the American comedian and writer Lindy West, 'I'm told, a constant barrage of abuse is just part of my job. Shrug. Nothing we can do. I'm asking for it, apparently.' If you can't take the heat, get out of the kitchen. Or rather, off the internet. 'That's a persistent refrain my colleagues and I hear when we confront our harassers. But why? Why don't YOU get off the internet? Why should I have to rearrange my life – and change careers, essentially – because you wet your pants every time a woman talks?' shoots back West.

I am not a provocateur. I do not, on the whole, 'take on' flammable issues or debate with people who are just looking for a reaction (although I sometimes feel tempted to). This unwelcome feedback can come through something as innocuous as a throwaway comment about replacing a book I loved and misplaced. 'The absolute privilege of buying a book twice – you make me sick,' read one email to our podcast inbox. It's not abuse. No one has offered to behead me with the sword of ISIS, as they have West. But it's a low-level nastiness that nips at your confidence and your conviction. People do not suddenly grow rhino hide when they start writing. Friends tell me to ignore it. It's shitty but it's inevitable, they say. *I never received the training for this*, I reply, bewildered. *Where's the sodding manual?* But of course, there isn't one. In the last few years, I've grown a bit of armour. But 'armour is heavy', writes West. And that protective shield requires daily maintenance.

There is a vast difference between disagreeing with what someone says and disagreeing with their existence. Yet somehow, the two have merged. I'm a fan of confrontation in everyday life, but when it comes to the internet, I feel compelled to ask: whatever happened to a good ol' bitch behind someone's back? Bring back the two-facedness! Make it three! Calling out someone on the internet doesn't make you a whistle-blower. Cancelling someone doesn't make you a moral vanguard. Making sure you @ someone in your tweet to tell them you think their work is rubbish doesn't make you an arbiter of taste. It just makes you a fuckwad.

Being a fuckwad on the internet is incredibly easy. There is no recourse, or retribution; absolutely no sense of risk. If you are not famous, what actual repercussion is there if you tweet something vile, except for a bunch of other avatars calling you a prick? You log off, with no impact on your day. There is just not enough of an incentive to avoid acting like this, and there absolutely should be. As Hugh Grant tweeted drily in February 2020: 'I've got a sneaky feeling you'll find that hate actually *is* all around.'

Devastating news breaks in real time as I write this essay: the television presenter Caroline Flack has been found dead in her home. In the months preceding her death, the forty-year-old *Love Island* host was a regular tabloid headline as she awaited criminal trial for assaulting her boyfriend, Lewis Burton. I am eating lunch in front of my computer when my husband comes in to tell me the tragic news – that someone so seemingly vibrant and vital has taken her own life. In the immediate aftermath, social media is a sepulchre of pain and fury. The hashtag #CarolinesLaw begins trending, as people call for safeguarding around press coverage of celebrities. A little over a week later, a petition has 839,000 signatures. 'What price is a life?' reads its description. By the time you read this, the petition will have been debated in the House of Commons. But amid the finger-pointing, something is glaringly amiss.

I've never been a tabloid journalist, and I think the content of most red-tops is total snotgobble. But, as part of Trump's Fake! News! Media!, I am also inevitably biased. Or, rather, I am well-versed in the 'grotesque dance of misery and bitterness' as Sophie Wilkinson describes it, that exists right now between the public, the press and the celebrity. The only way to snuff out those outlets you believe are fuelled by vitriol and prejudice is, quite simply, to not buy or read them online. Yes, *you* – perusing the sidebar of shame while darkly muttering about *what tosh it all is*. Because the more you read it, the more it gets written. The ability for websites to see exactly which stories get the most traction shapes subsequent stories. Why do you think there are infinitely more stories about Trump than there are on the violence perpetuated by Erdoğan, Bolsonaro and al-Assad? Sure, it's partly because Trump's the leader of the free world, but it's also because stories about Trump get clicks. He is a comedy villain who we love to hate. He is without nuance – like celebrity gossip. News websites 'only make stories that people want to read. And it doesn't matter to the [data] analytics processors if users are reading out of titillation or revulsion', notes Wilkinson. The press might amp up the story arc, but they're reflecting the polyphonic dogpile we create on social media. Which means that this bilious discourse is shaped by the very same outraged people who are calling for change with #BeKind in the aftermath of Flack's death.

This complicated moral hypocrisy is pithily explained by an author called Craig Stone: '25k tweets telling Piers Morgan to fuck off and 4k tweets advocating change in how the media targets individuals highlights the problem. That should be 25k tweets advocating change. We cannot continue being the oxygen that complains about the flames.' Elsewhere, the magician Archie Manners writes, quite rightly, that 'things have got to change. This is just devastating'. But Manners is also one half of a YouTube stunt group that, in January 2020, pulled a prank on the right-wing provocateur Katie Hopkins, inviting her to a ceremony in Prague to receive a bogus award for which the acronym was – ho ho ho – C.U.N.T. Hopkins flew to Prague, accepted the award, beamed for a picture, and the prank went viral. Hopkins herself asks, 'Will #CarolinesLaw just be for people you agree with?' How do we decide who deserves safeguarding? Do we keep a running chit of which celeb does right, which does wrong – so that those who violate a moral code of conduct forgo our protection? I'm no fan of Katie Hopkins. But the issue is not as simple as it is being made out to be.

As much as we need policy, we also need something more fundamental. 'A seismic change in our mode of engagement is indeed vital,' writes Mumford. We need to be able to '[express] our convictions in the public square' while recognising the 'inextinguishable humanity of one's adversary'. If only we could feel a type of *liget*. The neuroscientist Lisa Feldman Barrett describes liget as a pleasantly aggressive emotion experienced by the Ilongot tribe in the Philippines, characterised by an 'intense focus, passion and energy' while competing with opponents. Liget is as basic an emotion to the Ilingots as happiness and sadness are to us. Now, the Ilingots are known for beheading people while amped up on liget, so I don't suggest we copy the *expression* of this emotion. But I wonder if experiencing a bit of pleasant, site-specific aggression, with a clear mode of conduct, would mean arguing might lose some of its bile, allowing us to depersonalise disagreements and help contain the debate more effectively. Once their, ahem, 'headhunting' session is over, so ends the

Ilongots' exuberant, bonding arousal. Imagine containing our emotional discourse in chapters like this. The stewing and festering would simply disappear.

Given that we develop our emotions at a young age, it's unlikely that we're going to add liget to our emotional register anytime soon. A more achievable, hopeful path out of the morass is the community website Change My View. A place for members to expose their points of view in order for them to be challenged in constructive discussion, it has almost a million members. The topics are red-hot and the political positions diverse. A recipe for disaster, right? Joyfully, no. It is politically neutral and not age-specific. It is, unlike almost every other website I can think of, a melting-pot of identities – but populated by people who have the self-awareness to know they may not be unequivocally right. Topics include the most incendiary – abortion, gender, gun ownership and the death penalty – and yet strangers with radically different views manage to converse civilly. I've never been tempted to post on community websites like Mumsnet or Reddit, but I sign up to Change My View immediately, digging out an old eBay username to give me the freedom to learn and query without being shamed. It's one of the most galvanising things I've discovered online in a long time.

IV.

There is a rather horrible newspaper saying – 'If it bleeds, it leads' – meaning that violent news gets top billing. It sounds manipulative and morbid, but is actually a reflection of human nature: we are primed to look for and remember the bad over the good. Because of our *negativity bias*, the media is disproportionately skewed towards bad news. Thanks to more television channels and a host of social-media outlets and news apps firing tiny arrows of devastation at us all day long, we now have a 24/7 news cycle to match our high-octane, never-really-switching-off lifestyles. I'm frequently jolted awake in the night by a BBC alert on my iPad (that I have forgotten to silence), which reverberates in my skull, stopping me from returning to sleep.

In a short-cut, instant-gratification world, we often fail to appreciate long-term progress, frozen as we are in the rapid jaws of fear. So we forget that, for instance, you are more likely be crushed to death by a piece of furniture than you are to be killed by a terrorist. Or that you are infinitely more likely to die from asthma than in a tornado. Statistics like these are endless and often silly (did you know you're more likely to die from a coconut falling on your head than you are to be eaten by a shark?) but I think they are important to hold on to, especially if you consider the small but quickly growing group of people who choose to avoid the news entirely. They *can't deal with it any more*, they say. If they read it every day, they'd *never be able to leave the house*. I also frequently feel depressed and depleted after catching up on the news, but I think completely avoiding it leaves you more vulnerable. Like a horse wearing blinkers that cannot possibly see the ditch in its periphery. (After all, there is no such thing as avoidance therapy in psychotherapy.) I feel nervous when people write in to *The High Low* to tell us they stopped following the news and rely on our podcast to keep them abreast of current affairs – especially when the bulk of that week's segment is, say, about a highland cow named Doris that does the foxtrot. These news-dodgers are inevitably called snowflakes. But what if good news is crucial to our survival? And what if the negative bias is also causing us stress?

Bregman calls the 24/7 bad news cycle a *nocebo*. The opposite of a placebo, a nocebo is something with no physical impact but a negative psychological effect. A 2015 study found that people who consume a lot of rolling news are more likely to be irrational and pessimistic. While the world has gotten better – the late statistician Hans Rosling revealed that people are leading longer, healthier, richer, freer and more peaceful lives with global poverty halving in the last twenty years – the news cycle nocebo has us believing the world is getting more dangerous, unkind and untrustworthy. This nocebo has skewed our world-view and frayed the raw nerve. Rosling blames it on our 'overdramatic brains'. He prescribes a daily practice of *factfulness* – a theory and 2018 book of the same name – whereby you focus on long-term progress as a source of mental peace. Like a healthy diet and regular exercise, factfulness can help you make better decisions, stay alert to real dangers and possibilities, and avoid being constantly stressed about the wrong things.

Another idea is to limit our retention of bad news by reading printed newspapers, rather than scrolling through online news. You stay informed, but there is a finite amount of (tangible) pages. You don't fall down the rabbit holes of bad news and there is no depressing comments section. (I've heard of comment section moderators needing therapy to deal with the abuse they have to field and remove.) You simply shut the paper and move on. I have two newspapers delivered three times a week and I vow to read only them on those three days and to read the news online for the rest of the week. Another solution is to vary your news plan. There are outlets collating positive news from around the world, ensuring your daily practice of factfulness. My favourite is a website called Tank's Good News, which grew out of a popular meme account created by George Resch, a former fence-seller from Long Island. As I write, today's lead story is about the University of Sheffield scientists who have devised a system, aimed at refugee camps, for growing crops in discarded mattresses. After trialling them in the Zaatari refugee camp in Jordan, hydroponic experts hope the system could be rolled out all over the world. There's no need for pesticides and it requires up to 80% less water than growing plants in the soil. Seedlings are planted into the mattress foam with a carefully balanced nutrient solution to create 'desert gardens'. Another story is that of an oncology unit in North Carolina, which has received flowers from a mystery benefactor every Monday for the past twelve years, to give to 'the patient on your floor who needs cheering up the most'. They still don't know who the flowers come from, but they think they're from a man whose wife passed away on the ward many years ago.

Some of Resch's stories are basic heart-warmers; others tell of innovative scientific progress with potentially huge social impact. But it's hard not to read them and feel encouraged that the world is mostly good. That, as Bregman puts it, humans are actually 'pretty decent'. We don't always need to be the bearer of bad news to care (but we do need to read the stories). What we need is balance. Factfulness, writes Rosling, does not mean duping yourself into thinking everything is fine. It means acknowledging that it is unhealthy to not recognise the progress the world has made; otherwise 'the consequent loss of hope can be devastating'. A necessary component of a contented life is seeking out the good news as much as the bad and reading it offline as well as on screens. We need to rework our definition of self-care: Netflix and Chill and a face mask might make for a relaxing evening, but for long-term mental peace? My bet's on factfulness.

V.

Boosterism as a philosophy describes the enthusiastic promotion of something in order to make it more appealing. It is typically applied to politics – in July 2019, Boris Johnson said he would turbo-charge his spending on infrastructure with 'rocket boosters' – but it is written all over our exhaustive attempts to live our best life. Boosterism is about as subtle as Madonna. Things are forced down our throats as cures and solutions, transforming from an unknown entity into a constantly rolled-out hashtag before you can even blink. We do not dip a toe into a shallow pool of wellness, for example, so much as we are bogwashed by it. Boosterism is not always bad. Boosting something can be positive – come Wednesday, we could all do with a bit of a boost. But in boosting weighty things into buzzwords, or buzz*trends*, they become tired, distorted and flimsy. Drained of all meaning. The process of progress gets tossed aside and we jump straight to the end result: a profiterole which is aesthetically pleasing and easily to swallow – but prick it with a fork and it's mostly warm air.

A contemporary culture built on profiteroles that, once bitten into, have no lasting effect is fine – so long as we know that that's what they are. The problem is, we often don't. When applied to our lives as a whole, 'boosterishness is dangerous and cruel', says the philosopher Alain de Botton. 'We are angry whenever we believe that we are promised paradise and get a traffic jam, lost keys, a disappointing relationship, a less than optimal job. We are furious, and our sense of entitlement comes back to bite us.' Profiteroles are delicious (I personally prefer a glazed doughnut, but that's by the by) but they offer short-lived happiness that quite clearly won't sustain you beyond tea time. We're moving closer and closer towards a friction-free life – driverless cars, facial recognition, on-demand food, fashion and entertainment – and a monitored self – sleep-tracking, mood-tracking, period-tracking – which creates the illusion that life is something we can effortlessly bend to our will.

In *Happy Ever After*, the behavioural scientist Paul Dolan explains that there is a connection between 'perceived agency and happiness'. Feeling like you lack control, meanwhile, can be linked to stress, poor health and mental health conditions. But, as much as free will is a vital human right, we have gone past a healthy level of control. Whether consciously or not, so many of our decisions are not ones that necessarily serve us the best, but rather ones where we can exercise the most jurisdiction. 'Our anxiety does not come from thinking about the future,' noted the writer Kahlil Gibran, 'but from wanting to control it.' In trying to control everything, we are, paradoxically, left feeling *out* of control. It leaves us unable to tolerate things we have not predicted, or that we do not have power over. I think Bret Easton Ellis got one thing right in his takedown of millennials: that we expect life to be a 'smooth utopia'. But not for the reasons he thinks (that we were coddled as children and cannot tolerate a world which does not indulge us). I think we expect a smooth utopia because we have worked ourselves into the ground trying to create an ordered life, which we believe to be the right life. And if these apps and hacks and myths and tinctures – I've even heard of a pill in America that promises to alleviate the physical symptoms of heartbreak, for God's sake – don't result in the promised seamless life, then what was all that work *for*?

In early 2020, while we were all busily making New Year's resolutions to be happier, a study was published in *The Journal of Happiness Studies* suggesting that focusing on happiness could actually make you depressed. 'When you value happiness too much, you become too attentive to your emotions and you also struggle with regulating them in a good way,' said the co-author of the paper, Dr Julia Vogt. It shouldn't come as a surprise that self-surveillance – tracking our happiness like we do our sleep and our steps – does not lead to contentment. It can so quickly slide into pathology.

It is hardly a shock that in our boosterish age, where technicolour perfection is rewarded, we have become obsessed with happiness as the ultimate end goal. In fact, happiness begins to decline in your thirties, creeps back up in your fifties and peaks at the grand old age of eighty-two, says the cognitive psychologist Daniel Levitin. After analysing hundreds of studies, Levitin – who claims his finding 'holds true across 72 countries, from Albania to Zimbabwe' – concluded that the reason for this arc is that, as you grow older, you adjust your 'too high expectations' of youth and 'realise that life is pretty good'.

Levitin's analysis chimes with the much-reported theory that happiness is U-shaped: we're said to be happiest at the beginning and end of our lives. (By that measure, I am currently sliding down towards the U-bend.) Supposedly, we hit the trough in middle age because that's the point when, conventionally speaking, we have the most responsibilities and the most stress: kids, mortgages, career, elderly parents. But I'm not entirely convinced. My seventy-something parents, dealing with health issues and pining for the agility and sociability of younger years, are also sceptical. Yes, most likely your responsibilities are fewer near the start and end of your life – meaning you are forced to live in the present. But while some pensioners feel freed by this, I have known some who are unutterably depressed by the loss of a long-term future. I also wonder if being the *most stressed* necessarily means being the *least happy*. This is the kind of binary attitude we need to fight against in order to imagine that we can be simultaneously happy (about some things) and unhappy (about others).

To overcome the raw nerve, we need to fortify our nerve gliders. It's all very well saying that happiness eludes you when you chase it, but if striving for happiness is not the answer – then what is? Do we ignore it, as if it were a boy and you a teenage girl, hoping he might sidle into your life? Or is the answer to deconstruct what we think we know, in order to examine the components? Paul Dolan calls social narratives about what constitutes a perfect life *narrative traps*. 'Many of these stories end up creating a kind of social dissonance whereby, perversely, they cause more harm than good.' The narrative myth of being a banker, for example, is that it brings success, money and status and, therefore, the good life. 'It seems bizarre to me that most people will see it as a good thing when the son of a relatively happy builder becomes a less happy banker,' writes Dolan. If we consider happiness to be the primary objective of everything we do, then the myth doesn't make very much sense at all. Echoing Barry Schwartz's theory of the good enough, Dolan suggests we replace the accepted standard of *maximising* – weighing up each choice until we find the best possible one – and instead embrace a concept of *satisficing* – where we aim for satisfactory decisions, rather than the absolute very best. 'We need to bring back norms,' Davies tells me. 'What does your doctor say? He tells you when everything is normal.' Being *normal* used to be a good thing. But in our seemingly bespoke and optimisable age, we have begun to see being normal as subpar.

Sorting myth from fact is just the start. In writing this book, I have borrowed from the learnings of psychologists, neuroscientists, economists, culture critics, philosophers, epidemiologists, behavioural scientists, dieticians, among others – who often contradict one another. The one thing, the *only* thing, that I can conclude with certainty is that there is no such thing as the *right* life. But I expect you already knew that. I don't even think happiness is something we should be working towards. Sparks of joy are essential, but so are the low points – otherwise how do we know to value the peaks? I put my eggs in the basket of contentment, which is not about being passive, but about achieving an equilibrium from which we can peacefully assess the topography of our lives.

Malik argues there are so many ways – through narrative myth and the validation of social media – to reassure ourselves that we are doing things right, that it has meant the concept of rightness 'has been shorn of any meaning'. It has become mere lip service. Rather, living the right life means being 'in a state of questioning,' Malik tells me. It involves self-sacrifice. Making choices should not be risk-free – if they are, then we aren't considering the right options. 'We have to be okay with giving up capital: social capital, online capital and actual capital. And only then we can figure out how to be right.'

There is a Socratic saying, '[S]he who is not contented with what [s]he has, would not be contented with what [s]he would like to have.' (And yes, those square brackets are pointed, Socrates.) The progress of humankind depends on us striving for more. Otherwise we'd all stagnate. But the concept of 'more' is something we need to turn inward as much as outward. To accept that gain can involve loss; that to compromise is not the same as being compromised; that sensitivity does not eliminate resilience. While writing this book over the past year, I have been continuously interrogating my ideas not so much about what constitutes the *right* life, but a *rightful* one. I now realise that in doing so, I have moved one step closer towards it.

Notes

Prologue

xvi 'The misery is …', Zadie Smith, *Intimations: Six Essays* (London: Penguin, 2020), p. 9.

xvi 'The special trouble …', Oliver Burkeman, '"Focus on the things you can control": how to cope with radical uncertainty', *Guardian*, 28 March 2020.

xvii 'We're grieving the …', David Kessler, interviewed on the podcast *Unlocking Us with Brené Brown*, 31 March 2020.

xvii 'living losses', 'But you cannot …', from a conversation with Julia Samuel.

xvii 'There was recently …', Richard Lloyd Parry, 'Lonely, bored Japanese queue up to rent man who does nothing', *The Times*, 14 January 2021.

xix 'Friendship works best …', this paragraph adapted from a piece I wrote for *Grazia*, 'Pandora Sykes: "The Pandemic Has Made My Friendship Group Smaller, But Sharper"', 10 January 2021.

xix 'the twin babies …', 'Coronavirus: Twins born during India lockdown named "Corona and Covid"', *Sky News*, 4 April 2020.

xix 'schecession', '1.8 times that of …', Christine Ro, 'Why this recession disproportionately affects women', *BBC Worklife*, 27 October 2020.

xx 'I have learned …', Josie George, '"My personal lockdown has been much longer": on chronic illness, before and after Covid', *Guardian*, 6 February 2021.

xx   'Approach the future ...', 'What do we ...', Margaret Heffernan, *Uncharted: How to Map the Future Together* (London: Simon & Schuster, 2020).

xx   '"Hope" is the ...', Emily Dickinson, *Emily Dickinson: The Complete Poems*, ed. Thomas H. Johnson (London: Faber & Faber, 2016), p. 116.

Introduction

2   'The official dogma ...', Barry Schwartz, 'The paradox of choice', Ted Talk, 15 July 2005.

2   'Having no choice ...', Barry Schwartz, *The Paradox of Choice: Why More Is Less* (New York: Harper Perennial, 2004).

3   '83% of women ...', Alix Walker, 'Comparison culture is taking its toll on our self-esteem', Stylist.co.uk.

4   'Am I living ...', 'Grand Union: Zadie Smith in conversation with Diana Evans', at the Royal Institution, 2 October 2019.

5   'I thought how ...', Virginia Woolf, *A Room of One's Own* (London: Hogarth Press, 1929).

The Dream Catchers

7   'They drink their ...', Reeves Wiedeman, 'Who Killed Tulum?', *The Cut*, 20 February 2019.

8   'a holistic approach ...', Halbert L. Dunn, 'High-Level Wellness for Man and Society', *American Journal of Public Health*, 49(6), June 1959.

8   'an exchange between ...', Halbert L. Dunn, *High Level Wellness* (Arlington, VA: Beatty, 1961).

9   'Yoga in the park ...', Taffy Brodesser-Akner, 'How Goop's Haters Made Gwyneth Paltrow's Company Worth $250 Million', *New York Times Magazine*, 25 July 2018.

10   'You're all here ...', Russell Brand, quoted in James Hamblin, 'The Art of Woke Wellness', *The Atlantic*, 19 November 2018.

10   'it's not unlike ...', William Davies, *The Happiness Industry* (London: Verso, 2015), p. 116.

11 'regularly going into …', Zoltan Istvan, quoted in, Richard Godwin, '"We will get regular body upgrades": what will humans look like in 100 years?', *Guardian*, 22 September 2018.

11 'nearly any activity …', André Spicer, '"Self-care": how a radical feminist idea was stripped of politics for the mass market', *Guardian*, 21 August 2019.

12 'use self-care language …', @AnnieKNK on Twitter, 3 December 2019.

13 'The penthouse apartment …', Hadley Keller, 'This New York Condo Is Designed for the Health Obsessed', *House Beautiful*, 18 July 2019.

13 'having nice things …', Amanda Mull, 'I Gooped Myself', *The Atlantic*, 26 August 2019.

14 'Don Draper sits …', Andrew Marantz, 'Silicon Valley's Crisis of Conscience', *New Yorker*, 19 August 2019.

14 'entire society is …', Ronald E. Purser, *McMindfulness: How Mindfulness Became the New Capitalist Spirituality* (London: Watkins Media, 2019), p. 9.

15 'unplugging by plugging …', Andy Puddicombe, quoted in Kate Pickert, 'The Mindful Revolution', *TIME*, 3 February 2014.

15 '"mumbo jumbo" of …', Purser, op. cit., p. 15.

15 'moral worldview', David Forbes, *Mindfulness and Its Discontents: Education, Self, and Social Transformation* (Nova Scotia: Fernwood, 2019).

15 'sharp social critique', 'becoming a reinforcement …', Bhikku Bodhi, quoted in Purser, *McMindfulness*, p. 15.

16 'brain rewiring', from a conversation with Barbara Ehrenreich.

16 'As if anyone …', Barbara Ehrenreich, *Natural Causes: Life, Death and the Illusion of Control* (London: Granta, 2018), p. 86.

17 'Not only is …', Eva Wiseman interview with Jennifer Gunter, 'Women Are Being Told Lies About Their Bodies', *Guardian*, 8 September 2019.

17 'The implicit notion …', Alex Blasdel, 'Bowel movement: the push to change the way you poo', *Guardian* long read, 30 November 2018.

18 'Elimination is love', ibid.

18 '52% in 2017 …', according to a 2017 study by the Pew Research Center.

18 'we reject religion …', Jean M. Twenge, *Generation Me: Why Today's Young Americans Are More Confident, Assertive, Entitled—and More Miserable—than Ever Before* (New York: Free Press, 2006).

18 'Wellness comes with …', from an email exchange with Maxine Ali.

19 'The minute the …', Brodesser-Akner, op. cit.

19 'women are less …', Jennifer Billock, 'Pain bias: the pain inequality rarely discussed', BBC Future, 22 May 2018.

20 'There is a …', Jean Anthelme Brillat-Savarin, *The Physiology of Taste* (translated by Fayette Robinson) (Philadelphia: Lindsay & Blackiston, 1854).

20 'free of cancer …', Belle Gibson, *The Whole Pantry* (London: Penguin, 2014).

22 'Reading that Gwyneth …', James Wong (@Botanygeek), on Twitter, 9 September 2019.

22 'I wonder if …', Yvette d'Entremont, 'The "Food Babe" Blogger Is Full of Shit', Gawker.com, 6 April 2015.

22 'Cosmic Ginger Rose …', 'healthy, flavorful brew', https://www.moonandspoonandyum.com/blog/cosmic-ginger-rose-activated-charcoal-latte-vegan-gluten-free.

23 'if you just …', from an email exchange with Laura Thomas.

24 'A recent survey …', Andrew Ellson, 'Rise of fat as feminist issue shames dieters into silence', *The Times*, 11 January 2020.

24 'A woman's body …', Taffy Brodesser-Akner, 'Losing It in the Anti-Dieting Age', *New York Times Magazine*, 2 August 2017.

24 'orthorexic tendencies were …', Pixie G. Turner and Carmen E. Lefevre, 'Instagram use is linked to increased symptoms of orthorexia nervosa', *Eating and Weight Disorders – Studies on Anorexia, Bulimia and Obesity* 22 (2017).

24 'Sufferers may appear …', 'in search of …', Scarlett Thomas, '"I have more than 100 different food rules": how healthy eating became an obsession', *Guardian*, 25 October 2019.

25 'because the iambic …', ibid.

25 'Instead of saying …', Susie Orbach, quoted in Alexandra Jones, 'I was on a diet for 18 years. Here's what I learned …', bbc.co.uk, 1 October 2018.

26 'In April 2019 …', Jack Dorsey, interviewed on the podcast *Ben Greenfield Fitness: Diet, Fat Loss and Performance*, transcript

at https://bengreenfieldfitness.com/transcripts/transcript-time-saving-workouts/.

27 'When teenage girls ...', Virginia Sole-Smith, quoted in Alex Kuczynski, 'Inside Silicon Valley's Dangerous New Obsession with Fasting', *Harper's Bazaar*, 17 August 2019.

27 'This home manufacturing ...', Rob Rhinehart, 'How I Gave Up Alternating Current', robrhinehart.com, 3 August 2015.

27 'But Rhinehart wants ...', Lizzie Widdicombe, 'The End of Food', *New Yorker*, 5 May 2014.

28 'There is a ...', Laura Thomas, 'Opinion: We'll never achieve "true wellness" if we're all too hungry to get the job done', *Metro*, 29 June 2019.

28 'proposed ban on ...', Helen West and Rosie Saunt, 'Opinion: Only the privileged can afford not to eat on public transport', *Metro*, 10 October 2019.

29 'privileged pseudo-science', from a conversation with Rosie Saunt.

29 '29% of adults ...', NHS Statistics on Obesity, Physical Activity and Diet, England, 2019.

29 'affordable, nutritious, easy ...', from a conversation with Rosie Saunt.

29 'I suspect that ...', from an email exchange with Laura Thomas.

32 'we are constantly ...', Stuart McGurk, 'The Business of Sleep', *GQ*, 29 July 2019.

33 'We've never known ...', ibid.

33 'worth £100 billion ...', Marco Hafner, Martin Stepanek, Jirka Taylor, Wendy M. Troxel, Christian Van Stolk, *Why sleep matters – the economic costs of insufficient sleep: A cross-country comparative analysis* (Santa Monica, CA: RAND Corporation, 2016).

33 'get more sleep ...', Jonathan Gershuny and Oriel Sullivan, *What We Really Do All Day*, (London: Pelican, 2019), p. 42.

33 'patient who believed ...', Guy Leschziner, *The Nocturnal Brain: Nightmares, Neuroscience and the Secret World of Sleep* (London: Simon & Schuster, 2019).

35 'hundreds of giddy ...', Kuczynski, op. cit.

35 'curious self-alienation', 'there is the ...', 'Transcendant Oneness does ...', 'cannot levitate ourselves ...', Barbara Ehrenreich, *Smile or Die: How Positive Thinking Fooled America and the World* (London: Granta, 2009).

36 'wellest among us', Mull, op. cit.

36 'Purser nods to …', Purser, op. cit

36 'one in three …', Patrick Collinson, 'One in three UK millennials will never own a home – report', *Guardian*, 17 April 2018; and Donna Ferguson, 'Twenty years on – the winners and losers of Britain's property boom', *Guardian*, 23 January 2016.

36 'self-coddling', 'If we spend …', Spicer, op. cit.

37 'political warfare', 'Caring for myself …', Audre Lorde, *A Burst of Light* (London: Sheba, 1988).

37 'radical feminist act …', Evette Dionne, 'For Black Women, Self-Care Is a Radical Act', Ravishly, 6 March 2015.

37 'Continued political shocks …', Spicer, op. cit.

39 'Away from the …', Wiedeman, op. cit.

39 'On Self-Respect', Joan Didion, 'Self-respect: Its Source, Its Power' [original title], *Vogue*, 1 August 1961.

Get The Look

40 'She loves a …', Elizabeth Paton, 'The $50 Dress That Conquered Britain', *New York Times*, 11 June 2019.

41 'engages in typical …', urbandictionary.com, 2015 entry.

41 'Part of my …', Sirin Kale, 'The story of The Dress: how a £40 Zara frock stole the summer', *Guardian*, 11 August 2019.

42 '"modern variation" of …', 'combing, brushing and …', Pamela Church Gibson, *Fashion and Celebrity Culture* (London: Berg Publishers, 2013), p. 127.

42 'discussions of "agency"…', 'self-expression through dress', ibid.

42 'one in three …', according to a 2015 survey by Barnardo's.

42 'Cinderella Syndrome', Dana Thomas, *Fashionopolis: The Price of Fast Fashion – and the Future of Clothes* (London: Apollo Library, 2019), p. 244.

43 'By 2014, the …', James Wallman, *Stuffocation: Living More With Less* (London: Penguin, 2014).

43 'By 2019, she …', report by the Environmental Audit Committee, 'Fixing fashion: clothing consumption and sustainability', 19 February 2019.

43 'the average lifetime …', Paula Cocozza, '"Don't feed the monster!" The people who have stopped buying new clothes', *Guardian*, 19 February 2019.

43   'the term *neophilia* …', J. D. Salinger, 'Hapworth 16, 1924', *New Yorker*, 19 June 1965.

43   'the word *kipple* …', Philip K. Dick, *Do Androids Dream of Electric Sheep?* (New York: Doubleday, 1968).

43   'only seven times …', Barnardo's, 2015.

44   'tax every garment …', Damian Carrington, 'Ministers reject plans for 1p per garment levy to tackle fast fashion', *Guardian*, 18 June 2019.

44   '3 billion people …', 'America's Dopamine-Fueled Shopping Addiction', video by *The Atlantic*, 22 February 2019, available at https://www.theatlantic.com/video/index/598867/tree-poaching/.

45   'It was Gap …', Elizabeth L. Cline, *Overdressed: The Shockingly High Cost of Cheap Fashion* (New York: Portfolio/Penguin, 2012), p. 17.

45   'Her whole being …', Edith Wharton, *The House of Mirth* (New York: Charles Scribner's Sons, 1905).

45   'That instant when …', Sophie Kinsella, *The Secret Dreamworld of a Shopaholic* (London: Black Swan, 2000), p. 35.

47   'At its zenith …', from asosplc.com/corporate-responsibility/our-customers.

47   'two things happened …', from a conversation with Lucy Siegle.

48   'Moss accused Miller …', Laura Antonia Jordan, 'The Art of Copyquette: Is it Ever OK to Copy Someone's Outfit?', *Grazia*, 21 August 2019.

49   'first fashion blog …', 'fashion news cycle', Trey Taylor, 'Where Fashion Blogging Began', *New York Times*, 1 February 2017.

51   '43% of clothing …', according to Royal Mail's 2019 'Delivery Matters' report.

51   'hunter gatherer instinct …', from a conversation with Lucy Siegle.

52   'You see them …', Freya Drohan, 'An Investigation into the Influencer Frenzy Around "New Bottega"', fashionista.com, 24 September 2019.

52   'roughly four times …', Thomas, op. cit., p. 36.

53   'economy of sameness', Brenda Weber, quoted in Church Gibson, *Fashion and Celebrity Culture*, p. 148.

54   '66% of online …', according to the Hitwise UK Fashion Report 2019, available at https://www.hitwise.com/en/gated/uk-fashion-report-19/.

56 'Brands that affiliate ...', 'Boohoo.com's UK sales ...', Sirin Kale, '"They can sell anything": how the Kardashians changed fashion', *Guardian*, 28 January 2019.

56 'self-proclaimed "minimalist monastery" ...', 'Keeping Up With the Wests: Kim, Kanye (and Their Kids!) Answer 73 Questions', video by Vogue.com, 11 April 2019, available at https:// www. vogue.com/article/73-questions-with-kim-kardashian-west.

57 '*enclothed cognition*', Hajo Adam and Adam D. Galinsky, 'Enclothed Cognition', *Journal of Experimental Social Psychology*, 48(4), July 2012.

58 'Yomi Adegoke dubs ...', Kale, op. cit.

58 'Latin, Black, Arab ...', Joanna Fuertes, 'The New Beauty Is from Everywhere and Nowhere', Zora.Medium.com, 12 November 2018.

58 'five and a half ...', Anna Johnstone, 'This is the UK city where women take longest to get ready to go out ... and you won't believe how long they take', *Sun*, 16 February 2018.

59 'blackfishing', Kameron Virk and Nesta McGregor, 'Blackfishing: The women accused of pretending to be black', bbc.co.uk, 5 December 2018.

59 'is as unattainable ...', 'black Jessica Rabbits', Reni Eddo-Lodge, 'Reni Eddo-Lodge on the "Blackfishing" Phenomenon', *Vogue*, 14 December 2018.

60 'are not necessarily ...', Church Gibson, op. cit., p. 145.

61 'micro-influencers have 25,000–100,000 ...', Bobby Chernev, 'Influencer Marketing Statistics in 2020', TechJury.net.

63 'We are obsessed ...', Yomi Adegoke, 'Fast fashion is so entrenched we're shocked when a royal rewears a dress', *Metro*, 18 October 2019.

63 'It's important to ...', Aria Hughes, 'How Fashion Nova Won the Internet', WWD.com, 28 February 2018.

63 'Brits now spend ...', Olivia Petter, 'Brits to Spend £2.7bn on Outfits They Wear Once This Summer', *Independent*, 10 July 2019.

63 'over one third ...', Grace Whelan, 'Used returns costing retailers £1.5bn', *Drapers Online*, 18 September 2019.

63 '*wardrobing* or *snap* ...', research by Barclaycard, 'Snap and send back', 10 August 2018, available at https://www.home. barclaycard/media-centre/press-releases/snap-and-send-back.html.

64 'The stresses of ...', 'Instagram Illusion: Behind the Scenes', CommonToff.com, 13 January 2018.

64 'When you're more ...', 'I want to ...', 'Instagram Illusions: I Don't Actually Have This Many Clothes', CommonToff.com, 30 April 2018.

64 'It is difficult ...', Upton Sinclair, *I, Candidate for Governor, and How I Got Licked* (1935) (Berkeley: University of California Press, 1994), p. 109.

64 'Woman racks up ...', headline of an article by Sarah Young, *Independent*, 5 March 2018.

67 'When I buy ...', Jess Cartner-Morley, 'The fashion editor's eco makeover: can I rethink my love affair with clothes?', *Guardian*, 6 October 2018.

67 'People don't want ...', Theodore Levitt, quoted in Clayton M. Christensen, Scott Cook and Taddy Hall, 'What Customers Want from Your Products', *Harvard Business Review* excerpt, hbs.edu, 16 January 2016.

68 'The things we ...', Ann Patchett, 'My Year of No Shopping', *New York Times*, 15 December 2017.

68 '$2.5 billion by 2023', according to a report by market research firm Global Data.

69 'Our subscribers spend ...', 'That's a lot ...', Alexandra Schwartz, 'Rent the Runway Wants to Lend You Your Look', *New Yorker*, 22 October 2018.

70 'more fun than ...', Harriet Walker, 'Could renting clothes spell the end of fast fashion?', *The Times*, 28 September 2019.

71 '"wanting" and "liking"', Phil Barden, *Decoded: The Science Behind Why We Buy* (Chichester: Wiley, 2013), p. 161.

71 'We choose what ...', Renata Salecl, 'The Paradox of Choice', talk at the Royal Society of Arts, 15 July 2010.

Little Pieces Everywhere

75 'Fleabag nearly inverts ...', Gaby Hinsliff, 'Fleabag has gloriously affirmed every woman's right to screw up in style', *Guardian*, 5 April 2019.

75 'so that to ...', Virginia Woolf, *Mrs Dalloway* (London: Hogarth Press, 1925).

75 'The Problem That ...', chapter title in Betty Friedan, *The Feminine Mystique* (London: Victor Gollancz, 1963).

75 'burst like a ...', ibid., p. 11.

75 'that food cannot ...', ibid., p. 15.

76 'One half of ...', Mary Gaitskill, *Bad Behavior* (New York: Vintage Books, 1988), p. 177.

76 'There's always someone ...', Karla M. Hammond, 'Audre Lorde: Interview', *Denver Quarterly*, 16(1), 1981.

76 'Breasts, feet, hips ...', Susan Sontag, 'A Woman's Beauty: Put Down or Power Source?', *Vogue*, April 1975.

77 'In men, good...', ibid.

77 'Never mind Brexit ...', headline of an article by Sarah Vine, *Daily Mail*, 28 March 2017.

77 'direct attempt at ...', ibid.

77 'Is that big ...', Candice Carty-Williams, *Queenie* (London: Trapeze, 2019), p. 23.

78 '"Guy, you know ...', ibid., p. 169.

78 'seen and understood ...', from an email exchange with Candice Carty-Williams.

79 'Being the Cool ...', Gillian Flynn, *Gone Girl* (New York: Crown, 2012).

79 'mass production's first ...', Elizabeth Wurtzel, *Bitch: In Praise of Difficult Women* (London: Quartet Books, 1998).

79 'Once upon a ...', Zadie Smith, interviewed on the podcast *Literary Friction*, 7 October 2019.

80 'sad-eyed brooders (Ryan ...', Michael Schulman, 'Adam Driver, the Original Man', *New Yorker*, 21 October 2019.

80 'Men are less ...', 'interrogate the roles ...', from a conversation with Candice Carty-Williams.

81 'disappear and to ...', Rebecca Solnit, *Recollections of My Non-Existence* (London: Granta, 2020), p. 3.

82 'a good danger ...', 'Don't get me ...', Sophie Heawood, 'Sophie Heawood confronts the reality of growing older', *Evening Standard*, 23 October 2019.

83 '"It's not going ...', Pandora Sykes, 'The Response to Meghan Markle's Bump-Cradle Says So Much About How We View Pregnancy', Elle.com, 13 December 2018.

84 'I wanted to ...', Rachel Cusk, 'I was only being honest', *Guardian*, 21 March 2008.

85 'No one can …', Nigel Farndale, 'Doris Lessing: her last Telegraph interview', *Telegraph*, 17 November 2013.

86 'There's a logical …', Tessa Hadley, 'Mothers by Jacqueline Rose review – an indignant defence', *Guardian*, 20 April 2018.

86 'legislate for complexity', 'In motherhood the …', Cusk, op. cit.

86 'the neo-liberal intensification …', Angela McRobbie, 'Notes on the Perfect: Competitive Femininity in Neoliberal Times', *Australian Feminist Studies*, 30(83), 2015.

86 'I wasn't a …', Mikki Kendall, *Hood Feminism: Notes From the Women That White Feminists Forgot* (London: Bloomsbury, 2020), p. 238.

87 'to be poor …', ibid., p. 241.

87 'we don't really …', Glynnis MacNicol, 'I'm in my 40s, Child-Free and Happy. Why Won't Anyone Believe Me?', *New York Times*, 5 July 2018.

87 'There's vanishingly little …', Elizabeth Day, 'Other people's kids … do I really have to?', *Mail on Sunday*, 28 July 2019.

87 'flattened into either …', from an email exchange with Sophie Wilkinson.

88 'Here's what a …', Nora Ephron, 'Parenting in Three Stages', in *I Feel Bad About My Neck: And Other Thoughts About Being a Woman* (London: Black Swan, 2006).

89 'When my son …', from an email exchange with Nell Frizzell.

90 'the acknowledgement of …', Olivia Sudjic, *Exposure* (London: Peninsula Press, 2018).

91 'My life is …', Taffy Brodesser-Akner, 'How Taffy Brodesser-Akner Thrives on Stress', realsimple.com, 19 July 2019.

91 'Young Millennial Woman', Rebecca Liu, 'The Making of a Millennial Woman', anothergaze.com, 12 June 2019.

92 'flattening and deceptively …', 'deeply variegated class', ibid.

92 'There's something so …', James Rampton, 'Killing Eve: Why Villanelle is different from other baddies', Stuff.co.nz, 28 March 2019.

92 'you can't mess …', 'A lot of …', Candice Carty-Williams, '*Queenie* by Candice Carty-Williams', interview on BBC Radio 4, 15 April 2019.

93 'unruly bodies', Roxane Gay, 'The Body Is Unruly', Gay.Medium.com, 2 April 2018.

93 'womanhood has been …', Jia Tolentino, *Trick Mirror* (London: Fourth Estate, 2019), p. 252.

93 'binary fatalism', ibid., p. 91.

94 'To create a ...', Chimamanda Ngozi Adichie, 'The danger of a single story', TED Talk, 16 October 2009.

94 'I ceased being ...', Monica Lewinsky, 'The price of shame', TED Talk, 20 March 2015.

95 'An internship at ...', @MonicaLewinsky, on Twitter, 14 July 2019.

95 'Another day, another ...', @diet_prada, on Instagram, 28 February 2019.

96 'I don't live ...', Grace Shutti, 'Chidera Eggerue, Playboy and the New Rules of Feminism', *Playboy*, 21 August 2019.

98 'I could survive ...', Taylor Swift, '30 Things I Learned Before Turning 30', *Elle*, 6 March 2019.

98 'She said that ...', 'What I choose ...', Elena Ferrante, *Frantumaglia: A Writer's Journey* (New York: Europa Editions, 2016).

98 'Women need to ...', from an email exchange with Candice Carty-Williams.

99 'We can deal ...', Alain de Botton, interviewed on the podcast *How to Fail with Elizabeth Day*, 2 October 2019.

99 'Only by learning ...', Hammond, op. cit.

100 'You've had everything ...', Anna Hope, *Expectation* (London: Doubleday, 2019).

Work to Get Happy

102 'life-size doll named ...', 'a rotund stomach ...', Fellowes.com, 'Meet Emma Our Work Colleague of the Future', available at https://www.fellowes.com/gb/en/resources/fellowes-introduces/work-colleague-of-the-future.aspx.

102 'unemployment is cited ...', see Chapter 4: 'Work and Unemployment', in Andrew E. Clark, Sarah Flèche, Richard Layard, Nattavudh Powdthavee and George Ward, *The Origins of Happiness: The Science of Well-Being Over the Life Course* (Princeton: Princeton University Press, 2018).

103 'a fifteen-hour week ...', John Maynard Keynes, 'Economic Possibilities for Our Grandchildren', *Nation and Athenaeum*, 11 October 1930 and 18 October 1930.

103 'longest average working ...', Christine Armstrong, *The Mother of All Jobs: How to Have Children and a Career and Stay Sane(ish)* (London: Green Tree, 2018), p. ix.

104 'The Easterlin Paradox', coined by economist Richard A. Easterlin: see 'Does Economic Growth Improve the Human Lot? Some Empirical Evidence', in Paul A. David and Melvin W. Reder (eds), *Nations and Households in Economic Growth: Essays in Honor of Moses Abramovitz* (New York; London: Academic Press, 1974).

104 'the theory, first ...', Derek Thompson, 'Workism Is Making Americans Miserable', *The Atlantic*, 24 February 2019.

104 'walls between work ...', the term 'context collapse' is thought to have been coined by technologist danah boyd, something she says she could take credit for (the timing is feasible) but she's not entirely sure (more here: http://www.zephoria.org/thoughts/archives/2013/12/08/coining-context-collapse.html).

105 'A job has ...', Ezra Klein, 'Work as Identity, Burnout as Lifestyle', *The Ezra Klein Show* podcast, 22 April 2019.

105 'the idea that ...', Natasha Gillezeau, 'The burnout generation', *Financial Review*, 12 July 2019.

105 'Conclude the German ...', Verena C. Hahn and Christian Dormann, 'The Role of Partners and Children for Employees' Psychological Detachment from Work and Well-Being', *Journal of Applied Psychology*, 98(1), January 2013.

105 'One person's after-hours ...', Christian Jarrett, 'Work/Life Separation Is Impossible. Here's How to Deal With It', 99u.adobe.com, 4 September 2014.

105 'our base temperature ...', Anne Helen Petersen, 'How Millennials Became the Burnout Generation', Buzzfeed, 5 January 2019.

106 'idea that [you] ...', ibid.

106 'The notion of ...', Sir Michael Marmot, quoted in Johann Hari, *Lost Connections: Uncovering the Real Causes of Depression – and the Unexpected Solutions* (London: Bloomsbury, 2018), p. 83.

106 'People patching together ...', Petersen, op. cit.

106 'burn themselves out', David Graeber, *Bullshit Jobs: A Theory* (London: Penguin, 2018), p. xix.

107 'Hell is a ...', 'I would not ...', ibid.

107 'poll in 2015 ...', Will Dahlgreen, '37% of British workers think their jobs are meaningless', YouGov.co.uk, 12 August 2015.

107 'wellbeing is higher ...', William Davies, *The Happiness Industry* (London: Verso, 2015).

107 'Who gets up ...', Andrew Anthony, 'Bullshit Jobs: A Theory review – labored rant about the world of work', *Guardian*, 27 May 2018.

108 'the most facile ...', Anne Helen Petersen discussing her essay with *On Point*: '"Existing on a Plane of Burnout": An Intersectional Discussion on Millennials and More', wbur.org, 14 January 2019.

108 'During the boom ...', from an email exchange with Anna Codrea-Rado.

108 'the [clenching] and ...', Tiana Clark, 'This Is What Black Burnout Feels Like', Buzzfeed, 11 January 2019.

110 '"folk narrative" about ...', Jonathan Gershuny and Oriel Sullivan, *What We Really Do All Day*, (London: Pelican, 2019), p. 305.

110 'a boast disguised ...', Tim Kreider, 'The "Busy" Trap', *New York Times*, 30 June 2012.

110 'When we think ...', Gershuny and Sullivan, op. cit.

110 'lamented busyness is ...', Kreider, op. cit.

110 'likely to shape ...', Jerry A. Jacobs and Kathleen Gerson, quoted in Gershuny and Sullivan, op. cit.

111 'who had a ...', 'Pepys works, makes ...', Adam Gopnik, 'Bumping into Mr. Ravioli', *New Yorker*, 23 September 2002.

112 'the productivity market ...', IbisWorld, 'Operating Systems & Productivity Software Publishing Industry in the US – Market Research Report', January 2020, available at https://www.ibis world.com/united-states/market-research-reports/operating-systems-productivity-software-publishing-industry/.

113 'the way to ...', Tori Reid, 'Make Your Dreams a Reality with the WOOP Method', lifehacker.com, 15 January 2015.

113 'extremely old Dell ...', Lev Grossman, 'Jonathan Franzen: Great American Novelist', *TIME*, 12 August 2010.

113 'I can't write ...', Scott Feinberg, 'Last-Minute Honoree Quentin Tarantino Talks Writing in Santa Barbara', *Hollywood Reporter*, 31 January 2013.

113 'the most productive …', Hilary Potkewitz, 'Why 4 a.m. Is the Most Productive Hour', *Wall Street Journal*, 23 August 2016.

113 'shockingly productive', Dave Johnson, 'Apple CEO Tim Cook wakes up every day at 3:45 a.m. I tried doing it for a week, and it made me shockingly productive', businessinsider.com, 28 August 2019.

114 'it might sound …', Kristen Bateman, 'How I Get It Done: Audrey Gelman, Co-Founder and CEO of The Wing', *The Cut*, 16 April 2019.

115 'Are we the …', Kate Walbert, 'To Do', *New Yorker*, 26 August 2019.

115 'Things won are …', *Troilus and Cressida* (Act I, Scene 2).

116 'a dominant motif …', Oliver Burkeman, 'Why time management is ruining our lives', *Guardian* long read, 22 December 2016.

116 'It's easy to …', Oliver Burkeman, 'Members of the Uptighterati hate lateness: are we wrong?', *Guardian*, 2 August 2019.

117 'In a situation …', Jenny Odell, *How to Do Nothing: Resisting the Attention Economy* (New York: Melville House, 2019), p. 15.

118 'They exist up …', Anne Helen Petersen, speaking on the podcast *The Ezra Klein Show*, 22 April 2019.

118 'having fifteen jobs …', Emma Gannon, *The Multi-Hyphen Method: Work Less, Create More, and Design a Career that Works for You* (London: Hodder & Stoughton, 2018).

119 'Outside the walls …', 'LET'S DO THIS …', 'We want this …', Dave Eggers, *The Circle* (London: Penguin, 2013).

120 '3.3 million in 2017', Dan Hancox, 'Why we are all losing sleep', *New Statesman*, 6 November 2019.

120 'warm fuzzy feeling …', Jo Ellison, 'Revolutionary all-women workspace The Wing comes to London', *Financial Times*, 4 October 2019.

121 'safe, happy place …', Armstrong, op. cit., p. 69.

121 'The universe was …', Mihaly Csikszentmihalyi, *Flow: The Psychology of Optimal Experience* (New York: Harper & Row, 1990), p. 8.

122 '75% of children …', Jacob Dirnhuber, 'Vlog's a job: Children turn backs on traditional careers in favour of internet fame, study finds', *Sun*, 22 May 2017.

122 'The misguided idea …', from a conversation with Anna Codrea-Rado.

123 'Do you not …', Plutarch, *Caesar*, 11.6.

123 'British model Leomie …', this paragraph is adapted from a piece I wrote for the *Sunday Times Style*, 'Do You Have FOMOG? (… that's fear of missing out on goals)', 17 February 2019.

123 'There is no …', Csikszentmihalyi, op. cit., p. 10.

124 'I began to …', adapted from 'Do You Have FOMOG?'

124 '*autotelic self*', see Csikszentmihalyi, *Flow*.

124 'Desire hath no …', Robert Burton, *The Anatomy of Melancholy* (1621).

124 '*arrival fallacy*: the …', A. C. Shilton, 'You Accomplished Something Great. So Now What?', *New York Times*, 28 May 2019.

125 'addicted to busyness …', Kreider, op. cit.

125 'In order to …', David Sedaris, 'Laugh, Kookaburra', *New Yorker*, 17 August 2009

126 'men's flexible working …', Melissa Davey, 'Flexible working helps women succeed but makes men unhappy, study finds', *Guardian*, 3 February 2016.

126 'Only 1% of …', Ben Chapman, 'Shared parental leave: Government urged to overhaul systems as figures show only 1% of parents use it', *Independent*, 4 April 2019.

126 '75% of all …', 'Families and the labour market, UK: 2019', report by the Office for National Statistics, available at www.ons.gov.uk.

126 'a woman earns …', Eve Rodsky, *Fair Play: Share the Mental Load, Rebalance Your Relationship and Transform Your Life* (London: Quercus, 2019).

126 'companies with women …', '100 Women: Do women on boards increase company profits?', bbc.co.uk, 2 October 2017.

127 '53% more likely …', Caroline Criado-Perez, *Invisible Women: Exposing Data Bias in a World Designed for Men* (London: Chatto, 2019).

127 'bulk of housework …', Gershuny and Sullivan, op. cit., p. 132 (Chapter 6: 'Unpaid Work Matters' by Jooyeoun Suh and Christopher Payne).

128 'men's contribution to …', ibid.

128 'Famously progressive Finland …', Armstrong, op. cit.

128 'culturally "more intensive" …', Claire Cain Miller, 'Women Did Everything Right. Then Work Got "Greedy"', *New York Times*, 26 April 2019.

128 'women carry a ...', from an email exchange with Darby Saxbe.

129 'Women are often ...', ibid.

129 'It's easy to ...', Jessica Valenti, 'Kids Don't Damage Women's Careers—Men Do', Gen.Medium.com, 13 September 2018.

131 'Women are doing ...', Pat Levitt, quoted in Rodsky, op. cit.

132 'It is no ...', Erin Griffith, 'Why Are Young People Pretending to Love Work?', *New York Times*, 26 January 2019.

132 'are about "thinking" ...', 'Having to externalise ...', Derek Thompson, speaking on the podcast *The Ezra Klein Show*, 22 April 2019.

132 'the roots of ...', Csikszentmihalyi, op. cit., p. 12.

132 'Disempowerment occurs as ...', Davies, op. cit., p. 250.

132 'identifying and firing ...', ibid., p. 113.

Relentless Pleasure

135 'The term "infobesity" ...', coined by the consulting house Bain & Company, see Paul Rogers, Rudy Puryear and James Root, 'Infobesity: The enemy of good decisions', Bain.com, 11 June 2013.

136 'pancake people', 'Spread wide and ...', Richard Foreman, 'The Pancake People, Or, "The Gods Are Pounding My Head"', *Edge*, 8 March 2005.

136 '42% of millennials ...', David Dowling, *Immersive Longform Storytelling: Media, Technology, Audience* (New York: Routledge, 2019).

137 'Weird stuff happens ...', Mary H. K. Choi, 'In Praise of Binge TV Consumption', *Wired*, 27 December 2011.

137 'any instance in ...', Mary McNamara, 'Critic's Notebook: The side effects of binge television', *Los Angeles Times*, 15 January 2012.

138 '*I Love Lucy* ...', Tim Wu, *The Attention Merchants: The Epic Struggle to Get Inside our Heads* (London: Atlantic Books, 2017), p. 128.

138 'unparalleled significance in ...', ibid., p. 124

138 'regular attention was ...', ibid., p. 129.

139 'How lame is ...', Sam Levin, 'Netflix co-founder: "Blockbuster laughed at us ... Now there's one left"', *Guardian*, 14 September 2019.

140 '150 millions subscribers …', Guy Lodge, 'Streaming revolution: how do the new TV platforms stack up?', *Observer*, 13 October 2019.

141 'What we need …', Jamie East, 'Amazon, Netflix, Sky, Apple and Disney are taking streaming to the next level – for viewers with deep enough pockets', *The Times*, 29 September 2019.

141 'I was in …', Stendhal, *Naples and Florence: A Journey from Milan to Reggio* (1817).

141 'reasons for binge-watching …', Emil Steiner, 'Binge-Watching in Practice: The Rituals, Motives and Feelings of Streaming Video Viewers', in Cory Barker and Myc Wiatrowski (eds), *The Age of Netflix: Critical Essays on Streaming Media, Digital Delivery and Instant Access* (Jefferson, NC: McFarland & Company, 2017), p. 152.

142 'people start saying …', Soraya Roberts, 'When Did Pop Culture Become Homework?', Longreads.com, April 2019.

142 'Now members of …', from an email exchange with Jonathan Dean.

142 'It's the kind …', Samuel Fishwick, 'Hyperdrive on Netflix: Charlize Theron's car rodeo is a gloriously full-throttle joy ride', *Evening Standard*, 28 August 2019.

142 'reactance', Roberts, op. cit.

143 'the larger culture …', 'Essentialist pop culture …', ibid.

143 'Taste classifies the …', Neta Alexander, 'Catered to Your Future Self: Netflix's "Predictive Personalization" and the Mathematization of Taste', in Kevin McDonald and Daniel Smith-Rowsey (eds), *The Netflix Effect: Technology and Entertainment in the 21st Century* (New York: Bloomsbury Academic, 2016), p. 82.

143 'there are too …', from an email exchange with Jonathan Dean.

144 'non-event TV', 'dystopia'd out', Richard Godwin, 'The age of comfort TV: why people are secretly watching Friends and The Office on a loop', *Guardian*, 21 August 2019.

146 'Netflix is the …', Katherine Zoepf, 'The Unspeakable Cost of Parenthood', *New York Times*, 27 August 2019.

146 'bingey society', 'our souls aren't …', from an email exchange with Soraya Roberts.

147 'Netflix tripled the …', Kate Erbland, 'Netflix Has Almost Tripled Its Amount of Available Television Shows in Less Than a Decade', indiewire.com, 21 February 2018.

148 'homo distractus', Wu, op. cit., p. 6.

148 '67% of male ...', Nadia Whitehead, 'People would rather be electrically shocked than left alone with their thoughts', *Science*, 3 July 2014.

148 'vacancies of attention', Adam Phillips, *Attention Seeking* (London: Penguin, 2019).

149 'Certainly she was ...', Virginia Woolf, *To the Lighthouse* (London: Hogarth Press, 1927).

149 'modest, mouse-coloured people', Virginia Woolf, 'The Mark on the Wall' (1917).

149 'The story that ...', 'flesh cages', 'Grand Union: Zadie Smith in conversation with Diana Evans', at the Royal Institution, 2 October 2019.

149 'It seems to ...', Julia Hobsbawm, *Fully Connected: Surviving and Thriving in an Age of Overload* (London: Bloomsbury Business, 2017), p. 129.

150 'not a [sign] ...', Steven Johnson, *Everything Bad Is Good for You: How Today's Popular Culture Is Actually Making Us Smarter* (New York; London: Riverhead Books, 2005), p. 181.

150 'The Net delivers ...', Nicholas Carr, *The Shallows: How the Internet Is Changing the Way We Think, Read and Remember* (London Atlantic Books, 2010), p. 116.

151 'I was noticeably ...', Zachary Snider, 'The Cognitive Psychological Effects of Binge-Watching', in *The Netflix Effect*, p. 125.

152 'on weekends when ...', Seth Stephens-Davidowitz, *Everybody Lies: What the Internet Can Tell Us About Who We Really Are* (London: Bloomsbury, 2017).

152 'Goldfish, it is ...', Barbara Ehrenreich, *Natural Causes: Life, Death and the Illusion of Control* (London: Granta, 2018), p. 73.

152 'The goldfish metaphor ...', from an email exchange with Gina Rippon.

152 'task-dependent', Gemma Briggs, quoted in Simon Maybin, 'Busting the attention span myth', bbc.co.uk, 10 March 2017.

152 'the much-maligned goldfish ...', Aislinn Simpson, 'Fish's memories last for months, say scientists', *Telegraph*, 7 January 2009.

152 'the hyper-distracted glancing ...', Djoymi Baker, 'Terms of Excess: Binge-Viewing as Epic-Viewing in the Netflix Era',

in *The Age of Netflix*, p. 35, referencing Michael Z. Newman and Elana Levine, *Legitimating Television: Media Convergence and Cultural Status* (Abingdon: Routledge, 2012).

153 *'viewsing'*, Dan Harries, quoted in Djoymi Baker, 'Terms of Excess', in *The Age of Netflix*, p. 34.

153 'bland choice and …', from an email exchange with Soraya Roberts.

153 'Netflix is like …', Arwa Mahdawi, 'Netflix addiction is real – we are entertaining ourselves to death', *Guardian*, 20 June 2018.

154 'It does not …', ibid.

154 'We're competing with …', Reed Hastings, in a speech at Summit LA in November 2017.

154 'In 1918, a …', Adam Alter, *Irresistible: Why We Can't Stop Checking, Scrolling, Clicking and Watching* (London: Vintage, 2017).

154 'haven't buried any …', from an email exchange with Paul Flynn.

154 'Being dependent on …', Nir Eyal, speaking on the podcast *The Ezra Klein Show*, 7 August 2019.

155 'And diversion can …', ibid.

155 'tackle societal issues …', from an email exchange with Jonathan Dean.

155 'that there's a …', Tristan Harris, quoted in Bianca Bosker, 'The Binge Breaker', *The Atlantic*, November 2016.

156 'people's psychological vulnerabilities', 'There needs to …', 'Are we really …', from a conversation with Nir Eyal.

156 'It's no longer …', Peter Suderman, quoted in Carr, op. cit., p. 181.

156 'mental powers', Carr, op. cit., p. 196.

156 'cultural transmission', Pascal Boyer, quoted in Carr, op. cit.

157 'neuroticising', 'corporate culture to …', from an email exchange with Paul Flynn.

157 'It is becoming …', Anna North, 'When Novels Were Bad for You', *New York Times*, 14 September 2014.

158 'The person will …', ibid.

158 'A book never …', from an email exchange with Laura Freeman.

159 'Binge-watching can be …', 'seeing the forest …', Steiner, 'Binge-Watching in Practice', in *The Age of Netflix*, p. 158.

162 'the term *authentocrat*', Joe Kennedy, *Authentocrats: Culture, Politics and the New Seriousness* (London: Repeater, 2018).

164 'the observing ego', Louis Ormont, quoted in Richard Seymour, *The Twittering Machine* (London: The Indigo Press, 2019), p. 43.

164 'Having two identities …', Mark Zuckerberg, quoted in David Kirkpatrick, *The Facebook Effect: The Inside Story of the Company That Is Connecting the World* (New York: Simon & Schuster, 2010), p. 199.

164 '*The Looking-Glass Self*', Charles Horton Cooley, *Human Nature and the Social Order* (New York: Charles Scribner's Sons, 1902).

165 'distinction between an …', Lionel Trilling, *Sincerity and Authenticity* (London: Oxford University Press, 1972).

166 'reflect and construct …', Nicholas A. John, *The Age of Sharing* (Cambridge: Polity, 2017), p. 17.

166 '72% of followers …', Christian Rudder, *Dataclysm: Who We Are (When We Think No One's Looking)* (London: Fourth Estate, 2014).

166 'Sharing your life …', John, op. cit., p. 59.

167 '*Radical transparency*', for more, see Ray Dalio, *Principles* (New York: Simon & Schuster, 2017).

167 'Privacy is no …', Mark Zuckerberg, in a speech at the Crunchies Awards in January 2010.

167 'the more we …', John, op. cit, p. 65.

167 'Online sharing expands …', ibid, p. 149.

168 'honing [her] shareability …', Tavi Gevinson, 'Who Would I Be Without Instagram? An Investigation', *The Cut*, 16 September 2019.

169 'Somewhere along the …', ibid.

169 'self-consciously unadorned authenticity', Allegra Hobbs, 'The journalist as influencer: how we sell ourselves on social media', *Guardian*, 21 October 2019.

169 'the purity of …', Gevinson, op. cit.

169 'displays almost 1,000 …', 'Today's children will feature in almost 1,000 online photos by the time they reach age five', study conducted by Nominet in collaboration with ParentZone, available at www.nominet.uk.

170 'The woman who …', Mohadesa Najumi, 'Why the Woman Who Does Not Require Validation From Anyone Is the Most Feared Individual on the Planet', Huffington Post, 17 March 2014.

170 '74% of women …', Marisa Mahler, 'Women's Empowerment: Validation Comes from Within', psychcentral.com, 8 July 2018.

170 'It's like that …', Emma Jane Unsworth, *Adults* (London: The Borough Press, 2020).

172 'social responsibility', 'the authentic person …', 'there's a renewed …', from a conversation with Katherine Ormerod.

173 'very perfect and …', Jia Tolentino, 'The Quiet Protests of Sassy Mom Merch', *New Yorker*, 27 November 2019.

174 'If they are …', @fashionambitionist, on Instagram stories, 30 August 2019.

174 'veganism, creative imagery …', @essenaoneill, on Instagram, 3 November 2015.

175 'a cute vegan …', Alyx Gorman, 'From sponsors to socialism: the return of Instagram star Essena O'Neill', *Guardian*, 19 November 2019.

175 'Trust me, I …', Essena O'Neill, 'Positive Self Awareness A+', Authority Within [undated].

175 'I like the …', @essenaoneill, on Instagram, 16 April 2016.

175 'SOCIAL MEDIA IS …', ibid, 12 April 2016.

175 *'getting real moment'*, Carrie Battan, 'The Rise of the "Getting Real" Post on Instagram', *New Yorker*, 1 October 2019.

175 'combines digital culture …', John, op. cit., p. 154.

176 'brave and vulnerable', 'raw story', @KrisJenner, on Twitter, 5 January 2019.

176 *'superficial subversion'*, Seymour, op. cit.

176 'True authenticity …', Rebecca Liu, 'Influencer culture has turned vulnerability into a sales tool', gal-dem, 23 January 2019.

177 'Demi Lovato posted …', @ddlovato, on Instagram, 6 September 2019.

178 'I have such …', @jameelajamil, on Twitter, 25 June 2019.

182 'fake it until …', '"chutzpah"', '"moxie"', Edward Helmore, '"Fake it until you make it": the strange case of New York's socialite scammer', *Guardian*, 31 March 2019.

182 'She regretted nothing …', Emily Palmer, 'A Fake Heiress Called Anna Delvey Conned the City's Wealthy. "I'm Not Sorry," She Says', *New York Times*, 10 May 2019.

183 'Here's the hard …', @lilmiquela, on Instagram, 19 April 2018.

183 'fake-looking real humans …', 'Can you name …', Emilia Petrarca, 'Body Con Job', *New York Magazine*, 14 May 2018.

183 'Honestly, the fact …', Rhian Daly, 'Meet Lil Miquela, the real life Ashley O', *NME*, 17 July 2019.

185 'fear of the …', 'On social media …', 'fascination with catching …', Seymour, op. cit., p. 89.

186 'the high-status individual …', Mitch Prinstein, *Popular* (London: Vermilion, 2017).

186 'now so reciprocal …', Sean Redmond, *Celebrity* (London: Routledge, 2017).

186 'Authenticity has become …', from a conversation with Tina Brown.

187 'social media posts …', ibid.

187 'like a bloody …', 'At first it …', Allison P. Davis, '"Yeah, I'm Not For Everyone." Lena Dunham comes to terms with herself', *New York Magazine*, 16 November 2018.

187 'So, too persuasive …', Steven Poole, 'Why are we so obsessed with the pursuit of authenticity?', *New Statesman*, 7 March 2013.

188 'Keira Knightley opened …', Keira Knightley, interviewed on the 'Awards Chatter' podcast, 17 September 2018.

188 'The middle-class admiration …', Poole, op. cit.

189 'Who gets to …', Rebecca Traister (@rtraister), on Twitter, 9 May 2019.

190 'Authenticity is like …', Andrew Potter, *The Authenticity Hoax: How We Get Lost Finding Ourselves* (Toronto: McClelland & Stewart, 2010), p. 14.

190 'a self can …', Zadie Smith, 'Fascinated to Presume: In Defense of Fiction', *New York Review of Books*, 24 October 2019.

190 'Caroline was caught …', Natalie Beach, 'I Was Caroline Calloway', *The Cut*, 10 September 2019.

191 'a matter of …', Redmond, op. cit., p. 85.

191 'no way to …', Jean Baudrillard's theory of Simulacra and Simulation; see Jean Baudrillard, *Simulations*, translated by Paul Foss (New York: Semiotexte, 1983).

Looking Forward to Hearing Back

194 '*operant conditioning*', B. F. Skinner, *The Behavior of Organisms: An Experimental Analysis* (Oxford: Appleton-Century, 1938).

197 'Generation Mute', Hannah Jane Parkinson, 'Let's resurrect phone calls. Texting "hahaha" is no match for hearing a friend laugh', *Guardian*, 3 January 2020.

197 'possessed by a …', Richard Seymour, *The Twittering Machine* (London: The Indigo Press, 2019), p. 16.

197 'swimming in writing', ibid., p. 23.

197 'until they implant …', Julie Beck, 'How It Became Normal to Ignore Texts and Emails', *The Atlantic*, 11 January 2018.

198 'get to see …', Sherry Turkle, quoted in Beck, op. cit.

198 'suspended between a …', Josh Cohen, *Not Working: Why We Have to Stop* (London: Granta, 2018).

200 'when AOL would …', 'Gmail celebrates the …', Adrienne LaFrance, 'Is Email Evil?', *The Atlantic*, 12 November 2015.

200 'reservoir of your …', tweet by @sean_a_rose, quoted in ibid.

201 'average office email …', Adam Alter, *Irresistible: Why We Can't Stop Checking, Scrolling, Clicking and Watching* (London: The Bodley Head, 2017).

201 'required this kind …', John Freeman, *The Tyranny of E-Mail: The Four-Thousand-Year Journey to Your Inbox* (New York: Simon & Schuster, 2009), p. 7.

201 'out-of-office has thrived …', some of what follows also appears in a piece I wrote for Elle.co.uk: 'The "Out of Office" Is Now an Artform, But What Does That Say About How We Live Our Lives?', 8 March 2019.

201 'I'm not in …', tweeted by Helena Wilkinson (@BBCHelena), 25 February 2019.

202 'Dear person who …', Laurence Lessig, quoted in Freeman, op. cit.

202 'on a tour …', Thomas Barrie, '34 words and phrases that no one should ever use', *GQ*, 6 December 2019.

203 '*sending* messages actually …', Gloria Mack, quoted in Freeman, op. cit.

204 'It should cost …', Ivo Graham (@IvoGraham), on Twitter, 2 May 2018.

204 'ever question the …', Nikesh Shukla, 'The awful truth about family WhatsApp groups', *Observer*, 22 January 2018.

204 'university students at …', 'University of Warwick suspends 11 students over hate posts', bbc.co.uk, 9 May 2018; and 'Exeter university students expelled over racist comments', bbc.co.uk, 1 May 2018.

206 'Hello any woman …', Dolly Alderton, *Everything I Know About Love* (London: Penguin, 2018).

206 '*Hey Ladies!* lampoons …', Caroline Moss and Michelle Markowitz, *Hey Ladies!: The Story of 8 Best Friends, 1 Year, and Way, Way Too Many Emails* (New York: Abrams Image, 2018).

207 'Women use the …', Seth Stephens-Davidowitz, *Everybody Lies: What the Internet Can Tell Us About Who We Really Are* (London: Bloomsbury 2017).

208 '*phatic expressions*', Gretchen McCulloch, *Because Internet: Understanding the New Rules of Language* (London: Harvill Secker, 2019), p. 201.

208 'linguistic perpetual motion …', 'so we have …', from an email exchange with David Shariatmadari.

208 'engage in a …', David Shariatmadari, 'The hyperbole we love to hate', *Guardian*, 4 November 2014.

208 'The merchant goes …', W. E. Dodge, in a speech in 1868.

209 'in the words …', Tim Wu, *The Attention Merchants: The Epic Struggle to Get Inside Our Heads* (London: Atlantic, 2017), p. 184.

209 'the first major …', McCulloch, op. cit., p. 198.

210 'We stop seeing …', Sherry Turkle, *Alone Together: Why We Expect More From Technology and Less From Each Other* (London: Basic Books, 2011).

211 'Far too often …', 'If everyone is …' Priya Parker, *The Art of Gathering: How We Meet and Why It Matters* (London: Portfolio Penguin, 2018), p. 38.

211 'maximum of 150 …', Robert Dunbar, *How Many Friends Does One Person Need?: Dunbar's Number and Other Evolutionary Quirks* (London: Faber & Faber, 2010).

211 'where we navigate …', Turkle, op. cit.

212 'a shared hallucination', Jonathan Zittrain, quoted in LaFrance, 'Is Email Evil?'

212 'women are much …', Stephens-Davidowitz, op. cit.

213 'when women *didn't* …', Amelia Tait, 'Sorry for bothering you!: the emotional labour of female emails', *New Statesman*, 3 July 2017.

213 'non-verbal cues', 'Exclamation points, emoji …', 'can all help …', Victoria Turk, 'The Problem With Telling Women to Email Like Men', *Vice*, 11 March 2019.

213 'translate all your …', Freeman, op. cit., p. 106.

214 'hive mind', Seymour, op. cit., p. 24.

214 'We write to …', ibid., p. 23.

215 'Sometimes I go …', Grace Dent, 'In this always-on era, I sometimes like to go missing. Please don't call a search party', *Guardian*, 7 September 2019.

216 'You put off …', 'Anecdata suggest that …', Katy Waldman, 'Can You Respond to an Email With a Phone Call? What About a Text Message?', *Slate*, 5 October 2016.

216 'stumble over one …', Henry David Thoreau, *Walden* (Boston: Ticknor & Fields, 1854).

216 'Texting "hahaha" is …', Parkinson, op. cit.

The Raw Nerve

219 'I was relieved …', 'Blind date: "I kept coughing into my elbow like a sick Victorian prostitute"', *Guardian*, 9 February 2019.

219 'Generation Wuss', Bret Easton Ellis, 'Generation Wuss', *Vanity Fair France*, 26 September 2014.

221 '264 million people …', report published by the World Health Organization, 30 January 2020, available at www.who.int.

221 'would therefore be …', 'our rage, glee …', William Davies, *Nervous States: How Feeling Took Over the World* (London: Jonathan Cape, 2018).

222 'A 2017 study …', ibid., p. xvi.

222 'a vast neural …', ibid., p. 11.

222 'It would be …', 'legitimised the role …', 'God forbid we …', Matthew d'Ancona, 'Diana showed that we needed emotion, but it's had a downside', *Guardian*, 28 August 2017.

223 'The biggest deficit ...', Barack Obama, in a speech at Ebenezer Baptist Church in Atlanta, 20 January 2008.

223 'everything good, as ...', Paul Bloom, *Against Empathy: The Case for Rational Compassion* (London: Vintage Digital, 2017).

224 'There are 1,198,500,000 ...', Annie Dillard, *For the Time Being* (New York: Knopf, 1999), p. 47.

225 '"package-deal" opinions', James Mumford, *Vexed: Ethics Beyond Political Tribes* (London: Bloomsbury, 2020).

226 'Outrage was once ...', Ashley 'Dotty' Charles, 'As a black, gay woman I have to be selective in my outrage. So should you', *Guardian*, 25 January 2018.

227 'An old man ...', Rutger Bregman, *Humankind: A Hopeful History* (London: Bloomsbury, 2020).

228 'And it's even ...', Amnesty International UK, 'Black and Asian women MPs abused more online', amnesty.org.uk.

228 'We can't carry ...', David Lammy, 'We can't carry on with this us-them tribalism', *Guardian*, 18 June 2016.

229 'The actual problem ...', Choire Sicha, 'Jon Ronson's "So You've Been Publicly Shamed"', *New York Times*, 17 April 2015.

229 'flatly ignores copious ...', Davies, op. cit., p. 115.

229 'Islamophobic incidents rose ...', Lizzie Dearden, 'Islamophobic incidents rose 375% after Boris Johnson compared Muslim women to "letterboxes", figures show', *Independent*, 2 September 2019.

230 'Because I choose ...', 'armour is heavy', Lindy West, 'What happened when I confronted my cruellest troll', *Guardian*, 2 February 2015.

231 'I've got a ...', Hugh Grant (@HackedOffHugh), on Twitter, 9 February 2020.

232 'grotesque dance of ...', 'only make stories ...', Sophie Wilkinson, 'Celebrities Get Treated So Badly By the Media Because You Keep Reading the Stories', Huffington Post, 18 February 2020.

232 '25k tweets telling ...', @craigstone, on Twitter, 16 February 2020.

233 'things have got ...', @archiemanners, on Twitter, 15 February 2020.

233 'Will #CarolinesLaw just …', Katie Hopkins (@KTHopkins), on Twitter, 16 February 2020.

233 'A seismic change …', Mumford, op. cit., p. 12.

233 'intense focus, passion …', Lisa Feldman Barrett, *How Emotions Are Made: The Secret Life of the Brain* (London: Macmillan, 2017), p. 139.

235 'A 2015 study …', Gabriel Arana, 'The Benefits of Positive News Ripple Far Beyond the First Smile', *Huffington Post*, 19 August 2015.

236 'overdramatic brains', Hans Rosling, *Factfulness: Ten Reasons We're Wrong About the World – and Why Things Are Better Than You Think* (London: Sceptre, 2019).

237 'pretty decent', Bregman, op. cit.

237 'the consequent loss …', Rosling, op. cit.

238 'boosterishness is dangerous …', 'We are angry …', Alain de Botton, in Steven Pinker, Matt Ridley, Alain de Botton and Malcolm Gladwell, *Do Humankind's Best Days Lie Ahead?* (London: Oneworld, 2016), p. 13.

238 'perceived agency and …', Paul Dolan, *Happy Ever After: Escaping the Myth of the Perfect Life* (London: Penguin, 2019).

239 'Our anxiety does …', quote attributed to Kahlil Gibran.

239 'smooth utopia', Bret Easton Ellis, *White* (London: Pan Macmillan, 2019).

239 'study was published …', B. Mahmoodi Kahriz, J. Bower, F. M. G. Q. Glover, and J. Vogt, 'Wanting to Be Happy But Not Knowing How: The Role of Poor Attentional Control and Emotion Regulation Abilities in the Link Between Valuing Happiness and Depression', *Journal of Happiness Studies*, 2019.

239 'When you value …', Nicola Davis, 'Trying to be happy could make you miserable, study finds', *Guardian*, 4 January 2020.

240 'holds true across …', Daniel Levitin, *The Changing Mind: A Neuroscientist's Guide to Ageing Well* (London: Penguin, 2020).

241 'Many of these …', Dolan, op. cit, p. vii.

241 'It seems bizarre ...', ibid., p. 3.

242 'has been shorn …', from a conversation with Nesrine Malik.

List of Epigraphs

p. viii   'In this Short Life' by Emily Dickinson.

p. 7   Quote from Aldous Huxley.

p. 40   'Black Marilyn' from *In Search of Equilibrium* © Theresa Lola. Nine Arches Press 2019.

p. 74   Elif Shafak quote from an interview in the *Financial Times*. Reproduced with permission of Curtis Brown Group Ltd, London, on behalf of Elif Shafak. Copyright © Elif Shafak, 2017.

p. 101   *In Praise of Idleness and Other Essays* (p. 3) by Bertrand Russell, Routledge Classics 2004. © 1996 The Bertrand Russell Peace Foundation.

p. 135   Quote from Thomas Jefferson.

p. 160   'Do I contradict myself...' from 'Song of Myself, 51' by Walt Whitman.

p. 193   'Text' from *Rapture* by Carol Ann Duffy. © Carol Ann Duffy 2005. Reproduced with permission of the Licensor through PLSclear.

p. 218   *Pilgrim at Tinker Creek* © Annie Dillard, Canterbury Press, 2011. Reproduced by permission of Hymns Ancient & Modern Ltd. Used by permission. rights@hymnsam.co.uk.

The author and publisher gratefully acknowledge the permission granted to reproduce the copyright material in this book. Every effort has been made to trace copyright holders and to obtain permission. The publisher apologises for any errors or omissions and, if notified of any corrections, will make suitable acknowledgement in future reprints or editions of this book.

Acknowledgements

Because I am as intrigued by the journey of something as much as I am curious about the finished product itself, I am obsessed with acknowledgements pages. I often flick straight to them, before I even start the book, to get a 'feel' for the author and their inevitable plight. (No acknowledgements have ever started, *This was extremely easy to write.*) This page comes in as many flavours as there are stories. The ten-page monologue that earnestly thanks specific Spotify playlists, particular condiments and the precise contortion of the author's cat on a late Saturday in June when the light hits it just so. The woo-woo one-liner: *I thank only the universe, for giving birth to me.* The bellicose rant: *This is a fuck-you to everyone who said I would never write this.* And the artfully pompous: *I doff my cap to Hillary Clinton, Bill Gates and Henry Kissinger for their support.* All are delicious to me.

And so it is with a certain amount of trepidation – performance anxiety, if you will – that I approach my own acknowledgements. The truth is that this book only exists thanks to the endless encouragement, wisdom and patience of a group of women, and scores of kind and helpful individuals, beyond. To my agent and tiger mom Nelle Andrew, who sifted through my clusterfuck of ideas, coined the title, booted me into the ring and then held my hand as we crested the waves of my pregnancy and post-partum hormones, together. To my editors, Jocasta Hamilton and Anna Argenio, for their generosity and optimism: graciously allowing me up to ten drafts of each essay (as I wasted precious time wrangling over commas and italics) and never once expressing anxiety over the fact that I filed my book two months after I said I would, thanks to an inconvenient birth, on my part. (To the person who told me that pregnancy is an 'ideal time to write a book' – I'll deal with you later.) To Laura Brooke, my publicist, for understanding so completely how I wanted to frame this book.

To all those who let me interview them – too many to list here, but eternal thanks to anyone featured within these pages, in particular Nesrine Malik, William Davies, Pamela Church Gibson, Gretchen McCulloch and Gina Rippon, who each gave me far more of their precious time than I deserved. To JP Watson and The Pound Project, for supporting my first attempt at essay writing. It was an invaluable exercise. To Elizabeth Day, Liz Engleheart and Lizzie Paton (in all your variations of the Queen's name), Josh Glancy, Sophie Wilkinson, Rosie Saunt and Marigold Atkey, for your introductions, your proofreading, your insider knowledge, your research and your scrutiny. To Dolly Alderton, for your endless encouragement throughout the writing of this and for building a business with me. Yours is a face I will never tire of.

To my best friends, who have known me forever and hold my heart carefully in their hands, even when it might feel like a burden. Annabelle, Ailsa, Lucy, Miranda, Emily, Jess, Georgie, Sophie, Lara, Orlando, Henry and many more (I fear it will begin to read like a hen-do email, should I continue). Thank you for wittering with me about many of the things in this book; and may our wittering continue ad infinitum. To my parents, who don't always understand me but who show me infinite love; and whom I do not always understand but I love, infinitely. To my sisters, Moo, Enna – you are my scaffolding. Please keep trying to teach me about retinol. To my brother, Sam, for fixing my computer since 2000 and for begging me to use a hard drive in the two decades thus. I'll back up next week, I promise. To Janie, for being my right-hand woman since 1987. To Mimi, for being the most wonderful nanny – perhaps more than anyone, this book would not exist if it weren't for your help. To Enzo, beautiful boy, never forgotten and always loved.

To my husband, Ollie, who I am told that I am 'lucky to have' with such regularity that I begin to suspect that I'm punching. Thank you for doing all the weekend childcare for three months so that I could hunch over this book, and for doing way more than your fair share of the mornings with the babies when insomnia left me too knackered to move. Thank you for living your life with such ease. For waking up every morning as if each day is just as good as the last. For sending me endless ridiculous memes from the *acres* of internet wilderness that you traverse every night. For loving me without complication. And to Zadie and Sasha, who contributed precisely nothing to this book (and more often than not manifested as miniature fleshy bulwarks against its completion) but who fill me up, fit to bust. You are wonders.